GARDEN CRAFTS for KIDS

GARDEN CRAFTS for KIDS

50 GREAT REASONS TO GET YOUR HANDS DIRTY

DIANE RHOADES

A Sterling/Lark Book
Sterling Publishing Co., Inc. New York

Editor: Chris Rich
Art Director: Kathleen Holmes
Production: Kathleen Holmes and Elaine Thompson
Illustrations: Diane Rhoades
Photography: Evan Bracken

Library of Congress Cataloging-in-Publication Data
Rhoades, Diane. 1952
    Garden crafts for kids : 50 great reasons to get your hands dirty /
by Diane Rhoades.
      p.   cm.
    "A Sterling/Lark Book."
    Includes index.
    ISBN 0-8069-0998-6
    1. Gardening—Juvenile literature.   2. Nature craft—Juvenile literature.
[1. Gardening.   2. Nature craft.] I. Title.
SB457.R47   1995
635.9—dc20   94-37108
                                       CIP
                                       AC

A Sterling/Lark Book

10 9 8 7 6 5 4 3 2 1

First paperback edition published in 1998 by
   Sterling Publishing Company, Inc.
   387 Park Avenue South, New York, NY 10016

Produced by Altamont Press, Inc.
   50 College Street, Asheville, NC 28801

Distributed in Canada by Sterling Publishing
   c/o Canadian Manda Group, One Atlantic Avenue, Suite 105
   Toronto, Ontario, Canada M6K 3E7

Distributed in Great Britain and Europe by Cassell PLC
   Wellington House, 125 Strand, London WC2R 0BB, England

Distributed in Australia by Capricorn Link (Australia) Pty Ltd.
   P.O. Box 6651, Baulkham Hills, Business Centre, NSW 2153, Australia

Sterling ISBN 0-8069-0998-6 Trade
              0-8069-0999-4 Paper

CONTENTS

GARDENING ADVENTURES

A garden is a place to grow. It's a place where you can take delight in the way nature has of transforming a handful of seeds into a habitat teeming with life, color, and things to discover. A garden is alive. The seeds that you plant will grow and color in their spaces. They'll bloom and attract bees, birds, bugs, and people. What will come out of your closely watched and tended garden is an adventure full of fresh food, surprises, and fun. My own garden is a playground, school, supermarket, theater, and a preview of coming attractions.

Imagine your own personal garden. Do you see it with neat rows of vegetables and flowers? Maybe you picture your garden planted in keyhole shapes like the gardens of the aborigines in Australia. Or maybe you imagine it planted in circles and hills just like the gardens of some Native Americans. Be inspired about the many ways you can plant your own garden! How about growing a bean tepee playhouse, or, if you'd like to entertain friends, a whole village of tepees?

If you don't have space for a garden, don't worry. Plant outdoors in all kinds of fun containers. An old boot planted with snapdragons will look wonderful. A bathtub full of pole beans will look great, too. Let the beans grow up to form a shower curtain. Grow potatoes in stacks of old tires or flowers and vegetables in window boxes. You can even seed the cracks in your sidewalk with creeping white alyssum.

Activities grow out of gardens, just as plants grow in them. Pick your edible flowers to decorate homemade cupcakes. Cut and paint your own plywood toads, fairies, and grinning frogs, and place them on exhibit among your plants. Create homemade cards with pressed flowers. Grow hanging birthday-present baskets to give to your friends and family. Plant real family trees to celebrate births and anniversaries. And why not grow a business for yourself by selling ripe homegrown tomatoes, edible flowers, and custom-made scarecrows at your own produce stand?

Learn how to invite others to help you. There's a lot of hard work in the garden, and it's good to have company that knows just what to do. Befriend the hardworking earthworms and microorganisms in the soil! They'll work with you.

Building vitality into the soil, growing food, and understanding relationships with nature give us an opportunity to be good land stewards. When you set foot in your garden, enjoy it as it responds to the rain, the sun, and the attention you bring. By caring for the health of the soil and our natural resources, we can also grow power-charged food for ourselves and our families—food that is rich in vitamins and minerals. This is the great recycling adventure: when we take care of plants, plants take care of us.

A good garden goes on all year long, so whatever season you're in, jump in! Great gardens go on for lifetimes, so take your time. You'll learn as you grow. Cooperate. Learn from your experience. Experiment. Watch closely. Enjoy!

Chapter One:
GROUNDWORK

When to Start in the Garden

It doesn't matter what time of the year it is when you get the urge to garden; there's always something to do. When it's too cold to plant or cultivate, you'll add leaves and manure to the soil. These will decompose, release nutrients, and provide your earthworms with a real banquet. While the garden is resting, you can have your soil tested (or test it yourself) so that you'll know what to add to make it healthier. You can also build trellises for your beans, construct a scarecrow, build a seed caddy to carry your seeds and hand tools, browse through seed catalogues, and fill your mind with sweet peas, fresh corn, and other vegetables that get your mouth to water.

The end of the growing season is the time to eat and preserve the fruits, vegetables, and flowers that you've grown. We eat year round, so it's a good idea to learn how to turn fresh produce into foods that will keep. As an introduction to the art of preserving, you'll learn how to turn fresh apples into delicious fruit leather.

During Cold Weather: Get Ready, Get Set...

During Warm Weather: Go!

Throughout the Seasons

LET'S GET STARTED!

Choosing a Garden Site

Have you ever watched a dog circling round and round as it searches for the perfect spot for an afternoon nap in the sun? You may feel a little like that dog as you look for the ideal garden site. Following are some things to consider as you check out each potential place:

Distance from Your Home

No one wants to spend hot afternoons trekking back and forth to a garden that's far away. Your garden should be close enough for you to run out and peek at, pick from, and play and work in easily. Choose a site close to your house. You and your garden will be better friends if you do.

Sunlight

Without plenty of sunlight, most gardens won't have a blooming chance, so be sure the spot you choose will get six to eight hours of direct sunlight each day of the growing season. If you search for your site during the cold months of the year, don't forget that once the warm months come along, the sun will be higher in the sky. Trees will leaf out, too, and the leaves will block the sun from any gardens around them.

Soil

Pick up a handful of soil from the site you have in mind. What kind of texture does it have? Does it sit in your hand like a dusty, rocklike lump of clay? Does it run through your fingers like sand? Healthy soil shouldn't do either. It should feel crumbly and loose. Are there earthworms in your soil? Healthy soil has a lot of them.

Choose the best soil available, but don't worry if it isn't perfect. A beautiful garden will grow in the desert if the gardener has friends in deep places. It's amazing what some compost, seeds, mulch, water, and those friends—the earthworms—can do.

Water and Drainage

How long is your garden hose? If you don't have one, how far are you willing to haul water? If the only available garden site is without a convenient water supply, set a large bucket or a barrel nearby, and let it fill with rainwater.

Choose a fairly level garden site so that water will soak in where it's needed instead of running down slopes and eroding the soil. Check the soil drainage, too. Very sandy soil doesn't hold water long enough, and water on clay soil tends to puddle too long before it soaks in. Light, fluffy soil that is full of **humus** (decomposed vegetable and animal matter) holds water long enough to let plant roots drink their fill but not so long that the plants get "wet feet."

To test how well your soil drains, dig a small hole, and fill it up with water. Start counting slowly, and watch what happens. If the water remains in a puddle after you've counted to twenty-five or if it flows right through before you can even get to five or six, you'll need to improve the soil by digging in plenty of compost, peat moss, or other organic matter. If you don't already know how, this book will teach you.

GARDEN TOOLS AND SUPPLIES

Centuries ago, our primitive ancestors used sticks and stones as gardening tools. You'll need tools, too, but you'll probably find gardening easier if you start collecting the ones listed here:

—A **shovel** for digging, preparing planting beds, and **transplanting** (transferring small, container-grown plants to your garden bed)

—A **garden rake** for smoothing out garden beds before you plant seeds

—A **hoe** for making hills in your garden bed and for weeding

—A **hand trowel** for making furrows in the soil, for transplanting, and for use in container planting

—A **hose** or some **water barrels** for watering seedlings, seeds, and plants—and for sprinkling yourself

—A **wheelbarrow** for hauling leaves, manure, lime, plants, trees, small children, and rocks

Some garden stores and catalogues carry child-sized tools, but if you're strong, save some money by buying used, adult-sized tools at a yard sale. Check to make sure that the handles of used tools are fastened securely to the metal tool heads, and don't buy tools that are badly rusted. This book will teach you how to perk them up.

Although you can get along without them, the tools listed next will come in handy:

—A **spading fork** for harvesting potatoes and turning compost

—A pair of **hand clippers** or **scissors** for cutting the stems of vegetables and flowers

—A **cultivator** (or **potato hoe**) for loosening up the soil in your garden bed

—A **lawn rake** for gathering leaves and grass clippings

What about gardening supplies? Some important ones are:

—Heavy-duty **string** or **light rope** for making trellises

—A **spray bottle** for applying homemade bug spray

—**Garden markers** (you'll learn how to make them) or small **stakes** and **permanent-ink markers** for recording where you've placed each type of plant

—**Stakes**, **poles**, or **trellises** for supporting plants that grow upward. Don't buy trellises! You'll learn how to make these, too.

—**Compost**

You'll see the word **compost** many times in this book. What is this mysterious stuff? It's decayed organic matter. When you make compost, (turn to pages 108 to 109 to find out how), you turn your kitchen scraps, grass clippings, raked leaves, and even your own hair into a fantastically rich fertilizer for your garden and a gourmet meal for the earthworms and soil microbes that live in it.

PERSONAL TOOLS AND SUPPLIES

To avoid exposing yourself to too much sun, wear a floppy gardening hat that will shade your head and face. Use protection for your skin, too. If you want to keep your hands smooth and clean, wear gloves.

An old camera lens or a magnifying glass is worthwhile for people who enjoy being able to see what is fantastic in what is ordinary. We use our camera lens when we want to see things in crisp detail. With it, we study aphids, the moist, vein-covered surfaces of lettuce, the soft powdery beauty of peonies and roses, and the faces of sinister Japanese beetles.

A garden journal is useful, too. In it, you'll record all kinds of garden information: when and what you've planted; when you expect to harvest it; how sweet it was to nap in the flower bed surrounded by morning glories and singing birds. You'll also write about any bugs you see so that you'll remember to watch out for

them next year. Have you noticed any tiny yellow bumps under your bean leaves? They're Mexican bean beetle larvae. Describe them and the damage they do!

Capture the colors and images of your growing garden by drawing in a sketch pad or by taking photos at regular intervals. You'll learn how to turn these images into animated garden cartoons, and you can also use them to make a garden calendar for the following year.

You'll also need some common household tools and supplies for building projects. These are listed in the projects themselves.

DECIDING WHAT TO GROW

When it comes to what to plant, I have three simple rules:

—**I plant what I like to eat.**
—**I plant what I like to smell.**
—**I plant what I like to look at.**

Choosing plants gets especially exciting when garden catalogues start arriving, often while the weather is still cold. Look for catalogues at garden-supply stores, borrow them from friends, or request them from seed companies by writing letters. Catalogue photos and written descriptions will help you decide what you want to plant. Do you have fences? Consider what you'd like to grow on them. What are the staples in your meals? Can you grow them? If you like cut flowers, grow plenty. If the colors purple, green, and white delight you, plant your garden with a color theme of flowers and vegetables.

Ten Easy-to-Grow Vegetables

If you have a hard time deciding which vegetables to plant, this section may help you. In it, you'll find descriptions of ten popular garden vegetables. More information about them—how far apart to plant them, what kind of weather they like, and how long they take to grow, for example—can be found in Chart One, which starts on page 133. If you want to grow plants that aren't included among these ten, pay a visit to your local library, and check out some good gardening books.

Beans

Beans! There are many different kinds: snap, kidney, wax, purple, lima, garbanzo, navy, pinto, cranberry, Yankee, soy, and even yard-long asparagus beans.

Snap beans are the crunchy beans that you pick and eat fresh, either raw or cooked. (When the gate to our garden is left unlocked, our dog Lucy strolls in, picks snap beans right off the bush, and eats them. She eats raw carrots, too.) Though other kinds of beans can also be eaten green, many are better if they're dried and eaten year round.

Both snap beans and beans for drying come in two different varieties: **bush beans** and **pole beans**. Bush-bean plants are short and self-supporting; they don't require a trellis or stake. Pole-bean plants are much taller. They need support and take longer to mature, but they produce over a longer period of time and in greater amounts. Plant some of both varieties. Your bush beans will ripen and finish bearing just as the pole beans start to mature.

Carrots

Pull up a Queen Anne's lace weed, and smell its roots. You've just introduced yourself to a wild carrot. Don't eat it, though! Queen Anne's Lace is poisonous. Cultivated carrots, the ones we grow to eat, come in many shapes and sizes, all sweet and plump. There are varieties for every type of soil and every length of growing season.

Corn

Besides growing ears of sweet yellow or white corn, you can also grow the tiny corn cobs that you sometimes see in Chinese food. This "baby corn" is available as a specialty seed. You'll feel like Alice in

Wonderland as you nibble on the finger-sized cobs. Pack them up for school lunches, or varnish them, and turn them into earrings and jewelry. Grow popcorn, and explode some snacks, too; popcorn seed is easy to find in catalogues.

Cucumbers

Some cucumber varieties are grown for eating fresh, and some are grown for pickling. Some varieties grow to be three feet long! Lemon cucumbers are crisp and yellow and taste absolutely wonderful in salads with purple beans and tasty nasturtiums. They really do look like little lemons growing on the vine. Your seed catalogues will let you know which variety is which.

Try this gardening trick. While it's still tiny, place a growing cucumber into an empty bottle, and rest the bottle flat on the ground. Let the cucumber grow until it fills the bottle completely. See how many of your friends can guess how you got it in there!

Lettuce

Homegrown lettuce comes in many more shapes (oak leaves and rosettes) and many more colors (red, bronze, and purple) than most people get to experience if they eat only store-bought lettuce. There are two main types of lettuce: **head lettuce**, which grows in a big round clump; and **leaf lettuce**, with leaves that aren't attached as firmly to the center of the plant.

Lettuces usually grow best during cool weather, but some varieties can also be grown during warm weather and even during the coldest months.

Plant a window box with lettuce, parsley, and flowers. You'll enjoy looking at this tiny garden as much as you enjoy the harvest from it.

Peas

Peas are **legumes**—plants that pull nitrogen out of the air and fix it in the soil where other plants can feed on it. Like all legumes, peas work magic in your garden.

Green peas or **English peas** are peas that are meant to be eaten fresh rather than dried for later use. **Sugar peas** (also called **sugar snaps**) are a delicious, no-fuss choice for your garden. Their pods are just as tender and tasty as the peas themselves. **Chinese snow peas** have juicy, crisp pods. In fact, the pods, not the tiny undeveloped peas, are the tasty parts.

Potatoes

Potatoes were first cultivated in Peru around 750 B.C. (French fries came a lot later.) Even though they're inexpensive to buy, these root crops are such fun to harvest that you really should plant some anyway. Sinking your hand into the soil and coming up with fresh potatoes is a kind of shopping-spree-in-the-earth.

Did you know that "new potatoes" are not a special variety of potato? These delicacies are potatoes that have been harvested early, while they're still immature.

Pumpkins

How would you like to grow something bigger than your head—something you can eat, draw on, or make into a huge candleholder? Grow a giant pumpkin. Many varieties are available.

Pumpkins are thirsty, hungry, sprawling plants. They like rich, well-watered soil and a lot of space. If your garden bed is small, grow pumpkins right in the compost pile. There they'll enjoy a 24-hour all-you-can-eat arrangement.

Tomatoes

Because tomatoes are members of the deadly nightshade family, people used to think that they were poisonous, but "Apples of Love," as they're sometimes called, are now the most popular vegetable-garden plant.

Tomatoes grow on bushes and up vines. Different kinds are pear shaped, large and round, or small and bite sized. Colors range from yellow and orange to red.

Tomatoes are fragrantly delicious when they're picked ripe and eaten right away. Slice them into salads, layer them on sandwiches, or pop them into your mouth for a tasty explosion.

Zucchini

Zucchini (a type of summer squash) are easy to grow and very productive. I lock my car when zucchini are in season because I'm afraid that if I don't, I'll come back to find it filled up with my friends' and neighbors' extra zucchini! If you find yourself with more zucchini than you can eat right away, make zucchini cake (see page 121), and freeze it.

Five Easy-to-Grow Flowers

In olden days, people ate more flowers than they do today. Because kitchens didn't have refrigerators, cooks used fragrant flowers to disguise the unpleasant smells of aging food. They made violet vinegars, cooked with daylilies and chrysanthemums, stewed primroses, and put marigolds in their lamb stews. Today we use flowers to add color and fragrance and to enhance taste. I like to see the surprised looks on people's faces when they discover flowers in my salads.

Many flowers are edible, beautiful, fragrant, decorative, healthy, vitamin- and mineral-rich delights. Unless they've been sprayed with chemicals or are grown near a busy highway, every plant in the rose and mint families, for example, is edible. Just as many flowers, however, aren't safe to eat. The key word here is "safe." How do you tell which plants are safe and which aren't?

Plants that are poisonous, such as foxglove, sometimes taste and smell so bad that you wouldn't even be tempted to try them. Plants that are full of goodness are often sweet and tasty. But never, ever judge by taste. There are dangerous exceptions to the "taste" rule!

—Always identify each flower or plant that you're thinking about eating, and find out if it's classified as an edible plant.

—Never pop a plant into your mouth without finding out exactly what it is and whether or not it's poisonous. If it's poisonous, don't eat it!

Let's look at five favorite flowers, four of which are nourishing, tasty, and safe to eat. For more information on how to grow each of them, see Chart Two on pages 139 to 141.

Nasturtiums

The peppery taste of nasturtiums gives a welcome "kick" to salads, and the blossoms make beautiful hors d'oeuvre baskets when they're served with an herb and cream-cheese filling (see page 122). Suspend them in clear gelatin molds with a bed of shredded carrots, and serve them to your family.

Bugs dislike the smell of nasturtiums and avoid anything growing around them, so by all means plant at least one in each vegetable-and-flower bed. They're easy to grow, eager to be picked, and keep growing all summer long.

WHEN IS A VEGETABLE A FRUIT?

When we think about fruits, we think about sweet, juicy treats that grow on trees and bushes, but the dictionary defines a fruit as the part of a plant that develops from a flower and contains one or more seeds. What does that make a tomato? A fruit! Squash, cucumbers, and pumpkins are also fruits.

The dictionary also tells us that a vegetable is any part of a plant that is customarily eaten and is not developed from a flower. Edible roots, leaves, and stems are vegetables.

Test yourself. What is a beet? What is spinach? What are beans?

Bee Balm

These strong, tall fragrant plants want to be planted where they can be wild. Hummingbirds and butterflies love their sweet blossoms, which taste like oranges. The long, slender, tubular petals can be used to decorate cakes; just arrange them to make words, numbers, and designs. The flowers' red, purple, pink, and white colors are a quiet surprise in any salad, and the flowers are a good source of vitamin C.

Borage

Borage attracts bees, and the bees act as a dating service for plants by pollinating flowers. This bushy, knee-high plant is also supposed to inspire cheerfulness. (Maybe you'd like to feed some to the grownups in your household?) The blue, star-shaped flowers taste like cucumbers, are delicious in salads, and are a popular part of the decorations on the birthday cakes I make. To season your cold drinks with ice-cold stars, put some borage flowers in your ice-cube trays (see page 122).

Sunflowers

Sunflowers are giants and can grow up to ten feet tall. If you can't imagine ten-foot-tall stalks in your garden, plant one of the five-foot "dwarf" varieties. Even these smaller varieties will look like radar in your garden.

Sunflower oil is used in cooking, the flower heads are used to make dyes, and the stalks are used in weaving. Birds love to eat the seeds, and so will you. Shelled sunflower seeds make a nourishing addition to homemade granola and breads, and when they're roasted and lightly salted, they make a tasty, wholesome snack.

Zinnias (Are Not for Eating!)

Zinnias are easy to grow, and birds and butterflies love them. They come plain, ruffled, single, double, and in almost every color. The flowers bloom throughout the summer, and bouquets made from them last longer than almost any other cut flower. The more you cut them, the more they grow back. Both dwarf and giant zinnias will put on a show in your garden. The one thing you can't do with these wonderful flowers is eat them.

CHAPTER TWO:

DESIGNING YOUR GARDEN

Now that you've chosen a garden site, gathered your tools and supplies, and decided what you want to plant, it's time to plan your garden. At the end of this chapter, you'll find some garden designs; choose one of them if you'd like. If you'd rather design your own garden plan, you'll want to get some questions answered before you begin:

—How many of each plant will you need?

—What are the different ways to grow these plants? Some, for example, will grow straight up in the air, and others will spread across the ground.

—How much space will each plant take up?

—Will your plants do better if they grow next to special companion plants?

—What will the overall shape of your garden be?

In your notebook or journal, write down the name of each plant that you want to grow, one name per page so that you'll have plenty of space for notes. Then read on for answers to these questions and for ideas on how to get your garden off (or into) the ground. Every time you read a bit of information that applies to your list of selected plants, jot it down on the right notebook page.

How Many Plants or Seeds?

If you were to plant every seed in a packet of pumpkin seeds, you'd have enough jack-o'-lanterns to light up your house like an airport, but is this how you want to use your garden space? Probably not. Some vegetables, such as tomatoes, squash, and pumpkins, produce so much per plant that you'll only need a few plants.

Turn to Charts One and Two in the back of this book. For every vegetable in Chart One, there's an entry called "How Many Plants Per Person." Record in your notebook how many plants you'll need. Also check these charts to see how close together your vegetables or flowers can grow. Write down the answers.

Growing Methods

Your next decision will be to choose the growing method that's best for each plant on your list. In this section, we'll focus on several methods, each of which will give your plants plenty of room to grow and give you plenty of room to be creative. You'll find tips on:

—Plants that grow best in hills.

—Plants that can be grown vertically (straight up in the air).

—Plants that make good companions when they grow next to each other.

—Plants that can be grown in containers instead of in garden beds.

—Plants that can be grown in the same space as other, faster growing plants.

All of this information will help you picture how you want your garden to look. As you read about these planting methods, keep taking notes.

Planting in Hills

Years ago, Native Americans didn't have tillers, but they saved on labor by making small hills and planting squash, corn, and other crops in them. To improve the soil in each hill, they dug in fish heads, wood ashes, and other soil and plant nutrients.

Fertile garden mini-hills are great places to plant vegetables that like a lot of space. Cucumbers, watermelons, zucchini, pumpkins, and squash are all space-eaters and will sprawl out from the hills where you plant them. Making hills is easy. To find out how, see Chapter Four.

Vertical Planting

Have you ever wondered why some beans are called **pole beans**? It's because they're grown up poles—vertically, with support. Some plants do best when they have a chance to grow straight up in the air instead of straight out on the ground. They have higher yields and take up much less space than when they're allowed to sprawl out, and they also create a living wall of greenery. Soil preparation, weeding, and watering are also simplified, and because you'll be able to see insect pests more easily on a vertical plant, you'll also find it easier to control insect damage. During your daily "bug patrol," you'll be able to see the undersides of leaves and pick off the bugs that shouldn't be there. Plants that do well on supports include cucumbers, some tomato varieties, peas, zucchini, and some squash varieties.

To make supports for tall plants, you can use any sturdy, tall frame of piping, conduit, or wood, with a horizontal bar across the top. By attaching string or netting to the bar, you'll give your plants something to climb. Bed frames, bathtubs with shower poles, old gates, screen doors, bicycle wheels attached to the tops of poles, or a bunch of poles will all work well as sup-

Some plants act as bug traps. Bugs are attracted to them and eat them up, while nearby vegetables, flowers, and fruits are spared. We always plant borage as a companion near tomatoes and potatoes, because the beetles head straight for the borage. The leaves of our borage plants are lacy from Japanese-beetle feeding frenzies, while the tomatoes next to them are almost undamaged. (Fortunately, the bugs don't seem to like the blue borage flowers, and the flowers are what we like to eat!)

Cabbage is also a great bug trap. Almost every nasty bug enjoys chewing on it. Plant one cabbage in or near your garden, and watch it turn into green lace. If it doesn't become a hangout for bugs, eat it. You can't lose. To keep Mexican bean beetles off beans, try planting potatoes near the beans. The potatoes will repel the beetles.

Some companion plants work well together in the soil. **Heavy feeders** (plants that like to eat a lot) do well with legumes (plants that actually make food by taking nitrogen from the air and fixing it in the soil). Corn with beans, for example, is a marriage made in heaven—and in soil. Corn needs a lot of nitrogen. Beans, which are legumes, simply whip it up out of the air. What's more, beans like to climb up the corn to get a better view.

ports. Look around your home for something to recycle for your vertical planting. Instructions for a basic pole support are given in Chapter Four. If you'd prefer a rustic look, try the trellis project on pages 80 to 81.

Companion Planting

If you were a bean plant, you'd want at least one of your allies—corn, chives, potatoes, and nasturtiums—to be planted next to you. These companions of yours would discourage Mexican bean beetles and would confuse the rabbits who love to eat juicy beans. **Companion planting**, as it's called, is a way of designing your garden so that vegetable and flower friends can help one another.

Good plant companions protect each other from bugs. They're nature's own line of insect repellents. Years ago, before chemical pesticides were invented, farmers used to plant garlic in their orchards because the strong smelling garlic plants gave off an odor that kept bugs away. Chives perform the same trick as garlic, and both are good companions for a number of other plants.

Companion planting can also keep your garden looking beautiful. Cottage gardens used to be filled with lush combinations of flowers, vegetables, and herbs. The "good-neighbor" theme of these planting designs not only added strength and flavor to the plants and controlled garden pests, but also added color and natural beauty.

Chart Three on page 142 lists some companion plants. Use the list as you design your garden. Experiment, too. Keep track of which plants grow especially well, and remember the names of their neighbors.

Gardening Without a Garden

Have you ever walked through a city street and seen a little plant climbing its way out of a crack in the sidewalk? Some plants seem so eager to grow that they would probably jump at the chance to live in warm containers, with all the sun, food, and attention they needed.

Many edible plants lend themselves beautifully to container gardening. Charts One and Two at the back of this book describe some of them. Whether you have a "real" garden or not, there are some advantages to planting in containers.

—When your tomatoes and basil are sitting right next to you as you eat out on the patio or deck, you can watch their progress very closely.

—The wonderful fragrances of potted herbs and flowers will always be nearby.

—When container-grown plants finish growing, the containers can be moved, and other containers can take their place.

—When temperatures are too cold, your tub of rosemary or your dwarf fruit tree can be carried into the warm house or garage.

—Planting in containers is a great way for people in wheelchairs to enjoy gardening (see page 74).

—People without yards can use containers to grow some of their own produce and flowers.

If you want to try container gardening, you'll need to study your sun and shade situations carefully and choose plants that will do well with the sunlight that you have. Before you put any heavy containers on your roof, you or an adult in your household will also need to check with your local building inspector to make sure that the roof won't collapse!

Garden Relationships

Some plants grow really quickly. Others are much slower to mature. Parsley, for example, takes a long time to sprout, while radishes seem to leap out of the ground a few hours after a heavy rain. By planting your radishes in the same place as you plant your parsley, you'll not only get two crops from the same

company is burrowing around in the blossoms to get nectar, it's also transferring pollen from the **stamen** (the male part of the flower) to the **pistil** (the female part). This process is known as **pollination**. Without it, flowers couldn't reproduce.

You have a relationship with your garden, too, and once you're aware of it, you can keep your garden healthy. You can help attract the creatures that pollinate plants so that your harvests will be larger. You can set up environments in quiet corners of the garden to house hungry toads and their families, toads that will feed on pests such as aphids, leaf hoppers, cutworms, and beetles. You can develop balance and grace in your gardening relationship with nature.

GARDEN DESIGNS

There are as many ways to plant a garden as there are to dance. Now that you have some idea of what you'd like to plant and how to plant it, the next step is to draw a plan for your garden, one that will show the shape and size of your garden bed and the location of the plants in it. Before you do this, however, you should know which end of your garden bed is south and which is north. Why? Because tall plants such as sunflowers and corn should be at the north end, and short plants should be at the south. This way, the shadows cast by the tall plants won't block sunlight from the shorter plants. What's an easy way to find north and south? Get up at dawn, and stand outdoors facing the sun as it comes up. Stretch your arms out at your sides. Your right hand will be pointing south.

Make some sample sketches of your garden plan. If you're in the mood for precision, make them on graph paper. Is your picture of your own garden taking shape? Good. Use all the information that you've found in this chapter and in the charts at the back of the book. Be sure you have a good eraser on hand, and don't be afraid to use it. No matter what shape you'd like your garden to be, try to keep your plan simple and small. Big gardens look great on paper, but when it's hot outside and you'd rather go swimming, big gardens tend to be forgotten. Besides, what would you do with all the food that a big garden produces?

If you have trouble coming up with a garden design that pleases you, just pick one of the designs that come next.

space, (a process known as **staggering**), but you'll also be able to keep track of where you planted your slow-growing parsley. Your radishes will mark the spot. When the radishes are harvested, the emerging parsley seedlings will have plenty of breathing room.

Beets, which are slow growing, can be planted with lettuce, which grows quickly. The lettuce will be ready to harvest before the beets have started to form, so every time you pick some lettuce, you'll be giving the beets more space to grow in.

Parsley and radishes, beets and lettuce—the relationships between them are relationships of time and space. What about work-sharing relationships in the garden? Here's a mysterious one: Have you ever seen ants walking all over swollen peony buds that are just about to bloom? One year, my mother sprayed the ants so that she could bring the peony blooms indoors, but the flowers never blossomed. Books say that ants feed on the sweet secretions of the flower buds and that they don't do any harm, but what do ants do, if anything, to trigger peonies to bloom?

Flowers and bees have a strong work-sharing relationship. Flowers perform a song and dance of color and fragrance, and their dance attracts bees, butterflies, bats, and hummingbirds. While this drop-in

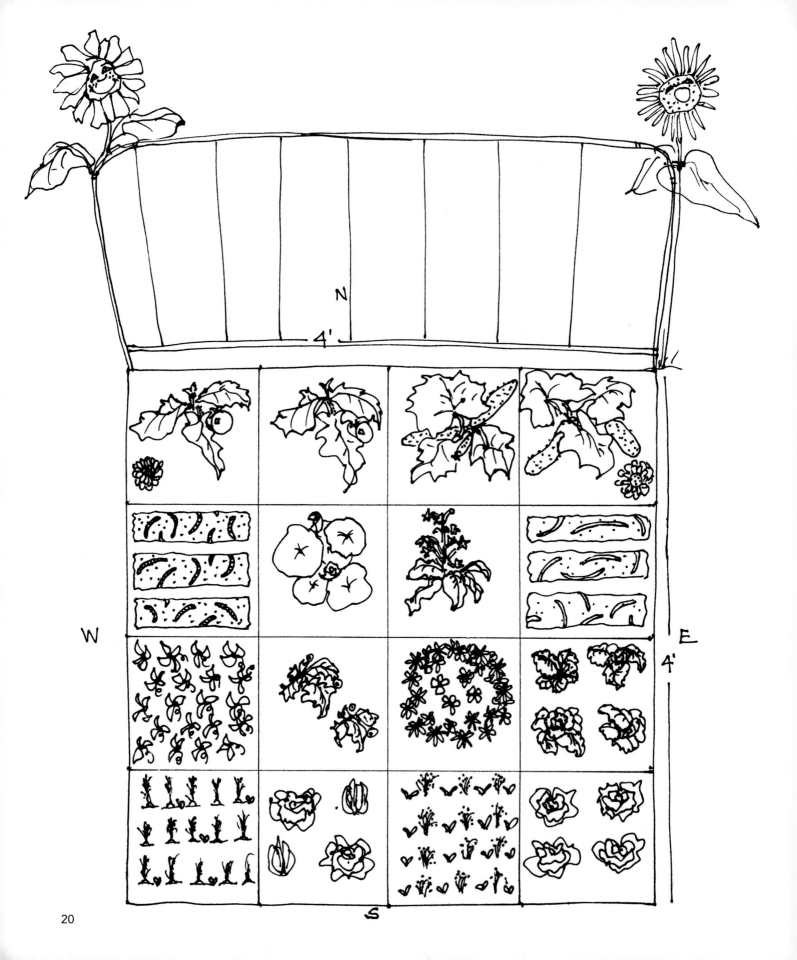

N

4'

W

E

4'

S

Square-Meal Garden
(with a Side of Hills, Tires, and Corn Rows)

Imagine a four-foot by four-foot garden as a group of one-foot by one-foot squares. Four lettuce seeds planted in one square would provide enough lettuce for one or two people. In another square, you might set out a tomato plant, and in the square next to it, four bean plants. Why design a garden this way? Besides looking pretty, a square-meal garden helps you save on seeds, and it's a great way to keep things simple and productive.

When you plant in rows, you often end up sowing more seeds than necessary. After all, the row is there, the seed packet is in your hand, so why not? With a square-meal garden, you know exactly how many seeds to plant in each square, so seeds aren't wasted. And when plants are surrounded by other types of plants, as they are in this garden design, the bugs who would like to eat them will be confused or repelled by the variety of odors, colors, and plant locations.

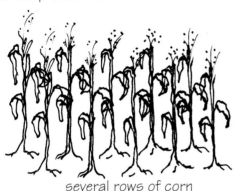

several rows of corn

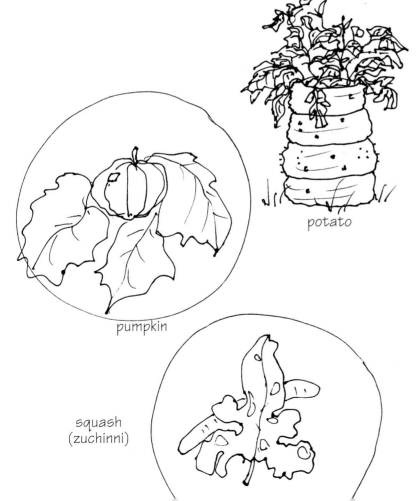

pumpkin

squash
(zuchinni)

potato

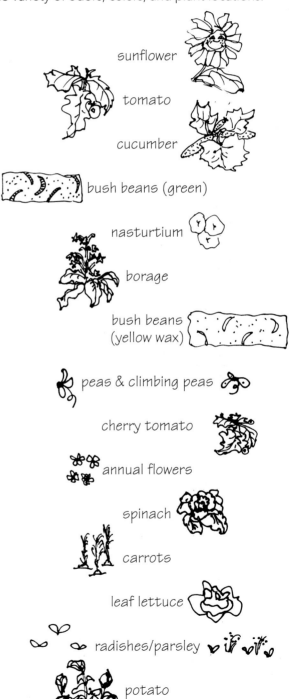

sunflower

tomato

cucumber

bush beans (green)

nasturtium

borage

bush beans
(yellow wax)

peas & climbing peas

cherry tomato

annual flowers

spinach

carrots

leaf lettuce

radishes/parsley

potato

21

Keyhole Garden

The concept of **permaculture** (or permanent agriculture) was inspired by the garden designs of native Australians, who garden as they live, in harmony with animals, plants, and nature. The aborigines made companion planting a practical art form. The beauty of their snail-shaped and S-shaped garden designs is that the variety and placement of the plants naturally discourages pests. The garden's keyhole shapes, which have clearly defined walks, make it easy to reach every planted area.

The garden in this illustration is 22 feet long and 12 feet across.

enough food for a family of four

See the helpful symbols on page 21.

Circular Garden

Your garden can be any shape you like, from a single straight row to a profile of your dog, but the circular garden is a classical and very beautiful design, one that's been used for centuries. Formal gardens are often circular, with brick paths throughout.

To make this garden, first mark a circle that is 10 feet across. Then mark another circle, 3 feet across, in its center. Finally, divide the circular garden into sections as shown in the illustration below.

food for a family of two hungry people

See the helpful symbols on page 21.

rock

basil

birdbath

loofah

peppermint

butterfly bush

rosemary

rose

rue

hyssop

pineapple sage

beebalm   sage

lavender

lilac

Fragrant Crescent Garden (A Living Headboard for the Garden Camper)

The Square-Meal, Keyhole, and Circular Garden designs are all planted with **annual** flowers, which die back after one year. This fragrant garden, however, is made up of **perennials**, which are plants that live and grow year after year. Perennials like to live together in a permanent location, where their roots and the soil won't be disturbed. They want to grow old and beautiful together.

Plant this garden in a level spot, one where you and a friend can sleep out overnight. The fragrant herbs and flowers will please butterflies and birds just as much as they please you.

Now you know what you want to plant and how to plant it. In the next chapter, you'll learn more about what to plant in—your garden soil.

dimensions: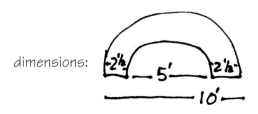

CHAPTER THREE:

SOIL

Before you dig into your garden soil and bring your garden design to life, let's take a look at the soil and its residents.

HEALTHY SOIL

Healthy plants need healthy soil—soil that is full of food for them, that allows their roots to move, and that holds water like a well-squeezed sponge. Fertile soil protects plants and keeps them from getting sick, just as our own healthy bodies help keep us from catching colds. Plants that are grown in well-balanced soil resist the "bugs" better—real ones as well as plant diseases.

The Vocabulary of Soil

Healthy soil contains

Water

Air

Microorganisms (living things too small to see without a microscope. Bacteria, some fungi, and algae are all microorganisms.)

Humus (from rotted plant and animal matter)

Minerals (from ground-up rocks)

A good balance of these things creates the rich, fertile soil that earthworms, microorganisms, plants, and gardeners love.

Microorganisms

Grab a handful of soil, and look at it. It looks still and quiet and not very alive, yet it's made up of millions of living things that you can't see. If you had your whole lifetime to count all the microorganisms in a small handful of soil, you'd count more of them than there are people alive today. Even a teaspoonful of healthy soil has over one million living residents. These creatures reproduce with amazing speed. One lonely microbe can become three hundred thousand microbes in a single day!

Microorganisms are the chemists of nature. The ones in soil turn nitrogen into nitrate, phosphorus into phosphate, and sulfur into sulphate, and all these "ates" are nutrients that plants love. Microorganisms feed humans, too. They live in our intestines, where they make it possible for us to absorb nutrients such as the iron in leafy green vegetables, the vitamin C in parsley, and the vitamin K in cabbage. When soil microbes die, their bodies make up a large part of

Earthworms

In 1881, Charles Darwin (Mr. Evolution) pointed out that without earthworms, vegetation would vanish from our planet. There would be no trees, grains, grasses, flowers, or vegetables—nothing! Worms are as essential to life as air. Yet who cares? We don't hear much about these humble creatures, do we? Have you ever spotted anyone in a night-crawler costume for Halloween? Seen any stuffed animal earthworms? Have you ever heard of boxes of redworms listed among the top gift-giving ideas? These bottom denominators of the food chain are rarely acknowledged.

the organic matter in the soil and are a part of the fertile humus that helps plants thrive.

It's clear that taking care of these little guys is a good idea. How do we do that? By feeding them what they like to eat—namely, garbage. That's right. What we think of as garbage, these tiny organisms think of as a feast. And as they feed on this garbage, they produce tons and tons of rich humus for our gardens. The more garbage (leaves, grass clippings, manure, egg shells, and vegetable scraps) we feed these microorganisms, the healthier our soil will be. Three of the projects in this book describe ways to make garbage feasts, otherwise known as compost. They start on pages 108, 109, and 110.

Humus

The dark brown, crumbly, earthily fragrant soil that earthworms, microorganisms, and gardeners thrive in is known as humus. It's rich in decayed organic matter and is soil's most important ingredient. Have you ever walked on the soft floor of the woods? The ground feels like a cushion because nature has provided years' worth of decaying plant materials to the forest floor. Microorganisms, earthworms, and other soil dwellers chew up and compost all this organic matter, transforming it into humus.

Soil that is rich in humus is also rich in the many nutrients that plants thrive on. What's more, the humus holds these nutrients and water where the plants can reach them.

When humus makes nutrients and minerals available to plants, plant-eaters benefit, too. How? By eating the vitamin- and mineral-rich plants. When a plant has its needs met by healthy, humus-rich soil, there's less work for gardeners and much more vitality for all of us.

Some people think that food chains are a line of supermarkets, but a **food chain** is actually an arrangement of organisms—plants and animals—in order of how they use or eat one another. From one-celled organisms to great white sharks, one plant or creature eats another. All living things are tied to each other by the food chain to which they belong.

Worms affect the food chain in a very basic way. As they eat, they provide nutrients for the plants that we eat later. Earthworms burrow through the soil, munching and making tunnels as they go and leaving behind digested organic matter called **castings**. These castings are like black gold. They contain thousands of useful bacteria and enzymes and are rich with nutrients for your plants, much richer than the soil that the worms eat. And the humic acid in castings serves as a storehouse for plant nutrients, a kind of 24-hour grocery store for your garden plants.

Worm castings make a wonderful addition to your garden soil.

To make castings, earthworms must have plenty of food to eat. Like microbes, they feed on organic matter in the soil. Compost is one of their favorite menu items.

The underground tunnels that worms make are also useful; they improve the soil structure and make it easier for oxygen and nutrients to penetrate to plant roots. If you live in an area where the soil is heavy clay, you've probably noticed that big puddles form whenever it rains. The packed clay makes it difficult for water to drain properly. Earthworm tunnels improve heavy clay soils. In fact, soils with healthy earthworm populations drain about four to ten times faster than soils where earthworms aren't present.

One of the reasons that worms are so productive is that they're so reproductive. Worms make big families, fast! When they mate, redworms create cocoons the size of rice grains. Three to four weeks later, two to five baby worms emerge from each cocoon. If this only happened once a year, the worm population would grow pretty slowly, but one worm can make two to three cocoons each week. Eight redworms can produce fifteen hundred more worms in only six months. Take a look at the worms in the photo on the opposite page. You'll see yellow bands around some of them. Once a worm is old enough to have this band, it can produce cocoons.

The facts about worms are so unusual, they're almost like science fiction.

—Worms aren't male or female; each worm is both.

—Worms attract each other by giving off **pheromones**, which are glandular secretions that other worms can smell and are attracted by. Human beings call this "chemistry!"

—When their rear ends are accidentally cut off by shovels, worms can grow whole new posteriors.

—Each day, one worm excretes the equivalent of its own weight in castings.

—Pound for pound, one worm is one thousand times stronger than one person.

—Night crawlers can live to be 12 years old.

—Every earthworm has about one thousand bristles that serve as feet.

—Earthworms "hear" by sensing vibrations through the soil.

—Earthworms have a strong sense of smell.

—A worm has three hundred kidneys and five sets of double hearts, but no lungs; it breathes through its skin.

ADVENTURE WITH NIGHT CRAWLERS

Go outside at night, and watch the evening activities of worms. Before you set off, use a rubber band to fasten a handkerchief around the face of a flashlight. The handkerchief will soften the light, making it less disturbing to the worms. It will also lend an atmosphere of espionage to your adventure. (A red handkerchief will work best; worms are very sensitive to white light.) If you want to collect some worms for your garden or compost pile, bring a container half filled with moist, shredded newspapers or leaves.

Tiptoe quietly outdoors, shining your flashlight on the ground ahead of you. Worms can feel the vibrations that your feet make as you walk, so step gently. See if you can spot any worms slithering back into their tunnels. When you catch one, don't yank at it while it's half in the ground and half out, or you might hurt it. Hold on to the worm gently for a second or two, until the muscular little creature stops resisting you and relaxes. Then pull the worm carefully out of the ground, and place it in your container.

During daylight hours, a perfect time to go looking for worms is after a heavy rain or storm. Because their tunnels tend to flood, the worms crawl up to the surface of the soil. Of course, there are dangers above ground, too. How many times have you seen dried-up worms in parking lots after a heavy rain? The poor worms risk drowning in puddles and being squashed by cars or feet. After the last hurricane, my daughter, Casey, and I gathered hundreds of worms in her school playground. They were very alive and are now living in our garden.

—In one year, one acre of worms in a healthy pasture will plow up about 50 tons of soil and contribute about five tons of rich castings. (If you've ever shoveled a truck full of manure onto your garden, you'll appreciate how much work worms do!)

WORM FARMING

Worm expert George Sroda operates the world's largest worm laboratory, in Amherst Junction, Wisconsin. Mr. Sroda has over two million redworms and many wonderful ideas about how worms can be used. One of his worms, Herman, is over 16 inches long and has appeared on a number of television shows in the United States!

A family of four, says Mr Sroda, can turn all its left-overs, kitchen scraps, and spoiled food into nutrient-rich garden compost by feeding them to worms. The city of Ontario, Canada, is experimenting with the use of worms in garbage-disposal systems, and Japan may use 125 tons of the wigglers to chew up wood pulp leftover from the wood industry. The country will then sell the worm castings to farmers and garden-ers. The day may come when canneries, lumber mills, breweries, wineries, and paper mills will all depend on earthworms for the efficient, clean breakdown of organic wastes.

My own family of three is **vermicomposting** (com-posting with the help of worms) with one thousand redworms. Our guest worms live in a box in our kitchen, where they're protected from the freezing temperatures outdoors. The box, which we've cleverly disguised (and use) as a seat, is virtually odor-free and bug-free and is perfectly placed when we want to scrape leftovers and food scraps into it. The worms are incredibly efficient, reproduce like crazy, and are great fun to watch. During warmer weather, we move our vermicomposter to the carport. If you'd like to start composting with worms, turn to the project on pages 110 to 113.

You might want to consider a career as an expert on worms. You'll be called an **oligochaetelogist** if you do.

Sweet and Sour: Soil pH

Soil can be **acidic** (sour), **alkaline** (sweet), or **neutral** (somewhere in between sour and sweet), depending on what's in it. By adding old coffee grounds to your soil, for example, you'll make it more acidic or sour, and by adding wood ashes from your fireplace, you'll make it more alkaline or sweet. Soil's sweetness or sourness is called its **pH factor**, which is measured as a number from 1 through 14. Take a look.

Acidic (Sour)   Neutral   Alkaline (Sweet)

1.0 .... 7 14

As you can see, soil with a pH of 1.0 is very acidic. Soil with a pH of 14.0 is very alkaline.

Why is soil pH important? Some plants grow best in soils of a specific pH. Blueberries like soil that's very acidic (4.5 to 5.0 pH). Carrots, prefer slightly sweet soil (6.5 to 8.0 pH). Most plants prefer a pH that's neutral or slightly acidic (6.5 to 7.0 pH). If your soil is rich in organic matter, with plenty of earthworms and microorganisms, the pH is probably fine for the plants in your garden.

SOIL TESTING WITH VIOLETS

In the first part of this project, you'll mix up an acidic violet solution and an alkaline violet solution. Once you've taken note of the different colors of these two sample solutions, you'll take soil samples from your garden. By adding ordinary violet solution to each soil sample and comparing the resulting solution colors with the sample solutions you made, you'll discover the pH levels of your garden soil.

What You'll Need

Violet blossoms
4 1-quart canning jars with lids
Boiling water
1 teaspoon lemon juice
1 teaspoon baking soda
Measuring spoons
Masking tape
A pen or marker
6 small glass containers
6 small plastic bags

Soil Tests

If you're new to gardening and you're curious about the nature of your soil, or if your garden didn't do very well last year, your local Cooperative Extension Service or other soil-testing professionals can test it for you. This test will cost a bit of money, but it will tell you whether your soil is sweet, sour, or neutral; which nutrients and minerals your soil contains; which are lacking; and what to add to improve your soil. This information is hard to find out just by looking at or touching the soil.

Even better than a soil test is a leaf test. This test will not only tell you which nutrients are in the soil but will also tell you which of these nutrients your plants are actually absorbing as they grow. Some minerals get "locked up" in the soil, so they can't reach your plants.

The best time to have your garden soil tested is just before the weather turns really cold. If the soil needs some help getting healthy, you'll have all those cold months before planting time to cook up some compost and a storm of worms and microorganisms.

Do-it-yourself soil-testing kits are available at many garden stores. Though they aren't usually as accurate as the tests done by professionals, they're still helpful. Following are instructions for using hydrangeas to find out if your soil is acid or alkaline. Try testing your soil with a violet solution, too.

What to Do

1. Fill two of the four jars with violet blossoms.

2. Bring some water to a boil, and pour it over the flowers to fill the two jars.

3. Put the lids on the jars, and let the violets steep overnight.

4. Set one jar of violet solution aside to use in the second part of this experiment.

5. Divide the contents of the other jar (flowers and all) into the two clean jars.

6. To one of the half-filled jars, add about 1 teaspoon of lemon juice. The solution will now be acidic and will be purplish-red in color. Use your marker and masking tape to label this jar "acidic," and set the jar aside.

7. To the other half-filled jar, add a teaspoon of baking soda. The solution will now be alkaline and will turn greenish-yellow. Label this jar "alkaline," and set it next to the acidic solution. Now that you know what acid and alkaline solutions look like, you're ready to test your garden soil.

8. Take the full jar of violet solution that you set aside in Step 4, and pour some of the solution into each of the six small containers.

9. Place a masking-tape label on each plastic bag.

10. Take your labeled bags, measuring spoon, and pen out into your garden. Place a teaspoonful of garden soil into a plastic bag. On the bag's label, write down which part of the garden the soil sample came from. Then move to another spot in the garden, collect another teaspoonful of soil, place it into another bag, and write down the garden location on this bag's label. Keep taking soil samples from different parts of the garden until all the bags are filled and labeled.

11. Go back indoors, and pour one soil sample into each of the small containers of violet solution. To help you keep track of which soil sample is which, keep each plastic bag right next to the container it belongs to.

12. Compare the colors of the soil-sample solutions to the two color-indicator solutions you made in the first part of this project. If your soil-sample solution turns reddish purple, you'll know that the soil from that part of your garden is acidic. If it turns greenish-yellow, you'll know that the soil is alkaline. If you want to calculate an average pH level for the whole garden, mix soil samples from several different garden areas, and add 1 teaspoon of the mixed soil to a small container of violet solution.

HYDRANGEA SOIL-TESTING EXPERIMENT

Hydrangeas will tell you the pH of your soil if you know how to listen. Can you guess how they do this? If the soil is acidic, their blooms are blue. If the soil is alkaline, their blooms are pink. When your hydrangeas send mixed messages, blooming pink and blue on the same bush, chances are good that months ago, someone sprinkled lime around the base of only one side of the bush. If you feed an established blue-blooming hydrangea with lime, its flowers will turn pink in 14 days. The timing of this color change is fairly reliable, so have a two-week countdown.

What You'll Need

1 pink hydrangea (in bloom) with stem attached
1 glass of water
Peat moss
Potting soil
1 terra-cotta planting pot

Hint

Peat moss is acidic.

What to Do

1. Place the hydrangea cutting in a glass of water. It will soon grow roots.

2. Make a mixture of 1/2 peat moss and 1/2 potting soil, and place it in your terra-cotta planting pot.

3. When the cutting has grown roots, plant it in the pot. Water the plant every day until cold weather comes.

4. Move the pot to a cool but frost-free spot for three months. During this time, the hydrangea will be hibernating and will need watering only once a week.

5. When the weather warms up again, give your plant a sunny spot in the home. What color do you think its flowers will be? Blue, of course (see the "Hint"). To make the flowers an even deeper shade of blue, once every two weeks, have an adult helper add a teaspoon of aluminum sulphate to the soil mixture.

6. Indoor hydrangea plants will live for many years if they're watered and fertilized properly, but if yours wants to lead a wilder life, plant it in a sunny garden spot. Next year, when it blooms, you'll have a living soil-tester.

Adjusting the Soil pH

If the pH of your soil needs to be adjusted, read on.

Soil is Too Acidic

Add about ten pounds of dolomitic limestone for every one hundred square feet of garden space. The best time to add limestone is just before the weather gets cold. During the really cold months, it will have plenty of time to break down and sweeten the soil. Bone meal and wood ashes will also raise the soil pH.

Soil is Too Alkaline

Dig in plenty of organic matter such as sawdust, peat moss, leaves, bark, and manure.

SOIL AND PLANT NUTRIENTS

When should you feed your soil and plants? When you first build your garden bed, during the growing season, and after the growing season is through. What should you feed them? Read on!

Plants live on about 16 basic elements in the soil, as well as hydrogen, oxygen, and carbon. The most important of these substances are nitrogen (N), phosphorus (P), and potassium (K). Calcium (Ca) is also very important. What does each of these do for your plants?

Nitrogen (N)

Nitrogen helps create deep green leaves, provides the energy to make plants grow quickly, and helps make strong stems. About 78% of the air we breathe is made up of this critical element, which is a gas. How does nitrogen get from the air to the soil? Aerobic (oxygen-using) bacteria in the soil take it from the air and "fix" it into the soil so that other plants can get to it. Soil gains nitrogen from the nitrogen-fixing bacteria of legumes, as well as from snow, lightning, and rain. In fact, one day's worth of rainy drizzle will make four pounds of nitrogen available to every acre of soil that is rained on.

Phosphate (P)

Phosphate is not an element, but a compound—a combination of phosphorus and oxygen. It helps plants to develop flowers and is very important because many of the vegetables and fruits that we like to eat are formed from flowers—squash, peppers, tomatoes, eggplants, peas, and beans, for example. Phosphates also help keep nitrogen in the soil. Nitrogen and phosphorus work together to boost each other's performance. In addition, phosphorus acts as a path along which necessary minerals are carried through plants. (When we eat plants rich in minerals, then we're well supplied with minerals, too.)

Potassium (K)

Potassium helps plants to develop strong roots, stems, and large fruits. Root crops such as carrots and beets need plenty of potassium.

Calcium (Ca)

Calcium feeds soil bacteria and sweetens acid soil. Plants use more of it than they do of any other element. Calcium can be found in limestone.

Not all soil has enough nutrients in it to keep microorganisms, worms, and plants healthy. Some soils are also too acid or alkaline for particular vegetables and flowers. Fortunately, if you know what's wrong with the soil in your garden, you can do a lot to improve it.

Chemical Fertilizers

Once you've discovered what your garden soil is lacking, how do you add the missing ingredients? Though many people use chemical fertilizers to boost plant growth and pesticides to control garden insects, I don't recommend them. These products are often **petroleum based** (made from oil), and there's a growing concern that the substances in them are reaching our water supplies and entering the food we eat.

I think of chemical fertilizers as the "junk food" of gardening. In the same way that a candy bar gives you a quick spurt of energy, a chemical fertilizer gives plants a growth spurt, but it doesn't feed the soil. In fact, chemical fertilizers sometimes run off the good guys in your garden—all those productive worms and microorganisms that help organic matter to decay and release its nutrients. When chemical fertilizers are applied, leaves, manure, and organic matter aren't, so the good guys have no reason to stick around. When they disappear, the soil can't balance and maintain itself properly and must continue to rely on more chemicals. Just say "no" to running off the worms!

Think about the food you eat. If you wanted to grow strong and healthy and live to win footraces with your grandchildren, would you change your eating habits? What do you eat when you're hungry, and what do you drink when you're thirsty? Your health and well-

TALKING PLANTS

If you're the scientific type, having your soil tested might be fun for you, but soil testing isn't absolutely necessary. You might want to watch and listen to your plants and weeds instead. Believe it or not, plants do talk to us.

When your lettuce leaves look wilted in the evening, and you know they're not hot because the sun's been down for awhile, what are those leaves saying? "Water! Give us water!" When your spinach leaves look pale or yellow, they're saying, "I'm hungry. I'll have some compost and a side order of manure tea, thank you." A plant that's full of bug bites registers its plea as "Pick these horrible beetles off me!"

Weeds talk, too. With the help of a weed identification book, you can translate their language. Take a look around your garden. If you see sorrels (see the photo above) or horsetail, they're telling you that your soil is probably too acid, too sandy, and too dry. You'll want to add organic matter for better drainage. Field mustard, horse nettle, morning glories, and cresses, on the other hand, send the opposite message: Your soil is crusty and draining poorly. Chickweed and lambs quarters both grow in fertile, well-cultivated soil. After you listen to what these last two have to say, eat them! They're both edible.

Top row: Sand, blood meal, commercial organic fertilizer, rock phosphate. Center row: Compost, sawdust, manure, bone meal. Bottom row: Lime, peat moss, wood ashes, green sand.

being are fueled by what you eat and drink. What your plants eat makes a big difference, too, so feeding the soil properly is important.

Before the Iroquois made important decisions, they considered how those decisions would affect the next seven generations. They wanted to be sure that their great, great, great, great, great grandchildren didn't suffer from their mistakes! If you want to make sure that your own descendants still have sparkling clean water to drink, fertile soil to cultivate, and spotted owls to watch, work with the time-honored, natural methods of gardening.

Organic Fertilizers and Soil Amendments

Organic fertilizers such as manure and compost release nutrients slowly and steadily as they decompose. They offer a complex balance of nutrients and minerals to the earthworms and microorganisms in the soil and to the animals and people who eat what is harvested from that soil. Adding organic matter to the soil keeps it fertile and offers us the simplest form of health insurance there is.

Compost and manure are among the best organic fertilizers, but there are many other organic materials that you can feed to your soil and plants. These **soil**

amendments will make your garden bed—and your plants—healthier and happier. Most are available at garden-supply stores. Some, such as sawdust, are often free for the asking. Think of these substances as food for your soil. By adding the right ones at the right time, you'll boost your garden's performance and keep all its residents full of life.

Following is a list of these fertilizers and soil amendments. In the next couple of chapters, you'll find out when to add them to your garden bed.

—**Blood meal** is dried blood that's been ground up. It's a great food for leafy crops such as lettuce and is a good source of nitrogen.

—**Bone meal** consists of crushed animal bones and contains about 28% calcium and 25% phosphate. Adding it to your soil will help your plants produce flowers.

—**Rock phosphate** makes the minerals in soil available to plants. Even when your soil is loaded with minerals, if there's not enough phosphate, your plants won't have the right password to get to them. Phosphate is especially good for root crops and plants that produce fruits and seeds. Manure and phosphate like working together, so whenever you add one, add the other, too. (Get colloidal phosphate if you can.)

—**Commercial organic fertilizers** aren't made from petroleum, but from animal and plant sources. They supply basic nitrogen (N), phosphorus (P), and potassium (K). Their ingredients are usually listed under the letters NPK. A 5-10-5 ratio of NPK fertilizer can be used at planting time, when you side-dress your growing plants (apply fertilizer to the soil around them), and when plants look like they could use a quick pick-me-up.

—**Dolomitic limestone** (or **calcium carbonate**) is loaded with calcium, which sweetens acid soils and helps repair calcium deficiencies. Use high-calcium lime that has a low magnesium content (less than 15%). Magnesium and nitrogen inhibit each other.

—**Greensand** is a mineral deposit found on the ocean floor and is a good source of potassium.

—**Manure** from cows, goats, horses, or chickens is a great source of nitrogen. This wonderful plant food shouldn't be added to the garden when it's fresh because fresh manure will "burn" the roots of your garden plants. Let manure (especially horse and chicken manure) age for at least four months before you dig it in. How can you tell when manure has aged? It looks black, and it doesn't smell like manure anymore. Cow and goat manure aren't as hot as horse and chicken manure, but you should let them age, too. Never use cat or dog manure because waste from meat-eating animals can carry harmful bacteria.

Manure is high in nitrogen but low in phosphate, so whenever you add manure to your soil, add something that provides phosphate, too.

—**Peat moss** is made up of plants that have decomposed very slowly in boggy places. It holds moisture well, improves drainage, and fluffs up hard, compacted soil. Peat moss is easy to find, lightweight, and inexpensive. Soak peat moss before adding it to the soil. If it's dry, it will take moisture away from your plants.

—**Sand** improves drainage and helps lighten up heavy soils. Some plants and flowers such as carrots and irises do especially well in sandy soils. Use **sharp builder's sand**, not beach sand, which is too rounded and which contains plant-unfriendly salt.

—**Sawdust** makes very alkaline soil more acidic. It's often used as a mulch.

—**Wood ashes** add potassium and sweeten acid soils. Save those hardwood ashes from your wood stove or fireplace, and add a handful when you plant deep-rooted perennials and root crops.

—**Compost** (see the next section)

Composting: The Whole Rotten Truth

Imagine trying to feed a baby a piece of hard, raw carrot instead of cooked, mashed carrots. Trying to feed your garden a buffet of fresh waste wouldn't be any easier. Garbage straight from your kitchen is often too "hot" (too fresh) or too plentiful to put directly into the soil. It needs to soften and break down to be most useful to the soil and plants.

Composting is a way to speed up this natural breaking-down process. By building a pile of layered garbage and letting the worms and microorganisms in it help to decompose all those egg shells, apple cores, hair, leaves, and grass clippings, you'll create fragrant, rich, black, luxurious humus. When the pile is built properly, it heats up as the microorganisms in it get to work.

When you add compost to your garden bed, you're:

—adding nutrients for your plants.

—improving soil drainage.

—providing leg room for plant roots.

—improving soil texture, which in turn will help prevent the soil from crusting over or eroding.

—helping the soil maintain even temperatures.

No gardener should be without a compost pile. As long as you keep eating and supplying the worms and little guys in your compost with good garbage, they'll keep eating and supplying you with fertile, composted soil. For instructions on how to make different kinds of compost piles, see the projects that start on pages 108 and 109.

Chapter Four: # STARTING YOUR GARDEN

Once the weather and soil have warmed up, it's time to prepare the garden site that you've chosen. Before you start, check the soil to see how damp it is. Working the soil before it's had a chance to dry out will make it hard and crusty. To test the moisture level of your soil, pick up a handful, and squeeze it in your fist. If it clumps up like a snowball, it's still too wet to work. Be patient. Even if you're compulsive about keeping busy, leave the soil to dry out. When you squeeze a fistful of soil and it's crumbly and loose, it's time to dig in!

SEEDS OR TRANSPLANTS?

To start your garden, you'll plant seeds, set out **transplants** (container-started plants), or do some of both. How do you decide which plants should be planted as seeds and which as transplants?

BUILDING A GARDEN BED

If you've never gardened before, chances are that the garden site you've selected is covered with weeds and/or grass. Create a brand-new garden bed by following the instructions that follow.

Use the same instructions to bring an old garden bed back to life. Ideally, garden beds should be made either very late or very early in the growing season, but unless the ground is frozen or flooded, you can make one any time.

What You'll Need

A spade or shovel
A tape measure
Stakes, sticks, rocks, or white flour
Soil amendments

Instructions

1. First, measure out your garden. Use a long tape measure, or pace off each side by measuring your foot, figuring out how many steps you'll need to take to walk along one edge of your garden, and then counting your steps as you pace. Or place a ruler down on the soil, and flop it over and over until you've covered the distance that you want the garden edge to be.

2. Once you've measured your garden bed, mark its outline with stakes, sticks, rocks, or sprinkled white flour.

3. If your garden site is covered with grass, use a spade (a straight-bladed one will work best) to cut an outline around the garden, through the grass, about 2 feet out from each edge of your measured plot. (The extra 2 feet will become a path.)

4. Think of the grass inside the cuts as a carpet that's attached to the soil by roots. You're going to roll up pieces of the carpet and take them away, but you'll have to cut through the roots first. Use your spade to dig under the carpet of grass, a little at a time, breaking off the roots about 1 or 2 inches below the surface. Roll up the pieces of *sod* (the grass, the roots, and the dirt beneath them) as you go. When you've rolled up a piece that's as big as you can lift, carry it off, and banish it to the woods or a garbage can. Don't compost it, or it may sprout right up in your compost pile. Keep digging, rolling, and carting away the sod until the soil inside the string lines is exposed.

Some people use a rototiller or plow to turn the sod under. I don't recommend this because perennial grasses and weeds tend to grow back up through the tilled earth. A good shovel and strong back work better here.

5. To make a path around the bed, start digging soil from the 2-foot-wide strip around it, and toss the earth into the center of the bed. Don't toss any outside. The path should be lower than the bed itself.

(continued on following page)

Some plants, such as tomatoes and peppers, shouldn't be started by sowing seeds outdoors. They start bearing earlier when they're started indoors and transplanted when the weather warms up. Purchase these transplants from nurseries or garden-supply stores. Tomatoes, peppers, and some other plants are also such generous producers that it would be a waste to plant an entire packet of seeds when you only need one or two plants, so purchasing transplants will save you money.

Other plants, such as lettuce, beans, and corn, are easy to start by planting seeds right in your garden bed, and because you'll eat up every bit of produce that a packet of seeds will provide, you won't waste

BUILDING A GARDEN BED
(continued from preceding page)

6. To loosen up the soil in the bed, dig it all up, and turn it over. This will make the soil inviting to hungry and helpful earthworms and microorganisms. If you have some aged manure, spread it on the heap, and mix it in by digging again. If you find that the soil is very hard to dig, if it doesn't look dark and rich, and if you don't see any earthworms while you're turning

it, now is the time to treat whatever ails your soil by adding some of the other amendments that you learned about in Chapter Three. Spread them on top of the soil, and dig them in.

Tip

A big, strong garden buddy will come in handy. If you don't have a buddy yet, just take it easy. Dig as much as you can, take a break or get a good night's sleep, and start again.

any of the seeds you buy. Some of these same plants can't handle the shock of being transplanted. They can only be grown by planting seeds directly in the garden.

To find out which method is best for each of the vegetables you want to grow, take a look at the lists that follow, or check at your local garden-supply store.

Plant Seeds Directly in Garden

Beans
Beets
Borage
Carrots
Corn
Peas
Radishes
Winter squash

Set Out Transplants

Broccoli
Cabbage
Cauliflower
Eggplant
Peppers
Tomatoes

Plant Seeds or Set Out Transplants

Bee balm	Pumpkins
Chives	Spinach
Cucumbers	Summer squash
Lettuce	Sunflowers
Marigolds	Swiss chard
Melons	Zinnias
Nasturtiums	Zucchini
Parsley	

Plant Sets Directly in Garden

Onions are available both as **sets**, which look like miniature ripe onions, and as seeds.

Tip

Potatoes are grown from seed potatoes, which look like pieces of potatoes. They're different from the potatoes you buy in the grocery store, which are sprayed with a substance that keeps their "eyes" from sprouting. Seed potatoes from garden-supply stores and catalogues have eyes that are meant to sprout.

Order your seed potatoes about one month before planting time. Put them in a warm, dry, lighted area to sprout. When the sprouts have grown, but before

MAKING HILLS

Hills can be made right inside your garden bed or can be used as Native Americans used them—as mini-gardens surrounded by uncultivated soil. The instructions here are for making hills on bare soil that hasn't yet been turned into a garden bed. If you want to place the hills inside the bed you've already prepared, you won't have as much digging to do!

What You'll Need

A shovel   Seeds or transplants
Soil amendments

What to Do

1. Mark a circle in the soil, about 4 feet in diameter.

2. Dig up the soil inside the circle, mixing it as you do. This will loosen the soil and make it inviting to worms and helpful microorganisms.

3. Dig up a 1-foot wide path around the outside of the circle. As you dig, pile up the dirt inside the circle to make a hill.

4. Add compost and any other amendments that the soil needs. Dig in a fish head if you have one. Everyone has fish heads lying around, right?

5. Plant your seeds or transplants in the hill.

6. Water the soil well.

Tips

If you're making more than one hill, be sure to leave enough space between them.

Cucumber hills should be 6 feet apart
Pumpkin hills should be 12 feet apart
Squash hills should be 8 feet apart
Watermelon hills should be 12 feet apart
Zucchini hills should be 8 feet apart

PLANTING BY THE MOON

Everything in nature has a relationship with everything else. When daylight hours start to dwindle, leaves know that it's time to fall off trees. When the days are no longer cold, the warmth in the soil tells bulbs to send up their shoots. Birds know when to build their nests and when to push their ready-to-fly babies out of them. When you look at a bowl of ice-cream, your brain prepares you to eat it by making your mouth water.

Many people find that paying attention to these relationships and rhythms is helpful to them, but sometimes they don't know why. Some people, for example, plant according to which phase the moon is in, without knowing what the facts are behind this centuries-old tradition.

The phases of the moon occur in a 28-day-plus cycle. Each month, there's a period of about two weeks (the **first** and **second** quarters) when the moon is **waxing**. During this period, the moon looks as if it's getting bigger. Towards the end of this period, the **new moon** becomes what we call a **full moon**.

After the moon is full, it starts to **wane**. The waning moon looks as if it's getting smaller because more and more of its dark side is facing the earth. This two-week-long waning period is made up of the **third** and **fourth quarters**.

Technically, the air is coolest and the soil is warmest when the moon is approaching its fullest stage. Because cool air is denser than warm air, it holds more minerals. Soil that has fewer minerals in it tends to be lighter around a full moon, which makes it easier for the tiny roots of new plants to establish themselves.

During other phases of the moon, the soil is heavy, and there are fewer nutrients and less moisture available to young plants.

If you'd like to try gardening by the phases of the moon, use these guidelines.

WAXING MOON (FIRST AND SECOND QUARTERS)

—Prepare your soil while it's light and fluffy. Digging up the soil during the third and fourth quarters, when it's heavier, may feel like more work.

—Plant crops that grow above ground.

WANING MOON (THIRD QUARTER)

—Plant crops that grow below ground.

—Hoe and weed.

—Fertilize your plants.

WANING MOON (FOURTH QUARTER)

—Hoe and weed.

—Fertilize your plants.

ANY QUARTER YOU LIKE

—Water your plants.

they're longer than three inches each, cut the seed potatoes into pieces, with an eye on each piece. Put the pieces in a brown paper bag, and let them "harden" for several days by keeping the bag in a warm, dry, dark place. Then they'll be ready for planting.

PLANTING

Different kinds of seeds and plants have different planting requirements. They like different temperatures and are planted at different depths and distances. Your seed packets will probably have planting instructions printed on them, but if they don't, turn to Charts One and Two at the back of this book. These charts give general guidelines for planting and looking after some popular vegetables and flowers. For information on plants that aren't listed, check out a good gardening book from your library.

When can you start planting? Plants that like a little frost should be started as early in the spring as the ground can be worked. These **cold-weather crops** (peas, lettuce, spinach, kale, cabbage, and collards, for example) will grow when you're still wearing two sweaters and wool socks. **Cool-weather crops**, such as beets, carrots, and parsley, will tolerate the cold, but they won't really grow much until the weather

warms up a little. Think of them as one-sweater plants. Then there are the T-shirt plants such as corn, sunflowers, and tomatoes. These **warm-weather plants** are tender, and they really enjoy hot weather.

If the sun is up, the soil is dry, you have your seeds or transplants, and you know how to plant them, what are you doing reading this page? Get out there and plant!

MAKING A POLE SUPPORT

 Now that you've prepared your garden bed and built some hills, you may want to set up supports for plants that like to grow upwards.

Tips

Your poles should be 6 to 9 feet long, and, if possible, should have slightly rough surfaces. If their surfaces are too smooth, the plants may think of them as slides. Bamboo and hardwood saplings are fine.

For especially fun ways to make vertical supports for your beans, see the projects on pages 55 and 81.

What You'll Need
A pole for each person in the family
A shovel
Soil amendments
Seeds

What To Do
1. Make sure that the soil is loose in an area about as wide as your outstretched arms.

2. Dig in any necessary soil amendments if you haven't already done this.

3. Dig a hole about 12 to 18 inches deep, and put your pole in it.

4. Fill up the hole with soil, one layer at a time, packing each layer down well with the rounded end of your shovel.

When to Water

—When you plant seeds or transplants, give them a drink to refresh them while they adjust to their new space.

—Watering is especially important during a seed's **germination** period. This is the period during which seeds break out of their hard, outer coatings and send shoots up into the light and roots down to shop for food, minerals, and moisture. By keeping the seed coatings moist, you'll help to soften them and will also help the seeds inside to swell up until they burst through their coatings.

—After your seeds have germinated, water regularly. Young seedlings of all types need a lot of moisture. As they grow, their moisture needs will vary. If you mulch, (see pages 43 and 44), you won't need to water as often. The mulch will help keep the soil moist and will also discourage weeds.

—When you set out transplants, water them to help them get over the shock of being moved from their containers to a garden bed or pots. A good watering will drive out any air pockets in the new soil and will settle it around each tiny root hair.

—It's better to water deeply and not too often than it is to give your plants a little water every day. Plant roots grow as much as they have to. When you water a little every day, the roots don't have to grow very far to reach moisture, so they aren't encouraged to grow deeply. When you water the roots thoroughly, but only once a week or so, they're encouraged to seek water deep in the soil, and they grow big and strong. Strong roots find it easier to survive droughts than roots that you've pampered by watering every day. Plants with strong root systems are also better equipped to search for minerals, food, and moisture. They take care of their own meals. Strong, healthy plants have greater resistance to freezing, too.

—Different kinds of soil "drink" water differently. Clay soil has a dense structure and requires less water than sandy soil or rich loam. It doesn't drain as well either, so don't water heavily or plant roots will drown. Sandy soil has a loose structure and drains too well, so you'll probably need to water the plants in it more frequently.

—Water in the early morning. This will keep plants from drying out later in the afternoon when the sun is hotter. If you water in the heat of the day, much of the water will evaporate before it reaches the plant roots.

—Water your plants a day before you fertilize them. They'll absorb the fertilizers better if they're not thirsty.

—Rain is the best water for newly planted seeds, but if you can't forecast the weather accurately when you plant, just give your seeds a gentle but thorough watering once they're in the ground. Make sure it's gentle! Seeds are small and light in weight. They'll be sent flying if you water them with a hose on full force.

How to Water

—Mulch and rely on rain. Water only when the weather has been very dry.

—Use a **soaker hose** to give the roots a thorough soaking. This is a hose with one end blocked and tiny holes all along its length. When you turn it on, the water comes out the tiny holes. Because soaker hoses moisten only the soil and the plant roots, they help prevent plant diseases, which tend to spread on wet leaves and stems.

To make a soaker, poke holes in the "nose" of an empty plastic jug. Fill it with water, screw the cap on tight, and turn the jug upside down in the garden bed. Water will drain slowly from the jug.

—Water barrels are a terrific way to store water when your garden is far away from a faucet. They're also handy for rinsing off dirt-encrusted hands. Set out one or two heavy-duty plastic barrels or garbage cans. If you have a shed near your garden, put the barrels under the gutter downspouts so that rainwater will funnel down into them. If there aren't any gutters near your garden, just put the barrels in the garden itself. They'll fill up eventually. To keep mosquitoes from breeding in the barrels, put a drop or two of detergent or oil in the water.

—What about ordinary hoses? If there's a water tap close to the garden, by all means hook up a hose, and shower your garden with it. Prop up the hose, and run through the spray yourself.

WEEDING

Many of the plants that we call weeds, such as hepatica and violets, are actually wildflowers, and others, such as dandelions, are nourishing and sometimes helpful in the garden. Their long roots bring up nutrients from deep in the soil to enrich the soil near your other plants. Chickweed and lamb's quarters are edible, and tell us that our soil is in good shape.

Some weeds do rob the soil and your plants of food and water. These can take over the garden. Smartweed, ragweed, and snakeroot are a few you can do without.

To find out which weeds are useful and which aren't, check out a good book on weeds from your library.

Take the book into your garden, and study the weeds that you see. If you still can't identify your weeds, bring some samples of them to your Cooperative Extension Service or university Department of Agriculture. You'll find people there to help you.

When you've decided which weeds need to be pulled, wait until the soil is a little damp. Pulling weeds from dry soil is hard work! Smothering the weeds with mulch is a good way to keep them from growing.

MULCHING

Mulching is covering the soil around your plants with a natural material such as straw, wood chips, newspaper, or shredded leaves. Mulches help keep soil temperatures even, help soil hold onto its moisture, and help keep down weeds. When soil isn't covered with a mulch, the water in it will evaporate in the heat of the sun.

You won't have to water mulched soil as frequently as bare soil because plant roots in mulched soil will grow deeply and find their own water. Train your plants to wait on themselves! Plants with big, strong roots produce larger, more mineral-rich harvests.

Mulch also keeps earthworms and microorganisms where you want them—near your garden plants. When the garden soil is bare, these friendly creatures are more likely to take off for greener pastures—or mulched ones.

FERTILIZING

Newly planted seeds don't need fertilizing. They supply their own nourishment until they get their first **true leaves**. (These are the first real leaves a seedling grows. Don't mistake them for the tiny leaflike coverings of the seed casing that come up with the sprout.) Transplants, however, which are the plants that you purchase or grow in indoor containers and then set out in your garden, will appreciate an energy boost. Let's investigate some ways to translate what your plants are telling you about their nutritional needs and then take a look at the different ways you can help them.

Foliar Feeding

Did you know that plants get about 80% of their food from the air? They take minerals from the atmosphere and deposit them in the soil. But **foliar feeding** (feeding plants through their leaves) actually works best when the soil is already fertile. If the soil is poor, the plant may act like a straw, sucking up nutrients from

Diagnosing Your Plants' Nutritional Needs

Plant Symptoms	Diagnosis	Prescription
Green leafy plants are stunted, and leaves are pale or yellow in color.	The soil needs nitrogen (N).	Add compost, manure, green manure crops, or blood meal. If you have access to them, fish emulsion, cottonseed meal, and alfalfa meal are also good sources of nitrogen. Planting legumes such as peas, beans, clover, and alfalfa will increase available nitrogen for next year's growth.
The flowers don't develop well.	The soil needs phosphate (P).	Add bone meal or colloidal phosphate.
Root crops are too small. Fruits are few or too small.	Soil needs potassium (K).	Add hardwood ashes, manure, sawdust, or greensand. Tobacco stems, pecan hulls, rice hulls, almond hulls, wheat and oat straw, granite dust, cottonseed meal, and fish scraps are all helpful, too.
Plants are tall, spindly, and unproductive.	There's too much shade in the garden or too much nitrogen in the soil.	Relocate the plants to a sunny area, and keep the soil free of weeds. Don't add any nitrogen-rich fertilizers.
Leathery-brown blemishes develop on the bottom ends of tomato fruits.	The plant has a disease known as blossom end rot.	Avoid overwatering and adding too much nitrogen.

the air, but sending them into the soil instead of retaining them. If the soil is healthy, the plant will absorb the nutrients.

The healthier a plant is, the thicker its leaves will be, and the more nourishment the plant can pick up through foliar feeding. Fill a spray bottle with manure tea, and spray the leaves just enough to dampen them. Spray early in the morning, when the dew is still on the plants.

The shorter the growing season, the more helpful foliar feeding will be. Foliar feeding helps speed up plant growth.

Applying Worm Castings

When you're planting your garden, sprinkle castings in the soil where you put the seeds, or mix a handful of castings into the garden soil that you put around new transplants. As the plants grow, apply worm castings as a top-dressing (right on top of the soil). Do this frequently when the plants are flowering or producing fruits and vegetables. For container-grown plants, sprinkle about 1/4 inch of castings on the potting soil, and then water the plants. Repeat every two months.

For the true story of worm castings, see pages 26 to 27.

Applying Compost

Finished compost should be applied to flowers, vegetables, houseplants, and container plants. When you're transplanting or planting seeds, mix some com-

post with the garden soil. For use in containers, mix the compost with potting soil. Side-dress garden plants by sprinkling compost around the plants' stems.

Tea Time

To make a healthy, nitrogen-rich drink for your plants, brew up some manure tea. Fill about 1/4 of any large, waterproof container with fresh or aged barnyard manure. Fill up the rest of the container with water, or let the rain do the honors. Let this "tea" brew for a day or two, and then offer the tea to your plants.

EVAPORATION EXPERIMENT

Mulches help keep moisture in the soil by slowing down evaporation. Here's an experiment to help you see how this works.

What You'll Need
2 glasses filled with water
Plastic wrap
A rubber band

What To Do
1. Cover one of the water-filled glasses with plastic wrap.

2. Put both glasses out in the sun.

3. Check the glasses a day or two later to see which one contains the most water. The glass with a plastic covering will probably have more water left in it because the covering stopped the water

from evaporating. On the underside of the plastic covering, you'll see the drops of water that couldn't escape into the air.

BUG AND CRITTER WARS

Fascinating creatures live in the garden, and if you spend time there, you'll probably get to know them. Some are helpful, and some aren't. Stroll through your garden every day, and get acquainted. Take out your magnifying glass, and study them. Match their faces with the pictures in books, and learn their names.

I treat bugs as if they were members of a science-fiction beauty pageant. I pick out the winners, disqualify the others, and watch them all for their talents and unusual good looks.

The Good Guys

To help you identify the beneficial creatures in the garden, read the descriptions that follow, find some pictures of these creatures, and copy the pictures by hand. If you'd like to draw giant versions on plywood, cut them out, paint them, and put them in your gar-

den, see the project that starts on page 105. Imagine a three-foot-tall praying mantis perched among your bean plants—a scarecrow for the insect world!

Ladybugs

Some ladies! These popular garden bugs eat like pigs. The ladybug received her name centuries ago, when vineyard farmers thought she was an answer to a prayer to the great lady, the Virgin Mary. The newly hatched young are flat, with orange and black markings; they have no shell. Though they don't look like their mothers, they can eat 40 aphids in an hour.

Some damaging bugs, such as cucumber beetles, resemble ladybugs. Both have spots, but if you look behind a ladybug's neck, you'll find a broken V that points towards her rear end. A cucumber beetle doesn't have this mark. Mexican bean beetles have 16 spots, while ladybugs never have more than 15 Squish the impostors!

Praying Mantises

These gorgeous, alien-looking insects are a blessing because they have enormous appetites and eat aphids, beetles, borers, and other garden enemies.

Female praying mantises have a reputation for eating their mates, but they only do this when they're hungry! And when they do, the act isn't a ritual. It's a passion for a good meal. (The praying mantis only eats creatures smaller than herself, so don't worry.) She grips her prey with sharp hooks on her legs.

Search for praying-mantis egg casings during the cool months of the year. They look like sand-colored pieces of foam, and they're attached to twigs, branches, and weeds. Pick the twigs carefully, and put them in your garden. You'll see the reddish-yellow **grubs** (or babies) when the weather warms up. The egg cases can also be bought through some garden-supply and seed catalogues.

When my daughter was two years old, a praying mantis moved into our home. We were delighted to have this large and attentive bug's company. It ate the spiders, so we didn't try to touch or catch it. At night, when I read to Casey, the praying mantis was almost always just a few feet away, head tilted as if it were listening. We missed it when it finally disappeared.

Lacewings

Turn on an outdoor light at night, and wait for these creatures to show up at the screen door. They love bright lights. Though they look delicate and dainty, with their lacy wings and iridescent eyes, they eat like truck drivers, devouring thrips, mites, caterpillar eggs, scales, and leafhopper nymphs as well as aphids and mealybugs. Their main defense is a foul-smelling substance they give off when they're attacked.

Lightning Bugs

Also called **fireflies** or **lampyrid beetles**, these shining flyers look like magic in the garden. The flat, long-jawed larvae have great appetites for slugs and snails, but the adults eat nothing at all.

Bees

Bees pollinate flowers so that fruits can develop. These buzzing insects love water. Fill a pie plate or shallow dish with water, and set it out in the garden. Be sure to plant a lot of flowers, too. Bee balm, butterfly weed, asters, and borage are all bee favorites.

Did you know that bees die after they sting someone? To avoid being stung, wear white or pastel colors, and don't wear perfume. If you do get stung, cover the sting with a paste made of baking soda and water.

Spiders

These eight-legged predators (which aren't insects, by the way) only eat insects that are alive. They're attracted by motion. **Wolf spiders** are especially fun to watch because they don't rely on webs to trap their food; they run after their prey. Spiders like dark locations. If you let an area of your garden get a bit wild, spiders will move in.

SONIC BLOOM

Imagine eating 325 tent caterpillars and 200 ants in a day. A bird can eat that many, so good gardeners welcome birds around their garden sites. There's another reason for you to attract birds to your garden; it's called "Sonic Bloom."

Some studies indicate that the frequencies and harmonies of the songs that birds sing may be what trigger a plant's **stomata** (a part of the leaf) to open up and absorb nutrients from the air. This opening-up at the sounds that birds make is called "Sonic Bloom."

Have you ever heard about experiments done with plants and music? Plants appear to respond to different kinds of music in different ways. They also seem to respond—and not very well—to a lack of certain harmonies and frequencies. In one experiment, orchards were treated to a sonic symphony. These orchards produced fruit that was unusually high in nutrients.

Birdsong is a natural soundtrack for your garden. How do you attract birds to sing your plants' stomata open? The Cherokee, who were fond of purple martins, discovered that they could attract these birds by hanging gourds on poles. The martins used the gourds as nesting sites and would return to them at the same time every year. Long ago, purple martins used to nest in abandoned woodpecker holes, but now they depend on nesting boxes provided by humans. (They will not nest where starlings and English sparrows have nested.)

Purple martins act as predawn alarm clocks. They're also watchdogs with high-pitched voices. Like chickadees, they learn to recognize the people around their habitats, and they get noisy when strangers arrive. Martins love to eat flies, mosquitoes, and other insect pests in the garden. If you'd like to attract some to your garden, see pages 95 to 96.

Toads

Toads should win the Most Helpful and Humble in the Garden Award. Under the safety of darkness, these creatures come out to make beautiful music and to chew up cutworms, potato beetles, cinch bugs, ants, slugs, and a lot of other obnoxious pests.

Encourage toads to move into your garden by providing simple toad luxuries such as a home with a pool. Turn to page 97 to find out more.

Bats

Bats don't deserve their bad reputation. They eat many undesirable insects, including mosquitoes, and they help to pollinate fruits and vegetables. Chances are you won't see many because they come out only at night and detect their meals by means of an internal radar system. Unless you make a habit of walking around with food in your hair, they'll avoid you and continue to shop for food in your garden. To attract them to your garden, buy a bat house at a garden-supply store.

The Bad Guys

There are three main types of bad guys: **sucking bugs**, **leaf eaters**, and **underground villains**.

Sucking bugs (insects that feed by piercing the tissues of plants and sucking out the sap) are known as suckers or sap-feeders. They lurk along tender stalks, leaves, and buds. One way to track them down is to look for their leavings: drops of a honey-like substance with tiny, black mold specks growing in them. Aphids, mealybugs, mites, red spiders, scale, spittlebugs, thrips, and whiteflies are all sucking bugs and will injure your plants. If you notice tiny, white, cottony insects or raised irregular surfaces on trunk, twigs, or buds, suspect these villains, and arrest them.

Leaf eaters eat holes in plants. Japanese beetles, corn earworms, cabbage worms, caterpillars, grasshoppers, snails, slugs, Mexican bean beetles, and potato beetles all love to chomp on leaves.

Underground bad guys aren't usually in sight, but you'll know they're there when your plants don't seem to grow or produce well.

Slugs

Slugs, which are related to octopuses, are especially fond of lettuce, cabbage, and delphiniums, but they also eat many other plants that you'd rather save for yourself. Shake salt on them to shrivel them up. Ask an adult in your home if you can have a bottle of beer. Then open the bottle, and sink it into the garden soil so that the lip is at soil level. Slugs and snails are boozers. They'll come for a drink and then drown in the beer. When the bottle is full of slugs and snails, empty it, clean it, and refill it with another round. Slimy slugs hate powdery ashes, so sprinkling wood ashes around each plant will also help.

Japanese and Potato Beetles

These highly visible, large shiny bugs eat many garden plants and can transform a healthy bean or potato plant into a lacy nothing in no time at all. To keep them under control, check for them often, pick them off, and squish them. They're slow, so they're easy to catch.

Mexican Bean Beetles

If you spot yellow fuzzy dots on the undersides of bean leaves, you've located the larvae of your enemy. The adult beetles look like large brown ladybugs with 16 spots. Catch them early, and stop their nasty appetites! Pull up every infested plant, and put the plants in the real garbage bin, not in the compost pile. Plant potatoes nearby to help control these beetles.

Aphids

These small, soft-bodied insects are shaped like tiny pears with antennae and excrete a substance that ants and flies love to eat. In fact, ants tend aphids just as we raise cows for food. To milk their "cattle," they stroke the aphids' bellies. Sometimes ants even bite off the wings of their little aphid prisoners to keep them from flying off.

Discouraging ants keeps aphids in check. To do this, sprinkle bone meal, powdered charcoal, or wood ashes around your plants. If you see a parade of ants in your garden, follow the parade to the ants' hole, squeeze some lemon juice in it, and place bits of lemon rind around the opening.

Spiders, assassin bugs, lacewings, and at least 14 species of fungus all enjoy a hearty aphid meal. So do ladybugs. Nasturtiums repel aphids. Try a strong homemade spray made with lime juice and water, or aim some Homemade Bug Spray (see page 88) at these sap-sucking pirates. Aphids are attracted to the color yellow, so set out a bright yellow dish filled with soapy water beneath infested plants. Placing aluminum foil around the base of the plants will keep flying aphids from landing on them.

Scale

These insects are so small that they're hard to see when they're in their early stages of development. After a short mobile life, the female loses her legs and most of her internal organs, and she produces about one thousand eggs. There isn't much of her left at this stage! The males don't do much better in their final stage of development. Their tiny wings will only carry them a few feet, and because they have no digestive systems, they don't eat. Neverthless, aphids are bad guys. A substance that they secrete attracts a black fungus, which blocks the light necessary to make the plants' food.

Chalcid wasps and ladybugs help control scale. The homemade bug spray that you'll learn how to make in Chapter Seven will also help, as will gently washing scale-damaged leaves and stems with soapy water.

Ants

Ants are unwelcome not because they damage plants but because they introduce aphids and scale to the garden when they carry these damaging bugs around as their personal food pantry! Pennyroyal, spearmint, southernwood, nasturtiums, and tansy all offend and repel ants. Plant them.

Weapons for Bug Wars

Resist any temptation to use bug-killing chemicals when you spot unwelcome bugs in your garden. Insects adapt to new poisons as quickly as people can invent them. A chemical spray that worked yesterday might not work next week. When even a few insects survive a pesticide, they pass on their tolerance to the next generation of bugs. Then you not only have stronger bad guys, you also have a lot of unnecessary poisons in your garden soil.

There are some safe substances that will control the bad guys in your garden. For sucking bugs, either buy an **insecticidal soap solution**, or make the one that's described on page 88. Insecticidal soaps won't harm mammals, but they will kill bugs. Spray the affected plant areas as often as it takes to get rid of the bugs.

Diatomaceous earth is also effective. Thirty million years ago, there were billions of one-celled plants called diatoms living in the ocean. Each diatom had a shell around it, made up of silica. When diatoms died, they drifted to the ocean floor. Over time, as the ocean floors shifted, they were gradually exposed to the air. Today, the fossilized layers of ancient diatoms are "harvested" or quarried and are ground up into what's known as diatomaceous earth, which is sold at garden-supply stores. When insects eat this earth, their insides are pierced by the tiny, razor-sharp particles of silica. This substance won't harm anything but bugs, so sprinkle it around your garden plants and on newly emerging corn silks.

Bacillus thuringiensis (or **BT**) is another safe bug-war weapon. It comes as a chalk-like powder and is available at garden-supply stores. Also called **milky-spore disease**, BT is actually a friendly bacteria. When the larvae of bad bugs eat it, it grows inside them and kills them. Then, when the dead larvae decompose in the soil, they release more good bacteria spores. Although it may take BT a few days to kill the larvae, BT will work! Apply it to the soil when the ground isn't frozen and when there isn't a strong wind. Look for application instructions on the package.

To help keep your plants healthy, rotate them by planting each one in a different place each year. Always remove diseased plants, and throw them in the garbage, not in the compost pile. Keep weeds down, too. Pick the big bad guys right off your plants, and squish them between your fingers, or crush them between two rocks.

The best protection you can give your plants is healthy soil. A garden with healthy soil will maintain a healthy balance in which beneficial bugs scare off or eat up the sucking, chewing intruders.

CHAPTER SIX:

HARVEST AND AFTER-SEASON CARE

In many areas of the world, a good harvest means being able to feed your family. In other areas, where supermarkets are stocked with food and people are wealthy enough to buy it, a good garden harvest is one that's grown in rich soil that will provide food more nutritious than the produce usually offered in stores.

HARVESTING

How do you know when to harvest your garden? Seed packets and catalogues often provide this information by telling you how long it will be from planting to picking. Having these facts is especially important when you're ready to pick a vegetable such as corn, which is hidden by its husks. (When in doubt, pick an ear of corn, strip away the husk, and taste a kernel or two.) Keep track of when you planted each type of plant by recording the dates in your garden journal.

Visiting the garden every day is another way to decide when it's time to pick vegetables and flowers. The descriptions that follow will also help:

Beans

Snap beans should be ready to harvest about eight weeks after you plant the seeds. You'll know they're ready when you can begin to see or feel the outlines of the seeds in their pods. Pick the beans when they're still young and tender by snapping them off at their stem ends. The plants will keep producing. Pole beans are usually harvested later, after the beans have started to develop inside the pods, but some varieties can be picked early. Use your taste buds to help make your decision.

Carrots

Carrots should be ready to harvest about ten weeks after planting the seeds, when the feathery green tops are about 12 inches high. To keep the greenery from coming off in your hand when you pull your carrots up, twist as you pull. Once the carrots are out of the ground, cut off the feathery leaves. If they're left on, these leaves will keep growing and will draw moisture and vitality out of the carrots. Carrots can stand a light frost, so don't hurry to pick them all. Harvest them as you need them until it gets really cold outside.

50

Corn

Corn is ready to eat when the silk turns brown and the husk has filled out, about nine to thirteen weeks after you sow the seeds. The kernels of ripe corn are sweet and milky. The natural sugar in corn turns to carbohydrate within hours, so pick only as much as you need, and bring your cooking water to a boil as you pick.

If you can't eat all the corn you've picked, freeze it. Bring some water to a boil as you strip the husk and silk from the ears. Boil the ears for four minutes, and as they're boiling, fill the sink with ice cubes and cold water. To keep the corn from cooking in its own steam, put it in the ice water as soon as you've taken it out of the boiling water. When they're cool to the touch, put the ears in freezer bags (a few ears per bag), and pop them into the freezer. The corn will still taste great when you reheat it.

Cucumbers

You'll have ripe cucumbers about 14 to 22 weeks after sowing the seeds. Different varieties are ripe at different sizes, so compare your cucumbers to the pictures on their seed packets. Pick cucumbers often! Eat them, give them away, or compost them, but keep picking the fully grown cucumbers before they ripen completely. The plants will keep producing enthusiastically.

Lettuce

Your leaf lettuce should be ready to pick in about seven weeks, when the leaves are at least 3 inches tall. Pick the outside leaves, leaf by leaf, and leave the inner ones to grow some more. Harvest head lettuce by picking the entire plant right out of the ground. Lettuce doesn't store well, so no matter which type you grow, pick only as much as you need.

Peas

Peas can be picked about ten weeks after planting. English peas are ready when you can see the round peas inside their pods. Snap peas should be picked while the pods are still flat. If you wait too long, the pods will be tough. The more you pick peas, the more they'll produce.

Eat peas as soon as you can. The **sucrose** (or sugar) in them that makes them taste sweet turns to starch quickly, so don't let them sit around for hours before you eat them.

Potatoes

As long as the plants are flowering, they're producing potatoes underground. When the leaves and flowers die back, the potatoes are ready to harvest. This will be about two months after you plant your seed potatoes. If you want what are known as "new" potatoes, just dig some up early. Keep harvested potatoes in a cool, dark, humid, frost-free place. If they're exposed to sunlight for long, they'll turn green and will be unfit to eat.

If you've planted potatoes in tires (see pages 62 and 63), you'll have a grab-bag easy time. Just lift up the tires, and pick the potatoes out of the soil. If you've planted potatoes in your garden bed, use a potato fork to gently dig up the soil around each plant.

Pumpkins

When they turn orange, they're ready to pick, usually about twelve weeks after planting. Cut the stems with a sharp knife or shears, leaving a short piece of stem on each pumpkin to help keep it from decaying. Store your extra pumpkins in a warm, dry place.

Tomatoes

Your tomatoes will be ripe about 22 to 24 weeks after the seed is sown. Spotting a ripe tomato is easy. It's bright red (or yellow or orange, depending on the type of tomato it is), and it's firm and juicy. Whether they're ripe or not, pick all the tomatoes before the first frost. Ripen any green ones by placing them on a windowsill indoors. Some people eat fried, green tomatoes.

Zucchini

Pick these about eight weeks after you've planted the seeds, when they're about 5 to 6 inches long and are still young and tender. The older and larger they get, the tougher and less tasty they are. The photo on page 138 shows a zucchini that's fun to look at—and that should be hammered into small pieces and aimed at the compost-pile target project on pages 115 amd 116.

Bee balm

The flowers can be picked within six to eight weeks after the last frost. Continue to harvest them throughout the summer.

Borage

Each plant puts out a profusion of flowers, which can be picked by midsummer.

Nasturtiums

It will be six weeks before you can pop hot, spicy nasturtium flowers into salads. The leaves will be ready in about four weeks. Both leaves and flowers are good to eat, and the more you pick them, the more they grow. Flowers bloom until frost.

Sunflowers

Your sunflowers will be ready to harvest eight to ten weeks after planting. To harvest the seeds, wait until they look dry and full. Then rub them off the flower head, and put them in an airtight container. Roast them with or without salt, or eat them plain. Save some plain ones for the birds!

Zinnias

The flowers will bloom and can be cut six to eight weeks after planting.

Tip

For fresh-cut flowers, pick them when they're in full bloom. If you'd like to dry them, pick them just before they reach the full-bloom stage.

CLEANING UP YOUR HARVESTED GARDEN

Cleaning up your garden bed is a little like cleaning up after a party. When you're finished, the party atmosphere will linger even though the garden bed will look completely different.

Gather all the old but healthy vines and stems, and throw them into the compost pile. If you find any plant materials from diseased plants, throw them in the regular garbage. Leave any mulch where it is.

COVER CROPS

When it's cold and sunny here at Crab Creek where I live, the worms hunker down deep in the soil, and my winter garden is blanketed in green rye grass. This grass is a **cover crop**—a crop that is planted to protect the soil instead of for eating. Cover crops are sometimes left in place all year to keep soil from eroding. Sometimes they're dug back into the soil to nourish it with organic matter when the weather warms up again.

Rye grass that is dug back into the garden is called a **green manure crop** because, like manure, it's rich in nutrients for the soil. Last September, my daughter, Casey, and her friend, Jennie, planted the rye by dancing a kind of broadcast ballet, tossing handfuls of seed onto the soil as they twirled and spun. Then they raked leaves onto a big sheet, dragged the sheet to the garden, and catapulted the leaves over the garden fence.

As soon as warm weather returns, all the rotted leaves, the rye grass, mulch from last summer's garden, and plenty of seasoned manure will be dug into the soil. On that day, the earthworms will surely be celebrating!

LEAVES AND LIME

Right after the cover crop is planted, we add leaves and a sprinkling of lime. Leaves are plentiful, and they're an inexpensive and wonderful food for earthworms and microorganisms. As they break down, they contribute organic matter to the soil. Most types, except for maple leaves, also make the soil more acid, so to neutralize the acidity, we sprinkle lime along with the leaves. Sweetening the soil in this way is like adding sugar to lemonade.

After the cover crop is established and growing, add more leaves and lime. Make compost piles with leaves and lime, too. You'll add this compost to the garden when the weather is warm again.

While the garden rests under its blanket of cover crop, leaves, and lime, it will break down these additions and fortify itself. When the weather warms up again, and you show up with your shovel and seeds, the worms will be ready to cheer you on.

MOVING ON

If you've been using this book as a field-action manual, you've been working hard, learning a lot, and probably eating more fresh vegetables than you ever have before. Maybe you're now a worm expert with a produce stand. Or maybe you designed an obstacle-course garden, where you leapt daily over potato-filled tires and hurdles made from vertically planted beans.

If you think it's been fun so far, let's see what comes out of your garden now that so much has gone into it. Your garden will always give you something to eat, create, do, share, examine, discover, and give away. In the next chapter, you'll find some of the many ideas and projects that can come out of a garden— yours or someone else's. Many more are waiting for you to discover them.

BEAN TEPEE

These practical, homegrown playhouses are easy to make, easy to grow, and fun to hang out in. Grow this shelter as your own personal habitat. It will offer you a quiet getaway spot within easy reach of healthy snacks. By planting a few tepees, you can provide shelters for your friends, too.

From the desk where I'm writing this, I can see a bean tepee that is missing an entire side. One day, we let out our goats (Rose and Sugar) for a bit of fresh fare. While we weren't looking, they wandered over to this tepee and had a gourmet treat. That's why we now plant more than one bean tepee each year!

What You'll Need

A medium-sized stick
A tape measure
4 or 5 7-foot-long saplings or poles
Sturdy cotton twine
A packet of pole-bean seeds
2 or 3 friends

What to Do

1. With your stick, draw a large circle in your garden bed. The circle should be about 7 feet across.

2. Prepare the soil inside the circle for planting (see Chapter Four).

3. Set the saplings or poles side by side on the ground, lining them all up at one end. Use your twine to tie them all together, about 12 inches down from the lined-up ends.

4. Have your friends help you lift the poles upright. Then spread the loose ends apart so that the bottom end of each pole rests on the outline of the circle. Adjust the tepee so that the legs are spaced equally.

5. Weaving the twine around the poles is easy once you get the hang of it. Start by tying the string to one pole, about 3 inches above the soil. Then unwind the roll of twine as you move to the next pole, and wrap the roll around that pole once or twice, 3 inches above the soil. Continue on to the next pole. When you get to the pole next to the one where you started, turn around, and start back in the other direction. Doing this will leave an open entrance to the tepee.

As you head back in the other direction, wind the twine around the poles about 8 inches higher than you did last time. When you get back to the first pole, turn around again. Keep repeating your web-weaving steps, winding the twine a little higher each time, until you reach halfway up the tepee. The opening for your tepee door will stop at this level. From here on up, you want beans to grow all around the tepee, so keep weaving, in one direction only, until you reach the top.

6. If you like, you can make the webbing more stable by weaving the twine up and down through the horizontal twine that's already in place.

7. Plant bean seeds around the entire outside base of the tepee, not just next to the poles. Bean seeds should be planted about 3 inches apart and 1/2 inch deep.

8. Enjoy! Do take care to avoid contact with the beans and leaves when they're wet, or they may catch diseases. Don't pick beans or cuddle up inside the tepee when the weather is rainy.

Kids who are more comfortable working with metric measurements will find a metric conversion chart on page 142.

TOILET-PAPER SEED TAPE

Some seeds are so small that they're difficult to handle, and even big seeds can spill out of your hands just when you don't want them to. Here's a project to take care of those problems. By gluing your seeds to a long, biodegradable tape and then planting the whole tape, you won't misplace a single seed. You won't need to remember how far apart to plant them, either, because the tape will do the remembering for you. You'll glue the seeds onto the tape at exactly the right distance apart.

Seed tapes are sold at gardening stores, but they cost money, and if you buy them, you'll miss the fun of making them. So let's get to work!

What You'll Need

Newspapers
Flour or gelatin
Water
A mixing bowl
A stirring spoon
Seeds
Spacing and depth-of-planting information
   for your seeds

A roll of plain white, unscented toilet paper
A ruler or tape measure
A waterproof marker
Cotton swabs or a narrow stick
A friend

Tips

Charts One and Two (see pages 133 to 141) provide seed-spacing information for ten vegetables and five flowers. You'll also find seed-spacing facts printed on seed packets and in some garden catalogues.

If you have to work outdoors on this project, wait for a still day without any breeze, or you'll end up casting yourself in toilet-paper mache!

Try to assemble your seed tapes right before you plan to "plant" them. The tapes can be rolled up and stored in empty jars or cans, but they're easily damaged.

What to Do

1. If your work surface needs to be protected, cover it with newspaper.

2. In your bowl, mix up the flour or gelatin with just enough water to make a thick mush. When the mixture feels and looks like soupy mashed potatoes, it's perfect.

3. Choose a packet of seeds, and decide how long you want the row of that vegetable or flower to be.

4. On top of your work surface, unroll a strip of toilet paper the length of your planned garden row.

5. Find out how far apart these particular seeds should be planted. Then, with your ruler and marker, measure down the center of the strip, and make a mark at the place each seed should go. If you're making a carrot-seed tape, for example, make marks every 2 to 3 inches.

6. Dip a cotton swab or narrow stick into the paste mixture, and dab a drop or two of it onto every mark on the tape. (If you're too impatient to bother with dabbing, just dribble a thin line of paste all the way down the strip.)

7. Place the seeds onto the paste, one at each mark you made. Then let the paste dry.

8. When it's time to plant, make a trench in your garden soil as deep as the planting depth for your seed. (For carrots, the trench should be about 1/2 inch deep.)

9. Have a friend help you set the tape down into the trench.

10. Cover the seed tape with fine soil. An orderly row of plants will sprout up in no time at all.

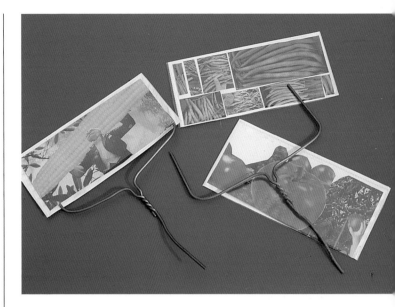

GARDEN MARKERS

Marking your garden rows will help you remember what you've planted—and where. Ice-cream sticks or stakes will work, of course, but making these colorful garden markers is much more fun and will provide something to do when it's still too cold outside to plant your vegetables and flowers.

What You'll Need

1 wire coat hanger for each marker

Wire cutters

Pliers

Clear plastic album sheets, 8-1/2 by 11 inches

Scissors

Heavy paper or poster board

Old seed packets, garden catalogues, or garden magazines

White craft glue

Permanent-ink markers

Waterproof tape

Tip

On the back of each marker or in your garden journal, be sure to record each variety of plant and where you got the seeds or transplants. Depending on how well each plant grows, you'll know whether or not to get it next year and where to buy it.

What to Do

1. To make a wire stake for each marker, use your wire cutters to clip off a coat hanger, about 7 inches down from the neck on each side.

2. Straighten out the hanger hook, and bend the 7-inch-long sides into a fork shape. If your hands aren't strong enough, use a pair of pliers, or ask for some help.

3. Cut a 3-inch-wide strip from the top or bottom of a plastic album page. Try not to cut into the folded seams; they'll help keep the inside of the plastic "envelope" dry.

4. Cut a rectangle from heavy paper or poster board, making it a little smaller than the plastic envelope. Test its fit by trying to slip it into the envelope. If it's too big, cut it down to size.

5. Cut out pictures of the vegetables and flowers that you're going to plant in your garden. Old seed packets, seed catalogues, and gardening magazines are filled with colorful pictures.

6. Arrange your pictures, and glue them onto the paper rectangle.

7. After the glue has dried, turn the rectangle over, and use a marker to write down some basic information about the plant—when to plant it, how deep to plant the seeds, and how long it will be until harvest time, for example. Add a poem or a drawing if you like. (Always use permanent-ink colors; damp gardens will make other kinds of ink get runny.)

8. Slip the decorated rectangle into the plastic envelope.

9. Slide the two prongs of the wire fork in through the open edge of the envelope.

10. Seal the bottom of each envelope with waterproof tape. Then push the marker into the soil next to a garden plant.

TOPIARY

Topiaries are plants that have been trained, cut, or trimmed into odd or ornamental shapes. The art of topiary was once more popular than it is today. People clipped entire gardens full of hedges in the shapes of animals such as elephants and dogs!

This simple project calls for training an ivy to wrap itself around a wire form.

What You'll Need

A terra-cotta pot, about 8 inches wide and deep

A metal topiary form

A handful of gravel

Potting soil

Worm castings, compost, or aged manure

Presoaked peat moss

2 ivy plants

Tips

Purchase the ivy plants at a nursery or gardening store. You may also find them in your own back yard. If you do, dig up a couple of plants with their roots intact.

Look at crafts-supply stores or florists for a topiary form, or make your own by bending a wire coat hanger into any shape you like. Don't be afraid to create a wild and wonderful shape!

What to Do

1. Place the metal form inside the terra-cotta pot, as shown in the photo. Its legs should rest in the bottom of the pot and should exert a little pressure against the sides. If the legs are too loose inside the pot, take the form out, bend the legs away from each other a little, and replace the form in the pot.

2. Place a handful of gravel in the bottom of the pot to assist with drainage.

3. Fill about 1/3 of the pot with a high-quality potting soil.

4. Place an ivy plant near each leg of the metal form, and fill the pot up with potting soil. Firm the soil well around the roots.

5. Water the plants well.

6. Now wind each plant around and up its half of the metal form. As the plants continue to grow, they'll cover the form completely. Check them once in awhile, and wrap any stray growing tips around the form. Ivy will grow indoors or out, so keep your topiary wherever you like.

7. Water the plants whenever they're dry, and offer them some manure tea or liquid organic fertilizer about once a month.

GROWING POTATOES IN TIRES

This project is a homegrown garden grab-bag and an easy way to grow a lot of potatoes even if you live in the city or have limited garden space. It's also a great way to recycle old tires.

What You'll Need

4 to 7 used car tires
Garden soil
Compost or presoaked peat moss
2 pounds sprouted seed potatoes
A shovel
Organic fertilizer or manure tea

Tips

For instructions on how to prepare seed potatoes for planting, see page 37.

For "new" potatoes, reach into the soil, and grab a few immature potatoes while the plants are still flowering.

What to Do

1. Pick a tire-sized outdoor spot that gets full sunlight. Make sure the spot is level. If it isn't, you'll end up with a "Leaning Tower of Potato."

2. Make a mixture of garden soil and either compost or presoaked peat moss.

3. Set two of the tires on the ground, one on top of the other, and fill them with the soil mixture.

4. Plant your seed potatoes in the tires.

5. Water the plants when the weather is dry. Add organic fertilizer or manure tea every other week.

6. As the plants begin to grow, add another tire to the stack, and fill the stack with more soil. Be careful not to break the potato plants' stems or leaves as you do this. You'll bury part of the plant, but make sure that some of the foliage remains above the soil.

7. Keep adding tires and soil as the plant grows, leaving some of the plant exposed each time. Stop when the stack is seven tires high or when the plants stop making flowers—whichever comes first. As long as flowers are growing above the stack of tires, potatoes are growing inside it! Fertilizing the plants is especially important while the plants are flowering.

8. After the flowers stop growing, the plant will die back. When it looks dead to you, it's harvest time. Have a friend or two help you lift the tires up and off the soil. As the tires are removed, push the dirt away to reveal your not-so-hard-earned rewards.

PAINTED GARDEN TOOLS

 Painted tools look distinctive, are easy to find when you've scattered them around, and are protected from the weather. Painting is fun, too.

What You'll Need

Newspapers or drop cloth
New or used garden tools
Rust-preventive primer and paint for metal
Exterior latex primer and paint
Paintbrushes
Turpentine
Jars for cleaning brushes
Gloves
Old clothes
Vegetable oil
Rags

Tips

Most hardware stores carry special rust-preventive primers for metal. Ask the salesperson to help you find a can of this. Apply the metal primer outdoors; its fumes aren't good for you.

You'll need two sets of brushes: one for the wood primer and latex paints, and another for the metal primer. To clean up your metal-primer brush, rinse it in turpentine. To clean the wood-primer and latex-paint brushes, rinse them in water. To clean up yourself, rub some vegetable oil onto any metal-primer spots on your skin. The oil will lift the primer right off. Latex primer and paint can be washed off with warm, soapy water.

If your tools are old and rusted, have your adult helper sand them down. This is a job that requires either muscles or power tools. Of course, if you want to develop upper body strength, this step's for you.

What to Do

1. Protect your work area by spreading a thick layer of newspapers or a drop cloth over it. Before you start, read the directions printed on the primer and paint cans.

2. Use a rag dipped in turpentine to wipe all the metal parts (even new ones) before you paint them. Wear gloves while you do this, and avoid inhaling any fumes.

3. Brush or spray one coat of rust-inhibiting primer onto the metal surfaces, and let the primer dry. Brush wood primer onto the wood surfaces, and let that primer dry, too.

4. Use latex paints to paint designs or solid colors on the primed surfaces, and set the tools aside to dry. Let each coat dry thoroughly before you apply the next.

5. Hang your tools on your tool station! Instructions for this handy tool rack start on page 86.

MOON-PLANTING CALENDAR

You don't have to stand outside at midnight to find out what phase the moon is in each time you want to plant seeds or hoe weeds. With the help of this calendar, you'll know when to plant root crops, when to plant crops that grow above ground, and when to do other work in the garden. Hang the calendar on a wall, and glance at it whenever you feel a surge of gardening energy coming on. (If you've forgotten how planting by the moon works, turn back to page 38.)

What You'll Need

A potato
A small knife
A large, blank calendar
A farmer's almanac
An ink pad with green ink
An ink pad with red ink
A colored marker

Tips

Make your moon-planting calendar during the cold months of the year so that you can use it as soon as the soil thaws.

Farmer's almanacs are available at many book stores.

What to Do

1. Use the knife to cut the potato in half.

2. On the flat side of one potato piece, carve away small bits of potato until a carrot shape stands out from the carved background.

3. On the flat side of the other piece of potato, carve until a head of lettuce or a spinach plant remains.

4. Open your blank calendar to the month when people in your area start working their garden soil. Open your almanac to the same month. The almanac will tell you which quarter the moon will be in on each day of that month.

5. For each day that the moon will be in the first and second quarters, use the lettuce stamp to stamp a green lettuce shape on the calendar. The lettuce shape will remind you that on those days, you should plant things that grow above the ground, such as lettuce, spinach, green beans, and pumpkins.

6. For each day that the moon will be in the third quarter, use your red carrot stamp. The carrot stamp will remind you that these are good days to plant below-ground crops such as carrots, beets, and potatoes.

7. Mark the fourth-quarter dates by using a colored marker to draw small hoes! You shouldn't plant anything during this phase of the moon, but it's a great time to weed, hoe, water, and fertilize.

8. Repeat Steps 4 through 7 to complete a moon-planting schedule for several months in your calendar. Skip the months when people in your area are toasting their toes by the fireplace!

GARDENING APRONS

Working in the garden is a great way to get dirty. When your hands are so crusted with soil that you can't even feel the seeds you're trying to plant, wipe off your fingers on this gardening apron. It's washable! What's more, its pockets will hold seed packets, hand tools, markers, labels, and twine. Carpenters have special aprons and tool belts, so why shouldn't gardeners have them, too?

For this project, you'll need a nail apron, which most hardware stores give away to their customers. If you don't want to buy a chain saw or drill just to get an apron, explain to the salesperson why you'd like one, and you might get some support for your gardening adventure.

What You'll Need
Newspapers
A nail apron
A pencil
Colored permanent-ink markers or acrylic paints
  and brushes

Tip
Because most nail aprons have printed advertisements on them, you'll decorate the back of yours and wear it backwards, too. When the pockets are pressed against your body, seed packets and other objects will be much less likely to drop out.

What to Do

1. Cover your work surface with newspapers, and place the apron on them, pocket-side down.

2. Sketch your design in pencil first. If you're stuck for ideas, try one of these:

—Draw a seed-spacing "cheat sheet" to remind yourself how far apart to plant each type of seed.

—Make a small layout of your garden plan to help you remember where to plant all those seeds.

—If you have a produce stand (see the project on page 130), paint an advertisement for it.

—Hide something wonderful in your garden, and then draw a treasure map. See if anyone's observant enough to figure out what those circles and lines on your apron are!

—Flowers, fairies, vegetables, worms, fruits, and bugs all make good subject matter.

3. Color in your design. (If you want your design to last, make sure you use markers or paints that are permanent and washable.)

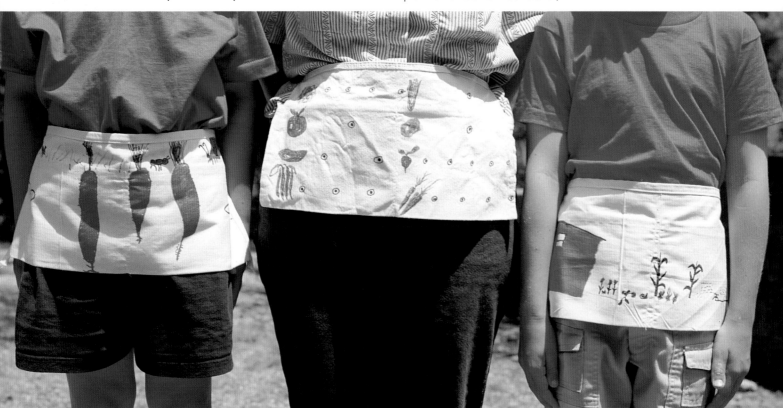

SEED CADDY

Living things are happier when they have what they need. This is just as true for gardeners as it is for earthworms and bees. When you're bent over your planting beds, with markers and pens falling out of your pockets and seed packets being trampled underfoot, you may feel that you're missing only one thing—an extra pair of hands. Gardening this way is frustrating. This project will hold much of what you need as you move about the garden.

What You'll Need

A 3/4 by 5-1/2 by 14-1/2-inch board (Handle)
2 3/4 by 3-1/2 by 16-inch boards (Sides)
2 3/4 by 3-1/2 by 10-3/4-inch boards (Ends)
2 3/4 by 3-1/2 by 5-inch boards (Dividers)
A piece of 1/4-inch-thick plywood, at least 17 by 17 inches
A tape measure
A pencil
A square
A crosscut handsaw
An electric drill and 1/4-inch bit
A hammer
A nail set
40 8-penny finishing nails
20 4-penny galvanized shingle nails
A coping saw
A rasp or wood file
A friend
100-grit sandpaper
Exterior latex primer and paint
Paintbrushes

Tips

Before they start this project, beginning woodworkers should turn to "Woodworking Highlights" on page 132.

The primer, paint, and paintbrushes are optional.

If your lumber supplier will cut the lumber pieces to length for you, he or she will save you a lot of hard work!

If you have a 1-inch hole saw, you can use it instead of the 1/4-inch drill bit.

What to Do

1. With your tape measure, pencil, and square, measure and mark the lumber pieces for cutting. Then use your handsaw to cut along the marked lines. Don't cut the plywood bottom just yet (see Photo 1).

Photo 1

2. Before you shape the handle piece, you'll need to mark it to show where the dividers will butt up against it when the project is assembled. Set the handle piece down flat in front of you. Using your tape measure and measuring from one end of the handle, make marks along the bottom edge at 4, 4-3/4, 9-3/4, and 10-1/2 inches.

3/4" x 5¹/2" x 14¹/2"
HANDLE PIECE

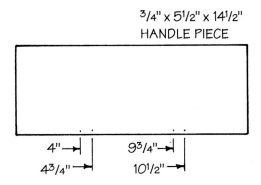

4"
4³/4"
9³/4"
10¹/2"

Kids who are more comfortable working with metric measurements will find a metric conversion chart on page 142.

3. With your pencil and square, draw a line from each mark up towards the top edge of the board.

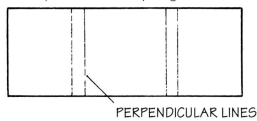

PERPENDICULAR LINES

4. To mark the finger slot in the handle, draw two 5-inch-long lines parallel to the top edge of the board, 1 inch and 2 inches down from that edge. Center these 5-inch-long lines between the lines you drew in Step 3.

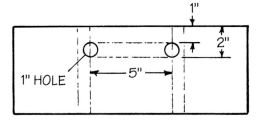

1"
2"
1" HOLE
5"

5. With your drill and 1/4-inch bit, bore two circles between the 5-inch-long lines, one at each end.

6. Draw the curved shape along the top edge of the handle (see Photo 2). Start the curved line 3-1/2 inches up from the bottom edge of the handle.

Photo 2

7. To cut out the handle slot, take the coping-saw blade out of one end of its frame, and slip the loose end of the blade through one of the holes you drilled. Tighten the blade back into the frame (see Photo 3). Make sure that its teeth are set at 90 degrees to the handle (see Photo 4), and then saw along the marked lines between the holes until the wood inside the finger slot drops out.

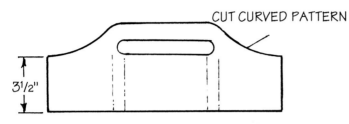

CUT CURVED PATTERN

3½"

Photo 3

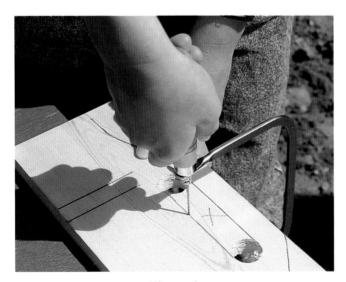

Photo 4

8. Also use your coping saw to cut away the curved shapes on the handle piece (see Photo 5).

Photo 5

9. With your rasp or file, smooth the rough edges on the top edge of the divider (see Photo 6).

Photo 6

10. Place a side piece flat down in front of you. Measuring from one end, make pencil marks along the bottom edge at 4-3/4, 5-1/2, 10-1/2, and 11-1/4 inches. Use your square and pencil to draw lines straight up from each mark. When you assemble the project, you'll use these lines to position the dividers.

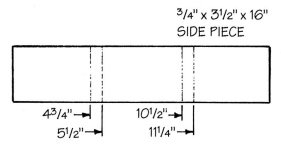

3/4" x 3¹/2" x 16"
SIDE PIECE

4³/4" → | 10¹/2" →
5¹/2" → | 11¹/4" →

11. Place an end piece flat down in front of you, and make two marks, 5 inches from one end and 5 inches from the other. Then draw lines straight up from the marks, just as you did with the other two pieces. Repeat with the other end piece. You'll use these lines to position the handle.

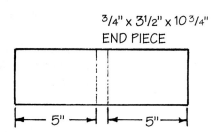

3/4" x 3¹/2" x 10 ³/4"
END PIECE

← 5" → | ← 5" →

12. Now it's time to assemble all the parts. First, place the dividers between the pairs of lines on the handle piece. Fasten them in place by using your nail set and hammer to drive 8-penny finishing nails through the handle and into each divider.

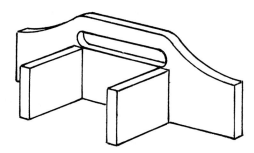

13. Attach the marked side piece to the other ends of the dividers, lining the dividers up inside the paired lines and hammering finishing nails through the side piece.

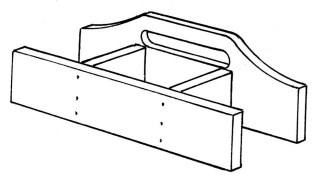

14. Attach the end pieces and the other side piece in a similar fashion.

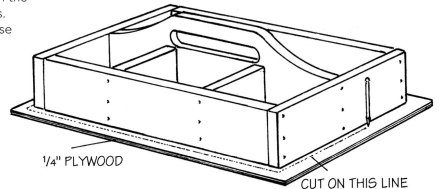

1/4" PLYWOOD

CUT ON THIS LINE

15. Place the assembled frame down on top of the plywood, and ask a friend to hold it steady. Trace the outline of the frame onto the plywood, holding your pencil straight up and down against the frame so that the plywood bottom will be slightly larger than the bottom of the frame.

16. Cut out the plywood bottom with your handsaw.

17. Sand all the parts well, especially the edges and corners.

18. Turn the frame upside down, and use 4-penny shingle nails to fasten the bottom piece to the bottom of the frame.

19. To protect your caddy from moisture and to make it more attractive, paint it with latex primer and a couple of coats of latex paint, letting each coat dry before you apply the next.

What You'll Need

A hanging basket
A plastic bag the size of your basket
1 cup aquarium charcoal
1 cup foam packing material (also known as "popcorn")
Potting soil
Compost or worm castings
A trowel
Presoaked sphagnum moss
Any of these started plants:
    Lobelia
    Geranium
    Ivy
    Vinca
    Portulaca
    Trailing nasturtium
    Trailing cherry tomato
    Petunia

Tips

Be sure to soak the moss in water for a few hours, so that it doesn't drain moisture from the basket after you drape it on top.

Choose plants that suit the location you've chosen for your basket: shade-loving plants for shady locations and sun-loving plants for sunny locations.

What to Do

1. In the bottom of the plastic bag, mix the charcoal and popcorn.

2. Add some soil, and place the plastic bag inside the basket, arranging it so that there are no folds in the plastic.

3. Set your plants into the soil. Add more soil, and firm it around the transplants. Tuck the top edges of the bag down where they can't be seen, and water the plants well.

4. To decorate the basket and disguise any visible parts of the plastic bag, drape the top of the soil with presoaked sphagnum moss.

5. To make a hanger for the basket, tie a loop of ribbon through its back.

6. Water the basket at least once a week, or whenever it dries out. Once a month, add 1/4 inch of earthworm castings or compost to the surface of the soil, or give your hanging plants some manure tea or commercial organic fertilizer.

HANGING GIFT BASKET

This is one of those homemade gifts that you'll like so much you won't want to give it away. Plan on making at least two! Tie a handwritten card to the basket you give away, with the names of the plants in the basket and instructions for watering and fertilizing. You might even want to include a gift-wrapped box of worm castings!

A list of some suitable plants are included with this project, but you can use almost any plant that will grow in a container.

GOURMET FLOWER CUPCAKES

Edible flowers can turn ordinary cupcakes into mysterious, funny, nourishing, and beautiful treats.

—Mysterious because eating flowers is a new experience for many people

—Funny because eating flowers may strike you as just that

—Nourishing because many flowers are full of vitamin C and minerals

—Beautiful because...Just look at the photo!

Kids in your class or neighborhood may be surprised to see you eating flowers on your cupcakes. Make enough to share, and your friends will be even more surprised to find themselves enjoying the taste!

If you've already planted edible flowers in your garden, you just need to pick them. If you haven't, plant some next year; you'll find some edible flowers described in Chapter One. Make sure that the flowers you pick are edible.

The fresher the flowers are, the better they'll look, so pick them right before you need them, or wrap them gently in a cotton towel, and keep them in a cooler or refrigerator until you're ready to use them.

Any cupcake and frosting recipes will work. The two here will get you started.

Carrot Cupcakes

3 cups unbleached all-purpose flour
2 cups sugar or 1-1/2 cups maple syrup
1 teaspoon salt
1 tablespoon baking soda
1 tablespoon ground cinnamon
1-1/2 cups canola or vegetable oil
4 large eggs, lightly beaten
1 tablespoon vanilla extract
1-1/2 cups walnuts, shelled and chopped
1 cup shredded coconut (without added sugar)
4 large raw carrots, pureed in blender or food processor, or 1-1/3 cups cooked, mashed carrots
3/4 cup crushed pineapple, drained
A blender or food processor
Measuring spoons
A measuring cup
Cupcake pans
Oil for pans (or paper cupcake liners)
A large mixing bowl
A stirring spoon or mixer
An egg beater
A knife
A cooling rack
Edible flowers (nasturtiums and bee balm)

What to Do

1. Preheat the oven to 350°F (177°C). Oil the cupcake pans, or insert paper liners.

2. Place the dry ingredients into the mixing bowl.

3. Add the oil, eggs, and vanilla. (If you're using maple syrup instead of sugar, add it now.) Beat the mixture well.

4. Fold in the walnuts, coconut, carrots, and pineapple.

5. Pour the batter into the cupcake pans. Bake for 20 to 25 minutes or until the edges have pulled away from the pan and the tops have browned a bit. To check, insert a knife into one cupcake; when the blade comes out clean, the cupcakes are done.

6. Remove the cupcakes from the pans, and cool them on a rack for one or two hours. Make the frosting while you're waiting (see the next recipe).

7. Ice the cupcakes.

8. Arrange the edible flowers on the icing, and keep the cupcakes refrigerated until it's time to eat.

Cream Cheese Icing

1 16-ounce package cream cheese
1 teaspoon vanilla extract
1-1/2 cups confectioners' sugar or 1 cup maple syrup
A blender (or a mixing bowl and stirring spoon)

What to Do

1. Blend the three ingredients, and the icing is done! Keep it refrigerated until you use it.

BATHTUB GARDENING

For everyone who enjoys gardening, warm weather brings a wild urge to participate in the growing season. For people in wheelchairs and for people who have no yards, this can pose a challenge. If a wheelchair keeps you from working comfortably at ground level, why not bring ground level up to you—by filling a bathtub with soil? If you don't have a yard, why not create a bathtub garden outside your apartment building? We have a bathtub planter right in the heart of our garden, and we've filled it with toad lilies, sedum, asters, and other flowers.

First, you'll need to find a tub. Most landfills and junkyards will let you have one for next to nothing. All you'll need is help hauling it and getting it set up. If the tub isn't quite high enough for you, place it on cinder blocks.

What You'll Need
A bathtub
2 to 4 cinder blocks
2 flat rocks
About 20 round rocks
Garden soil or potting soil
Presoaked peat moss or damp shredded newspaper
Compost, aged manure, or worm castings
A shovel
A few earthworms
Plants or seeds
2 or 3 muscular adult helpers

What to Do

1. Find a level spot for your bathtub garden.

2. If you're using cinder blocks, place them so that they'll support the weight of the tub.

3. Your tub must be lower at the drain-hole end so that rainwater will drain out instead of sitting in the tub. To raise the other end of the tub, set the flat rocks under it (or on the cinder blocks at that end).

4. Have your adult helpers set the tub in place, with the drain hole at the lower end.

5. To make sure the tub is stable, test it by trying to shake it. If it wobbles, adjust the rocks, or replace them with flatter ones.

6. Spread out the round rocks in the bottom of the tub. These will also help with drainage.

7. Make a mixture of 1/3 garden soil, 1/3 peat moss or shredded newspaper, and 1/3 compost, aged manure, or worm castings. Shovel the mixture into the tub, leaving about 4 inches unfilled at the top.

8. Add a few earthworms to the soil. You're ready to plant! (See the tips that follow these instructions.)

9. Give your tub the same care that you would give any container planter. Water it when it's dry, and every three weeks or so, add manure tea or liquid organic fertilizer. Just before the cold months come along, cover the soil in the tub with leaves, straw, animal bedding, or a crew-cut cover crop of rye grass.

Tips on What to Plant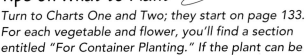

Turn to Charts One and Two; they start on page 133. For each vegetable and flower, you'll find a section entitled "For Container Planting." If the plant can be grown in a container, it can be grown in a bathtub.

Some plants such as mint and bee balm are invasive, which means that they spread quickly and can take over a garden in no time. Growing these plants in tubs keeps them from kidnapping precious garden space. Tubs also make great cutting gardens when they're planted with colorful flowers.

If your tub still has an old shower pipe attached to it, plant beans near the pipe, and they'll climb right up. If the old shower-curtain frame is attached, tie several pieces of twine to the frame, and the beans will climb up and look like a shower curtain.

Kids who are more comfortable working with metric measurements will find a metric conversion chart on page 142.

LOOFAH SPONGES

The loofah is a type of gourd. Its inner surface, once dried, makes a wonderful sponge for washing dishes, glasses, narrow jars, and our own bodies. In the tropics, absorbent loofahs are sometimes used as padding inside pith helmets; they absorb perspiration from sun-baked heads! Years ago, giant steamships used them as oil filters.

Washing your skin with a loofah is wonderfully refreshing, but there are other advantages to a good scrub with the lining of this gourd. First, it will gently scrape away the dead, outer cells of your skin and open up clogged pores. (Your skin cells are reproducing all the time. Though you may not have noticed, you're shedding old skin at this very minute!)

Second, stimulating your skin with exercise, sunshine, and a loofah sponge, can help to stimulate the fifty thousand miles of capillaries (or tiny blood vessels) just underneath the surface of your skin. When these vessels are stimulated, your blood flows

more easily through them and keeps your internal systems running smoothly. Vigorously scrubbed skin also stimulates hormone and oil-producing glands and helps skin to eliminate wastes.

What You'll Need

A loofah
A large canning kettle
Detergent

Tip

For planting and growing directions, turn to page 95. Loofahs are grown in the same way as other gourds.

What to Do

1. Leave the loofah gourds on the vine until they're ripe or until the vines are killed by frost.

2. Harvest the gourds, leaving a couple of inches on each stem. Tie a long piece of string to each stem, and hang the loofahs in a dry, warm, well-ventilated place for three to six months to dry.

3. When the loofahs are completely dry, soak them in a canning kettle filled with water until their coverings and insides soften. This may take several days.

4. When the loofahs start to fall apart, remove their outer coverings by rubbing the gourds together.

5. Remove the seeds.

6. Wash the loofahs thoroughly in soapy water, changing the water several times. Then rinse them well.

7. Hang the loofah sponges out to bleach and dry in the sun.

LIGHTNING BUG FLASHLIGHT

Lightning bugs (also called *fireflies)* are *nocturnal*, which means that they sleep during the day and are active at night. How convenient when you want them to cooperate and become a flashlight for you! Just for one evening. Just so that you can walk in the darkness with a bit of natural, mysterious light.

Have you ever wondered why these bugs light up? Their lights are mating signals. While they're flying, the males give off six quick flashes of light in a row. The females, usually resting on stems of grass, answer exactly two seconds later. Lightning bugs also light up when they're alarmed or hear loud noises. Clap your hands, and watch the response.

The light that lightning bugs give off is called *bioluminescence. Bio* means life and *luminescence* means glow. If you've ever touched a light bulb that's been burning for awhile, you know that it's hot. Most light gives off heat as well as light, but bioluminescence is cold.

What do lightning bugs eat? Nothing, if they're adults. Only the young larvae *(glow worms)* need food. These baby lightning bugs, which live and feed underground and which look like worms, are less than 1/8 inch long. Their jaws are curved and pointed. When they bite an earthworm or a snail, the poison in their digestive juices turns their prey into a liquid meal. During their second or third summer, they *metamorphose* (change into another form).

What You'll Need
2 plastic bags
A small can
A can opener
2 rubber bands
Lightning bugs

What to Do
1. Catch some lightning bugs. It's easiest to see them when the temperature is above 80°F (27°C) and the moon is hidden. When you catch them, put them gently into a jar, and watch to see if their flashing patterns change. Study them closely. Can you see their compound eyes? These eyes are made up of hundreds of small, flat eyes.

2. Remove both ends of the can, and wash it well.

3. Slip one of the plastic bags over one end of the can, and fasten it with a rubber band.

4. Place the lightning bugs in the open end of the can.

5. Slip the other plastic bag over the open end of the can, and secure it in place with a rubber band. If the bags droop, blow a little air into them before you fasten the second bag in place.

6. Think of this lightning-bug flashlight as a luxurious two-room mobile home with a hallway, but don't keep your lightning bugs in it for longer than an hour or two. Let them light your way around for an evening walk, thank them, and then set them free. Their mission is to lay eggs and reproduce, which they can't do when they're cooped up in a flashlight.

Cold Frame

One reason why people grow their own vegetables is to capture the special taste of food that's eaten right after it's picked. Much of the produce that we buy at the grocery store lacks this fresh taste because it's harvested before it matures; it ripens as it waits for you to buy it!

How can you guarantee that you'll have fresh vegetables when it's too cold to grow them in your garden bed? Build and use a cold frame. This sun-warmed box will extend your growing season by protecting the vegetables planted inside it. When you want minute-old lettuce for your sandwiches and salads, just dash out into the frosty garden, and harvest the lettuce from the cold frame.

You'll use your cold frame when the weather begins to warm up, too. To help your transplants adjust to outdoor weather (a process known as *hardening off*), place the containers inside the frame for a few days. Then transfer the plants to your garden bed.

During very cold weather, keep the lid closed so that heat from the sun will be trapped inside the frame. When the sun is shining and temperatures aren't quite as cold, use a stick to prop up the lid. If you don't do this, the plants inside may bake.

What You'll Need
A window sash from a double-hung window
A tape measure
A pencil and some paper
A square
A 1-1/2 by 9-1/2 by 96-inch board (Parts A, B, and C)
A 1-1/2 by 7-1/4 by 30-inch board (Part D)
A crosscut handsaw
An electric drill and 1/8-inch bit
12 No. 8 by 3-1/2-inch deck screws or 16-penny nails
2 pieces of drywall, 2 by 3 inches each, cut from an old tire (see "Tips")
8 No. 8 by 1-1/2-inch deck screws

RUSTIC TRELLIS

Make this project for upwardly mobile plants—the ones that want to live where there's a view! The rough bark on the branches you use will make climbing easy for your plants. Branches are free, of course, and their shapes look natural in the garden. Any branches will do, but branches from hardwoods, including oak, locust, maple, and birch, will last longer than softwood branches, which you'll have to replace each year.

What You'll Need

3 or 4 branches, each 4 inches thick and 7 to 9 feet tall
A few smaller branches
A pencil
Paper
Strong cotton or nylon twine
A hammer
Nails

Tip

To gather branches, look for a neighbor who's been cutting up firewood, or take a walk through the woods or a park after a heavy rain. Ask for some from a friend or family member who lives in the country.

What to Do

1. To design your trellis, first imagine it as a sturdy wall made up of big branches with smaller branches tied across them. Then spread your branches out on the ground so that you can see what each one looks like.

2. Play around with some designs by moving the branches around. The largest ones will form the basic structure, so arrange them in a row. Their thickest sections, which will be placed in the soil, should go at the bottom. The smaller branches will be fastened between the large branches to make a trellis pattern and to stabilize the trellis. Every small branch should stretch over at least one big branch, or better yet, two.

3. Sketch or memorize the design you like best, so you'll remember how to assemble the branches later.

4. One by one, dig 12-inch-deep holes in your garden bed, one for each of the main branches. Put the thickest part of each tall branch in its hole, and pack the dirt firmly around it.

5. Tie the smaller branches to the branches that are standing up. Hammer a few nails into the branches where they cross each other.

6. After you've tied the branches together, run some twine back and forth across the trellis as if you were making a spider web, tying the twine to the branches wherever it crosses them. By adding this web of twine to the trellis, you'll be giving your future bean plants some extra climbing surfaces.

7. Plant your seeds, and settle back to watch them make their ascent.

CLOTHES POOFS

Centuries ago, people thought that taking baths and showers was unhealthy. You can imagine what they smelled like! To disguise the bad odors in their clothes, they made *sachets* (cloth bags filled with sweet-smelling herbs), which they put in their closets. Their clothes picked up the wonderful herbal scents.

Though we don't need sachets for the same reasons today, we still use them to add fragrance to clothes and to rooms. They make great gifts, too, especially when you grow the herbs to put inside them. Toss a few poofs in with your stationery, fold a few into your linen, carry a couple in your purse or backpack, tie them to gift-wrapped packages, and tuck one under your pillow to sweeten your dreams.

What You'll Need

Fragrant dried herb-and-flower filler
Dried lemon or orange peels (optional)
String
A 12 by 24-inch piece of fabric
Pinking shears
A ruler
A pencil
A needle (or sewing machine) and thread
An adult helper
Straight pins

Tips

You won't need the sewing machine or adult helper if you know how to stitch by hand.

Fillers can be bought at crafts-supply stores. Ask the salesperson where to find potpourri, which is what mixed dried herbs are called. If you'd like to make your own potpourri, follow Steps 1 through 3 of the instructions. If you buy potpourri, start with Step 4.

What to Do

1. To make your own potpourri, first wait for a hot, dry day. Then cut some stems of several different herbs and flowers that smell good to you. Lavender, roses, and basil, for example, are all used to make potpourri. Keep each bunch of herbs separate.

2. Tie strings around the stems of each bunch, and hang the bunches upside down in a dry, well-ventilated place until the leaves and flowers are as dry as paper.

3. Remove the flowers and leaves to use as filler, and discard the stems. (Add some small pieces of dried orange or lemon peel if you like.)

4. Fold the fabric in half to make a 12 by 12-inch square, with the best-looking side of the fabric facing out. Then place the fabric in front of you, with the fold at the bottom.

5. Using your ruler and pencil, lightly draw three vertical lines and three horizontal lines on the fabric, to make sixteen 3 by 3-inch squares (four in each row).

6. Stitch a vertical line 1/4 inch away from each side of every vertical line that you drew. You should have six stitched lines when you're finished. Then stitch one vertical line 1/4 inch from the open right-hand edge of the folded fabric and another vertical line 1/4 inch from the open left-hand edge.

7. Stitch 1/4 inch above (but not below) each horizontal line you drew. Also stitch a line that's 1/4 inch up from the folded bottom edge of the fabric.

8. With your pinking shears, cut along the three horizontal lines you drew. You'll now have four strips of fabric "pockets." Each pocket will be open at the top. Use the shears to cut away the fold from the very

bottom row of pockets—the row that was located at the fold in the fabric.

9. Cut the rows into individual pockets. Each pocket should have one open edge and three closed edges.

10. Fill the pockets with the potpourri mix, but don't pack them too tightly.

11. Pin the pockets with straight pins to keep the filler in place. Then stitch a line 1/4 inch from each open edge to close every pocket.

12. The poofs can be decorated with ribbons and dried flowers, although your fabric may be so colorful that it doesn't need any decoration.

13. Before the poofs become your personal sachets or gifts for friends, try a game of hide-and-seek, or, in this case, hide-and-sniff!

DECORATED WATERING CAN

Let's say it's raining and cold outside. You've ordered your seeds from garden catalogues, and you're so anxious to get started that you're about to dive into those catalogue photos of fresh corn and watermelons. Here's a project to keep you busy until the soil dries out and warms up.

What you'll be doing when you make this project is called *decoupage*—the art of decorating surfaces with cutouts.

What You'll Need

Seed catalogues and garden magazines
Scissors
Newspaper
A plastic watering can
Clear waterproof glue
A small container for the glue
A 1-inch paintbrush
A waterproof marker

What to Do

1. Cut out some pictures that appeal to you—pictures of bugs, flowers, people eating popcorn, earthworms, violets—whatever you like.

2. Spread some newspaper out on your work surface.

3. Pour some glue into a small container, and use your paintbrush to apply the glue to the backs of your pictures.

4. Press the pictures onto the watering can, but leave the handle bare. Pictures there might wear off. Let the glue dry completely.

5. Paint a coat of glue over the pictures and the plastic watering-can parts around them, but don't get any on the handle. Let the glue dry again.

6. Sign the bottom of your decorated watering can, and date it. Who knows? You might become a famous artist someday. In the meantime, people will know who made the lovely and unusual watering can.

Electric Onion Experiment

All living and nonliving things are electric in nature—even you. This experiment, modeled on one from our local junior high school, will demonstrate how an onion can be used to generate electricity.

The science department at our junior high constructed a clock powered by onions—a clock that's been keeping time for over a year. Centuries ago, long before modern scientists studied electricity, Mayan civilizations appear to have used onions as batteries.

What You'll Need
1 large onion
A voltmeter
1 3-inch-long strip of zinc
1 3-inch-long piece of 12-gauge electrical wire

Tips

Ask someone in your school science department if you can borrow a voltmeter for a day. You might also ask your science teacher about helping you make an onion-powered clock.

Look for zinc at your local hardware store. While you're there, buy the 12-gauge wire, and ask the salesperson to expose about 1 inch of copper at each end by stripping away the plastic coating.

A lemon will work just as well as an onion. The man who invented the first electric cell used a piece of cardboard soaked in salt water!

What to Do

1. First, let's learn a little about electricity. Matter is made up of *protons*, which don't move around much, and *electrons*, which like to move around. Each material is made up of different electrons, and electrons are more attracted to some materials than to others.

When you take two different materials (such as copper and zinc) and provide a liquid contact between them (such as a juicy onion), the electrons will be more attracted to one material than to the other. In this case, they'll be more attracted to the zinc. When the two wires of a voltmeter are hooked up to the two materials, the electrons will flow from the copper, through the liquid in the onion, towards the zinc, through the voltmeter and back again, around and around. What you've done by connecting the two materials to the voltmeter is create an electric circuit. The movement of the electrons produces electricity, which is measured with the voltmeter.

2. Now let's put this theory into action. Stick one end of the strip of zinc into the onion.

3. Stick one bare copper end of 12-gauge wire into the onion.

4. You'll see that the voltmeter has wires attached to it: a red wire and a black wire. Turn the voltmeter on, and press the black wire tightly against the copper and the red wire against the zinc.

5. Watch the hand or digital readout on the voltmeter register the amount of electric charge. You've just created what's called an *electric cell*. When several electric cells operate together, they're called a battery.

Tip

When scientists first discovered electricity, they experimented using dead frogs. By creating a circuit just like the one in this onion experiment, they managed to get the leg of a dead frog to twitch. The scientists were tremendously excited because they thought that they might be able to bring dead things back to life. They didn't realize that although you can make the electrons in nonliving matter move, life involves more than moving electrons and twitching legs!

Tool Station

 Things of value deserve a special home. Good tools aren't easy to come by, so if you're fortunate enough to have some, take good care of them by putting them in this tool station when you're through for the day. You'll know just where to find them when you need them.

What You'll Need

1 3/4 by 5-1/2 by 60-inch board
1 36-inch length of 1/2-inch-thick dowel
A pencil
A square
A crosscut handsaw
A tape measure
An electric drill and 1/2-inch bit
Waterproof wood glue
A hammer
A damp rag
100-grit sandpaper
An adult helper
Wall-mounting hardware
Exterior latex primer and paint
Paintbrushes

Tips

If you're new to woodworking, see "Woodworking Highlights" on page 132.

The primer, paint, and paintbrushes are optional.

Before building this project, decide where you want to put it. (Locating it in a shed or under an overhang will protect your tools from rain.) Then take your adult helper with you to the hardware store, and ask the salesperson to help you find the hardware that you'll need to attach the tool station to the surface you've chosen.

Next to your station, set out a bucket filled with sand. Pour some used motor oil into the sand, and mix it up well. Every time you're ready to hang up a tool, plunge its metal head into the bucket a few times. The sand will scrub off the dirt, and the oil will protect the tools from rust.

What to Do

1. To decide how long to make the back of your tool station and where to put the dowel pegs, first place the 60-inch-long board flat on the ground.

2. Rest the heads of your tools on the board, starting about 4 inches from one end. Leave about 4 inches between each tool, and make sure you've placed the heads where they'll actually be positioned once the pegs are in place.

3. With your pencil, trace the outline of each tool onto the board. Then make a mark on each side of every handle, so that you'll know where to put the dowel pegs. Try to keep the marks even along the length of the board by imagining that you're making them all on one straight line.

4. Make a mark on the edge of the board, about 4 inches beyond the last tool shape. Then remove the tools.

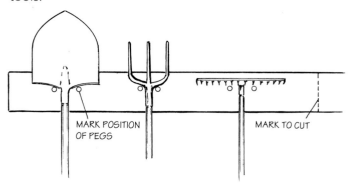

MARK POSITION OF PEGS   MARK TO CUT

5. Use your square and pencil to draw a line across the board at the mark you made in Step 4.

6. Use your handsaw to cut the board at the marked line.

7. With your drill and 1/2-inch bit, drill a hole all the way through the board at every peg mark you made in Step 3. Hold the drill at an angle so that the pegs will slant downward into the board.

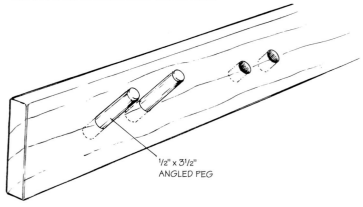

1/2" x 31/2" ANGLED PEG

Kids who are more comfortable working with metric measurements will find a metric conversion chart on page 142.

8. Count the number of peg holes. Then, using your tape measure and pencil, mark one 3-1/2-inch-long section on the long piece of dowel for every peg hole you counted.

9. To make the pegs, just cut the dowel at each mark you made in the last step.

10. Smear a little glue inside a hole in the base, and put a few drops on the end of a dowel peg. Then use your hammer to tap the glue-covered end of the dowel all the way into the hole. (Don't let the peg stick out the back of the board.) Repeat this step to glue all the dowels into the holes.

11. Use a damp rag to wipe up any smears of glue.

12. After the glue has dried, sand the tool station well.

13. If you want to paint this project, apply one coat of primer and two or three coats of paint. Be sure to let each coat dry thoroughly before you apply the next one. To keep track of which tool goes where, paint each tool shape on the station.

14. Have an adult helper attach the rack to the surface you've selected.

15. Hang up those tools!

HOMEMADE BUG SPRAY

When you notice tiny holes in your lettuce leaves and stinkbugs walking all over your loofahs, it's definitely time for action. To keep all your plants free of holes and footprints, you can pick off the bugs by hand, but it's easier to repel them with this basic (and very stinky) spray. Adjust the recipe if you like, and test your own concoction to see how well it works.

What You'll Need

1 gallon hot water
8 cloves garlic, peeled and crushed
1 tablespoon dried hot pepper (cayenne)
1 teaspoon pure soap
Measuring spoons
A 1-gallon jug
A piece of cheesecloth
A mixing bowl
A friend
A spray bottle
A homemade label for the spray bottle
Masking tape

Tips

Watch your plants closely so that you'll be ready to nip bug problems in the bud. Bugs multiply at amazing rates, and the longer they have to reproduce, the harder it is to stop them.

Don't use detergents or dish-washing liquids in this recipe. You'll find pure soap at many hardware and health-food stores.

What to Do

1. Mix the hot water, garlic, hot pepper, and soap in the jug. If you have an old blender that won't be used for anything else, blend these ingredients with a little water before placing them in the jug with the rest of the water. (Throw in a few of the bugs that you'd like to rid of, too. Some people believe that blended bugs scare off their insect relatives!)

2. Let the mixture sit for a day or two.

3. Ask your friend to hold the cheesecloth over the bowl while you pour the mixture through it.

4. Pour the strained liquid from the bowl back into the jug.

5. Fill your spray bottle with the solution. Make a label, and display it clearly on the bottle so that no one tries to clean windows with it by mistake!

6. Spray any garden plants that show evidence of bug damage, even if you can't see the bugs. The spray won't hurt the plants, but it will help keep the bugs away. Respray periodically.

Tussie Mussie

In England, during the early 1700s, *floriography*—the art of sending messages by flowers—was very popular. Different flowers and herbs came to represent different emotions. People actually communicated with each other by combining different flowers and herbs in small bouquets called *tussie mussies* and sending them to friends. By the nineteenth century, there were even floral dictionaries, and mothers taught daughters the language of flowers. Bouquets gathered from cutting gardens became ways to say things that people were too shy to say out loud.

Although not as popular today, the language of flowers and herbs is far from forgotten. Once you learn the language, you'll be able to send your own messages in tiny bouquets of fragrant flowers. Tussie mussies make delightful talking gifts!

The Language of Herbs and Flowers

Affection	Dianthus
Love	Rose
Passion	Myrtle
Devotion	Lavender
Courage and strength	Thyme
Worth beyond beauty	White alyssum
Long life and good health	Sage
Peace	Lily of the valley
Joy	Marjoram
Light	Rue
Hope	Daisy
Faith	Violet
The enchantress	Bee balm
Refinement	Butterfly bush
Profit	Cabbage
Riches	Corn
Grief and despair	Marigold
Benevolence	Potato
Haughtiness	Sunflower
Thoughts of absent friends	Zinnia

What You'll Need

Dried or fresh herbs and flowers
Adhesive floral tape
Paper doily
Scissors
Ribbon

What to Do

1. Decide what you want to say. What's the most important feeling, mood, or message you'd like to convey?

2. Select the flower or herb that matches your message, and place it in the center. In the tussie mussie shown in this photo, the main message being sent is "love." In the center of the bouquet are roses.

3. If you'd like to, add other flowers around the ones in the center, arranging them in any way that looks pretty to you. The roses in our bouquet are surrounded by rue and sage. Can you figure out what messages these herbs send?

4. Pull all the leaves off the bottoms of the stems, and wrap the stems together by winding a piece of adhesive floral tape around them.

5. Cut an X shape in the center of the doily.

6. Gently push the wrapped stems of the bouquet through the cut in the doily.

7. Just under the doily, tie a bow around the stems. Let the ribbons hang down from the sides.

8. Add a little card with a written translation of your message, or send your floral gift without any explanation, and let your friend enjoy the mystery.

GARDEN CARTOON

Imagine a film about building a house. Now imagine watching it backwards and at high speed. You'd see a lot of frantic men taking apart a house, packing the lumber onto a truck, and driving the truck backwards to the mill, where all the boards would snap back together into logs and then be trucked to the forest to become trees.

Recording sequences of events can be a playful way to watch change and growth. This project will show you three ways to make a cartoon about your garden and watch your garden's development (backwards or forwards) in a matter of seconds.

PROJECT ONE: SKETCHED CARTOON

What You'll Need

A place to sit in your garden
A spiral-bound sketch pad
A pencil
Crayons or colored markers
A few minutes, once every few days for several weeks

What to Do

1. Early in the gardening season, before you've planted anything, choose a spot to sit where you can see your garden well. Sit on the ground, or set up a special chair for yourself.

2. Sketch what you see—what you really see, not what you think things look like. Either focus on one small area of the garden, or catch as many of the garden shapes and colors as you can. Use crayons, markers, or paints to color in your sketch.

3. A few days later, sit in the same spot, at the same time of day, and on the next page of your sketch pad, sketch and color in exactly what you see.

4. Once every few days, make another drawing. Always sit in the same spot at the same time of day, sketch the same area of the garden, and use the next page of the same sketch pad.

5. At the end of the growing season, hold the sketch pad in one hand, and flip through the pages quickly with the other so that each page is visible for just a moment. The pages will move so quickly that what you see will look like an old movie being played backwards.

6. Give your cartoon a title.

Tip

Because the last picture you drew is the first picture you'll see when you flip through the pages, the cartoon will show your garden from finish to start, instead of from start to finish. If you'd like to end up with a cartoon that starts at the beginning of the gardening season and ends at the end, make your first drawing on the last page of the notebook, the next drawing on the page before, the next drawing on the page before that, and so on.

PROJECT TWO: PHOTOGRAPHED CARTOON

What You'll Need
A place to stand in your garden
A camera
A thirty-six-exposure roll of film
A small, spiral-bound notebook
Photo-mount corners
A few minutes, 3 times a week for 12 weeks

Tips

The camera and roll of film that you use shouldn't be used to take any other pictures for 12 weeks. This is a long time to hog the family camera, so consider using a disposable camera instead.

When you're tired of your photo cartoon, pick three of the best photos, and have them enlarged. Then make a three-month calendar with them for the next year.

What to Do

1. Early in the gardening season, find a good spot from which to take a picture of your garden.

2. Three times a week, at the same time each day, stand in the spot you've chosen, and take a picture of your garden. Always focus on exactly the same area.

3. After 12 weeks, you'll have finished the roll of film. Get it developed.

4. Arrange the photos in order, and mount one on each page of a small, spiral-bound notebook.

5. Now flip through the notebook pages quickly. If you mounted the first picture on the first page of the notebook, you'll see a backwards "film" of your garden. Lush tomatoes will become tiny transplants, and tall pole beans will disappear into bare soil! If you mounted the first photo on the last page, you'll see your garden grow to maturity in just a few seconds.

PROJECT THREE: FILMED CARTOON

What You'll Need
A place to stand in your garden
A video camera and film
A few minutes, once every few days for several weeks

What to Do
This project works just the way Projects One and Two do, but this time, you'll capture your garden on film for a few seconds once every few days. Hold the camera still, focus on the same area each time, and use the same film. (Make sure that no one uses that film for anything else.) Always stand in the same spot, at the same time of day.

When you play back your short clips as if they were a single movie, you'll see buds bursting into flowers, vegetables growing at amazing speeds, and butterflies appearing and disappearing.

Tip

While you're at it, use the video camera to make a video letter—a guided tour through your garden. Then mail the tape to a friend. Keep a copy for yourself; you may want to show it to your own children some day.

SHOE SCRAPER

Fresh-picked sweet corn and zinnias are two things you're likely to bring indoors from your garden. Dirt, mud, and other shoe-and-boot-loving substances are some others. To keep traffic from the garden into the house popular and to make less work for the person who cleans your floors, build this shoe scraper. You'll be recycling a can at the same time.

What You'll Need

An empty can
A can opener
A tape measure
A square
A pencil
A crosscut handsaw
1 3/4 by 5-1/2 by 16-inch board
1 3/4 by 3-1/2 by 5-1/2-inch board
An electric drill and 1/8" bit
3 No. 8 by 1-1/2-inch deck screws
A No. 2 Phillips screwdriver
A hammer
An adult helper

Tips

If you're new to woodworking, see "Woodworking Highlights" on page 132 before building this project.

After you've set up your scraper, place a big rock next to it. To help shake loose any caked mud on the soles of your shoes or boots, kick the rock after you've used the scraper.

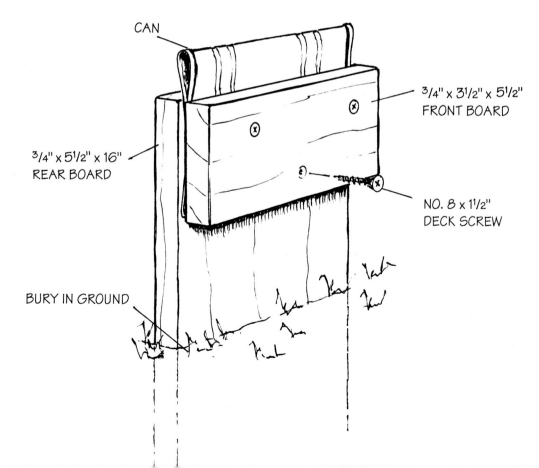

CAN

3/4" x 3¹/2" x 5¹/2"
FRONT BOARD

3/4" x 5¹/2" x 16"
REAR BOARD

NO. 8 x 1¹/2"
DECK SCREW

BURY IN GROUND

What to Do

1. Clean the can. Then use the can opener to remove its bottom.

2. Flatten the can as much as you can by stamping on it with your foot. Hammering it will also help.

3. If you haven't already cut your boards, use your square and pencil to mark across the 3/4 by 5-1/2-inch board at 16 inches. Mark across the 3/4 by 3-1/2-inch board at 5-1/2 inches. Then use your crosscut handsaw to cut the boards at the marked cutting lines.

4. With the help of an adult, use your drill and bit to bore three holes through the short piece of wood, placing the holes to form a triangle. These predrilled holes are for the screws and will make driving them into the wood much easier.

5. Place the 16-inch-long piece of wood flat down on a firm surface.

6. Place the can on the wood so that about 1 inch hangs over the end.

7. Make a can sandwich by placing the short piece of wood on top of the can. Line up one edge of the short piece with the top end of the long piece that's underneath the can.

8. Have your adult helper hold the pieces steady as you use your screwdriver to drive the screws into the holes in the small piece of wood. When the screw tips touch the can, strike them with a hammer to start them through the metal. Then use your screwdriver again to drive the screws on into the long piece of wood.

9. Bury about 10 inches of your scraper in the ground near the door to your house. Before you go indoors, run the soles of your shoes or boots across the can to scrape off the dirt.

FLOWER BED

Some time ago, we paid a visit to our friends—Suzette, Kevin, Kirsten, Chelsea, Eliana, Joshua, and their horses, chickens, dogs, cats, and rabbits. Their garden was magnificent. Just when I thought I'd seen everything a garden could offer, there it was—a flower bed! Not just any flower bed, but a real bed. Flowers had been planted in a patchwork-quilt pattern and were growing around and between a real headboard and footboard set up in the garden soil (see photo above). This bed was planted to look at, not to sleep on.

When we got home, we couldn't resist making our own version. We climbed up into the hayloft of our barn and lowered down an old metal bed frame. We set it up (springs, frame, and all) and planted climbing nasturtiums, snapdragons, and other flowers all around it. We left the area in the center bare so that we could sleep in it. Then we waited for our bed to make itself by blooming.

One night, we set up an inflatable mattress in the center of the bed, where we slept framed in moonlight and flowers. The night sounds provided the relaxing music of crickets chirping, frogs croaking, and the steady hum of a gentle breeze.

What You'll Need

A headboard and footboard or a metal bed frame with springs

Any or all of the following seeds:

Morning glories
Marigolds
Red salvia
Nasturtiums
Sweet peas
Zinnias
Snapdragons
Cosmos
Basil

A shovel
A trowel

Tips

The flowers we've listed are easy to grow and are beautiful, but choose any flowers you like. Do pick annuals, which will bloom for one season and then die back.

To make a variation of this project, set up a headboard, a footboard, frame, and springs. Then tie strings from the top of the headboard to the top of the footboard. Plant beans at both ends; they'll form a canopy when they grow over the strings.

What to Do

1. For a patchwork-quilt flower bed like the one in the photo, dig two deep trenches, 72 inches apart and about 48 inches long. Bury the bottom part of the headboard in one trench and the bottom of the footboard in the other.

2. Plant your seeds in a quilt pattern, arranging them so that the tallest plants will grow along the headboard, the medium-height ones will grow along the footboard, and the shortest ones will grow in the center.

GOURD PURPLE-MARTIN HOUSE

Gourds are old-timers in the garden. They've been found in Egyptian tombs dating back almost four thousand years and were probably used to make some of the first kitchen utensils, including water dippers and flasks. When families moved to new countries, gourd seeds were among their most treasured possessions. From the tiny, lightweight seeds, people could grow bowls, rattles, birdhouses, and shapes to stretch socks over when the socks needed darning. Gourds were also used as cider barrels, whiskey jugs, and—when soap was being made—lye kettles.

Because gourds come in many shapes and sizes, you can turn them into all sorts of things: salt-and-pepper shakers, containers, decorations for gift packages, toy whales, and birdhouses.

Dried gourds can often be purchased at crafts-supply shops and grocery stores, but the instructions that follow will teach you how to grow your own. Of course, if you buy a dried gourd, you won't need everything in the list that follows.

What You'll Need

Lagenaria gourd seed
A trellis or fence
A trowel
String
A compass (the kind used to draw circles)
A pencil
An electric drill and bits (1/8-inch and 3/8-inch)
An adult helper
A keyhole saw
A large canning kettle
Detergent
Steel wool
A bottle brush
A medium-sized screw eye
A piece of chain

Tips

Buy the screw eye and chain at a hardware store.

Other birds may very well nest in this birdhouse.

What to Do

1. Gourds need full sunlight and fertile, well-drained soil. Prepare a hill in your garden bed, by the compost pile, or next to a trellis or fence.

2. When the weather has warmed up, plant four seeds in each hill, 1 inch deep and 6 inches apart. (If your growing season is short, start your seeds indoors, and transplant the seedlings when the weather is warm.)

3. When the seedlings are 6 inches tall, thin out the two weakest looking ones. Cover the soil with mulch.

4. These plants are big eaters, so feed them once every two weeks after the gourds start to grow. They also need a lot of water. When the gourds turn creamy brown in color, they're mature. Stop watering at this point, so that the outer covering on each gourd will harden before the first frost.

5. Harvest your gourds after the first frost or after their shells are hard, whichever comes first. Leave a length of stem on each one. Tie some string to each stem, hang the gourds in a dry, well-ventilated place, and turn on your patience! Gourds take three to six months to dry.

6. Bring a dried gourd to your work area. Using your compass and pencil, mark a circle exactly 2-1/2 inches in diameter in the middle of one side of the gourd. This hole will be large enough to let purple martins bring in nesting materials, but not so large that the baby martins will fall out!

7. With help from an adult friend, use the electric drill and 3/8-inch bit to bore a hole just inside the marked circle. Then slip your keyhole-saw blade into the hole, and cut out the 2-1/2-inch circle.

8. Scoop out the seeds and pulp.

9. Fill a large canning kettle with warm water, and add a little detergent. Soak the gourd in the soapy water for fifteen minutes. Then use steel wool to scrub off the dirt and mold. Use your bottle brush to clean out the inside, too. Allow the gourd to dry completely.

10. With your drill and 1/8-inch bit, make several small holes in the bottom of the gourd. These will allow any water that gets inside the gourd to drain out.

11. Use your drill and 1/8-inch bit to make a small hole in the top of the gourd.

12. Insert the screw eye in the hole, and slip the chain over the screw eye. (You may need to open the "eye" a little by bending it with pliers. Be sure to close it again once the chain is in place.)

13. Hang your birdhouse in a sheltered area where nesting birds won't be disturbed by people, pets, or wild animals.

WILDLIFE SANCTUARY

If you supply fragrant and colorful flowers, all sorts of creatures will arrive to hover, sing, pollinate, eat, and be wild in the safety of your garden. In cities and suburbs, where development has interrupted natural habitats, it's especially important to provide wildlife with food, water, housing, and a safe place to raise young. During the colder months, when food and water aren't as plentiful, creatures appreciate them even more, so be dependable throughout the year.

Plants, which supply food and shelter naturally, are the keys to attracting wildlife. Water is especially important when cold temperatures freeze natural water sources. To provide unfrozen water during the winter, buy an outdoor water heater made for this purpose; garden-supply stores carry these.

TOAD VILLA

Have you ever looked closely at a toad's legs? They're so muscular and strong that their owner can jump up to ten feet high! Toads also have long sticky tongues that flick out to catch live insects and larvae. This makes them valuable for your garden bug wars. When word gets out that you've built this toad villa, toads will come from miles around.

What You'll Need
A shovel
2 terra-cotta flower pots

What to Do
1. Find a quiet, shady corner in your garden.

2. Turn the pots on their sides, and bury the lower side of each one (see photo).

3. Don't disturb these containers.

Tips

Another way to build a toad villa is to turn a flower pot upside down in the soil. Prop it up at an angle by slipping a small, flat rock under one edge. Toads will hop in through the crack.

If your garden lacks a pond or stream, provide a water source when you build the toad villa. Set an oil-changing pan or another shallow container in the soil near the villa so that its top is level with the soil. If the container is deeper than a toad is tall, put some rocks on the bottom so that toads can stand on them. Fill the container with fresh water.

PLANTS

Perennial and annual flowers provide nectar for butterflies, bees, and hummingbirds. Plant your flowers in large groupings, and choose ones that will bloom at different times so that flying creatures will have access to food throughout the growing season. There's one plant in particular that butterflies adore: the butterfly bush (see photo). Following are some other plants that are especially attractive to garden wildlife:

> Butterfly weed
>
> Purple coneflower
>
> Garden phlox
>
> Zinnia
>
> Marigold
>
> Cardinal flower (for hummingbirds)
>
> Pineapple sage (also for hummingbirds)

FEEDERS

Set up feeders and fill them with a sunflower, niger, and millet-seed mix during the cold months of the year. During warm weather, set out a nectar solution for hummingbirds.

SHELTER

Wildlife must have wild-looking areas in which to raise their young—areas where they'll feel safe and comfortable. Following are some ways you can help provide these:

—Plant evergreen trees and shrubs, which provide year-round protection from weather and predators.

—Plant deciduous shrubs and trees, the leaves of which fall off every season. These offer cover during warm weather.

—Set up birdhouses and toad villas (see the gourd birdhouse project that starts on page 95).

—Leave a few brush, log, and rock piles in your garden. Small animals, reptiles, amphibians, and a great variety of insects make their homes in these.

—Set up a habitat for yourself. Choose a garden spot where you can be quiet. Pay attention to the sounds and activities in your garden, or take a one-inch hike with your magnifying glass. (Keep your journal and a magnifying glass on site, and store them in a watertight container.) Sit on a comfortable rock, or, if you want shelter, make a bean tepee or canopied flower bed (see pages 55 and 94).

If you're the adventurous type, sleep out in the garden, and experience its nightlife. Brown bats are most active during the hour before sunset and the hour before sunrise; you'll probably see some. Throw a rock in the air near them, and they'll dive for it. Night owls, nighthawks, and toads will be out hunting. Crickets and katydids will sing you to sleep.

> Kids who are more comfortable working with metric measurements will find a metric conversion chart on page 142.

FOREST HONEY

The first time you taste this sweet and delicious forest honey, you'll think it was made by bees. Not so. You won't have to face any swarms when you make it. Instead, you'll take a walk in the forest when the weather is still cool and the plants are just beginning their growth cycles. Forest honey, which is full of vitamins and minerals, is made from the fresh shoots of hemlock trees or pine trees. In Germany, it's called "waldhonig," which means woods honey.

Keep in mind that the hemlock you're looking for is the hemlock tree, not the smaller, poisonous hemlock plant. Don't, don't, don't confuse the two! In fact, make sure that an informed adult helps you with this project, and stick to pine needles if you're the least bit doubtful about which hemlock is which.

What You'll Need
An adult helper
A paper grocery bag
Clippers
A stainless steel or ceramic pot
4 quarts cold water
A colander
A mixing bowl
3 cups sugar
A stirring spoon
Pine or hemlock-tree needles
A clean jar with lid

What to Do

1. Early in the growing season, fill half of a grocery bag with new hemlock-tree or pine-tree shoots. You'll find that these shoots, which grow at the tips of the branches, are a lighter shade of green than the older needles.

2. Place the needles in a big stainless steel or ceramic pot. Don't use an aluminum pot!

3. Cover the needles with the cold water.

4. Set the kettle over high heat until the water comes to a boil. Continue to boil the needles and water for about thirty minutes over medium heat. Then let the needles stand in the water overnight.

5. To remove the needles, strain the liquid through a colander and into a clean mixing bowl. Throw away the needles, and save the water.

6. Pour the water back into the pot, and heat it until it's almost boiling. Stir in three cups of sugar.

7. Turn the heat to low, and let the mixture simmer for several hours. Stir it every once in a while to make sure it doesn't stick to the bottom of the pan.

8. When the mixture is as thick as honey, it's done. Place your forest honey in a clean jar. If you don't eat this delicious project right away, place the lid on the jar, and keep the honey refrigerated.

SCARECROW

 Scarecrows keep a garden looking friendly. Crows and birds will sit on them as they enjoy the view of their buffet below.

What You'll Need for the Frame

1 3/4 by 3-1/2 by 72-inch board (Spine)
3 3/4 by 3-1/2 by 17-inch boards (Shoulders and Arms)
1 3/4 by 3-1/2 by 18-inch board (Hips)
2 3/4 by 3-1/2 by 36-inch boards (Legs)
A hammer
18 large nails
Old clothes, hat, shoes, and gloves for your scarecrow
Old clothes for you

Tips

You don't really have to measure each board for the frame. Custom design your scarecrow by scouting out scrap boards that look like a scarecrow waiting to happen.

How do you want to dress your scarecrow? A long-sleeved shirt or dress will hide its wooden arms, long skirts or pants will disguise its shapeless wooden legs, and gloves pulled up over the sleeves will cover the bare wooden "hands." Big old boots standing right underneath the costume will create the illusion that your scarecrow could run off an unwelcome guest if she or he wanted to.

What to Do

1. Look at the photo of the scarecrow frame. It's missing the arms because you need to dress the frame before you nail these pieces in place.

2. Arrange the wooden parts as shown in the photo, setting aside the arm pieces. Be sure to make the "neck" fairly long because some of it will disappear inside the scarecrow head. Fasten the parts together by hammering only one nail into each joint. Before you pound in the remaining nails, check to see that the clothes will fit. If they do, go ahead and pound two more nails into each joint. If they don't, pry apart the boards, and saw off the ones that are too long before nailing the parts together again.

3. Dress your scarecrow.

4. Push the sleeves of the scarecrow's costume up as far as they'll go.

5. Fasten the last two arm pieces in place, and roll down the sleeves.

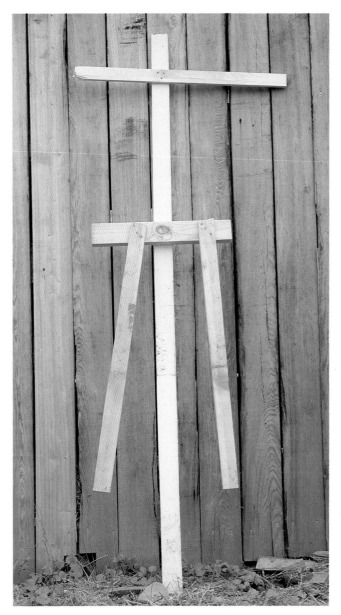

What You'll Need for the Head

Newspapers
A paper bag
A balloon
A large mixing bowl
Water
White craft glue or white flour
Acrylic paints
Exterior-grade polyurethane
Paintbrushes
A sharp knife
An adult helper
Your dressed scarecrow frame, looking for a head
A shovel

Tips

Make a head by stuffing an old pillowcase with hay, tying its open end tightly closed, and painting a face on it, or just use an existing mask. The head of the scarecrow shown on page 100 was made with a mask picked up at a yard sale. If you'd like an "airhead" scarecrow, proceed with these instructions, which will show you how to make a head by covering a blown-up balloon with paper mache.

To see a balloon-head scarecrow, turn to page 130. She's the one who's waving!

Work outdoors if you can, and wear old clothes. If you can't make your scarecrow-head outside, be sure to spread newspapers over your work surface and on the floor.

What to Do

1. Tear some newspaper into strips, and place the strips into a paper bag so that the wind won't blow them away.

2. Blow up the balloon.

3. In the mixing bowl, mix some glue or flour with water. The mixture should be as thick as syrup.

4. Dip a strip of newspaper into the mixture, and squeeze out the excess liquid by running the strip between the thumb and fingers of one hand.

5. Press the damp strip onto the inflated balloon. Keep applying strips until the whole balloon is coated with three or four layers of paper. Try to position the strips in each layer so that they run in a different direction from the strips in the previous layer.

6. Let these layers of paper mache dry completely in an airy, sheltered place, away from the rain and night air. In a day or two, the head will be dry to the touch.

7. Mix up another batch of paper mache, and use the strips to shape a nose, lips, eyes, and hair on your scarecrow head.

8. Let the head dry completely.

9. Using acrylic paints, design a face for your scarecrow, and unless you plan to put a wig on the head, paint on some hair, too! Set the head aside to dry again.

10. When the paint is completely dry, brush on one or two coats of polyurethane to protect the head from the effects of rain.

11. Have an adult helper stand by while you use a sharp knife to cut a hole in the bottom of the head. Make the hole about the size of the scarecrow's wooden neck.

12. Fit the head onto the neck.

13. Decide where you want to put the scarecrow. Then dig a hole that's deep enough to allow your scarecrow's "feet" to reach its shoes! Place the scarecrow's spine in the hole, and fill the hole up with soil again, packing the dirt down firmly with the rounded back of your shovel. Put the shoes just under the scarecrow's feet.

HANGING HEARTS

 Make these valentines for a mom, a dad, a special friend, or for the love of your life—yourself!

What You'll Need

A heart-shaped cookie cutter or a sharp knife and an adult helper

Rigid polystyrene plastic foam

Clean white paper or shelf liner

White craft glue

A 1-inch paintbrush

A small container for glue

1-1/2 cups dried lavender flowers

Assorted dried flowers and herbs

Dried rosebuds

Floral pins

1 yard of 1/4-inch-wide satin ribbon

Lavender oil (optional)

Tips

Look for the foam, dried flowers, dried herbs, and lavender oil at your local crafts-supply store.

Don't substitute newspaper for the white paper or shelf liner. Newsprint will run when it's wet and may stain your hearts.

A floral pin is just a U-shaped piece of wire.

What to Do

1. Use the cookie cutter (or the knife and your adult helper) to cut out two heart shapes from the foam.

2. Cover your work surface with white paper or shelf liner.

3. Squeeze some glue into the small container. Then, dipping your paintbrush into the container, paint the hearts with glue.

4. Sprinkle dried lavender flowers over the glue-covered hearts.

5. After the glue has dried, arrange and glue dried flowers and herbs on top of the lavender.

6. Let the hearts dry again. Then add the dried rosebuds.

7. Use a floral pin to fasten one end of the ribbon to the V-shaped cleft of each heart.

8. Add two drops of lavender oil to each heart.

9. Inhale. Look closely at the hearts. Isn't it amazing how the garden can find its way into your heart and home?

103

HOMEMADE GINGER SODA

 Commercial soda is not good news for our bones. At our local Health Adventure (a hands-on discovery center that operates out of our hospital), there's a real skeleton riding a bicycle. It demonstrates all the bone movements that pedaling a bike involves. There's also a skeleton puzzle made up of real human bones, some of which are brittle and flaky and look as if they might break easily. These are bones from people who had a disease called *osteoporosis*, which occurs when living bodies lack calcium.

In healthy bodies, calcium and phosphorus are balanced. When we consume too much phosphorus, which we do every time we drink a phosphorus-loaded commercial soda, our bodies must have extra calcium to balance the phosphorus properly. The extra phosphorus in our bodies searches for and binds with calcium. If it can't find that calcium in what we eat, it robs calcium from our bones!

Just as our plants don't thrive when the soil they grow in is too acidic or too alkaline, our bones have a difficult time when we eat and drink in an imbalanced way. Why not make a soda that tastes good and that will keep our bones energetically riding bicycles? This thirst-quenching recipe won't play hide-and-seek with the calcium in our skeletons.

What You'll Need (for 4 glasses of soda)

4 tablespoons honey

4 tablespoons apple-cider vinegar

A large glass jar or pitcher

A stirring spoon

4 glasses natural sparkling water

6 thin slices fresh ginger

Tip

Don't let the mention of vinegar prevent you from trying this delicious, sparkling drink!

What to Do

1. Place the honey and vinegar in the glass jar or pitcher. Stir until the honey has dissolved.

2. Add the sparkling water.

3. Add the fresh ginger to the sweet-and-sour water.

4. Taste the soda. What do you think? Add more honey if you like.

Kids who are more comfortable working with metric measurements will find a metric conversion chart on page 142.

104

GARDEN ART

Ever since electricity was invented, most kids' art has been exhibited behind magnets on refrigerators. That's fine, but unless your friends take walking tours of refrigerators, who gets to see your creations?

As long as you're spending time in your garden, why not plant some creative energy there by making works of garden art? Make a huge fairy-tale creature to prop up in your pumpkin patch, a larger-that-life lizard to hang on the fence with your loofahs, some earthworms to set out where they'll look as though they're burrowing into the soil, and some oversized ladybugs to threaten the aphids. People will begin to slow down as they pass your garden plot.

The best subjects for garden art are those that excite you. Get silly if you like. Make a painted fish to stand in the corn. How about heads and hands reaching out of the soil, or giant chickens and snails? You might even find that turning small, every-day things into huge garden-art creations makes them hilariously funny. What about a praying mantis the size of a pony?

What You'll Need

An adult helper

1 48 by 48-inch sheet of 1/4-inch-thick exterior-grade plywood

1 scrap board, at least 24 inches long
2 sawhorses or wooden boxes
A pencil
An eraser
A coping saw (or, with adult supervision, a jigsaw)
A hammer
3 or 4 nails
Fine sandpaper
Latex primer and paintbrush
Acrylic paints and paintbrushes
Exterior-grade polyurethane and a paintbrush

Tip

Before they start, beginning woodworkers might want to read "Woodworking Highlights" on page 132.

What to Do

1. Think about what you'd like to draw, and how to make good use of the plywood when you draw on it. Then sketch your drawing on the plywood. Make sure that the outline of the shape is especially clear.

2. Place the plywood across the sawhorses or boxes, and have an adult helper help brace it as you use your coping saw to cut along the outlines you drew. To reach each part of the outline, you'll probably need to move the plywood once in awhile. If your grown-up helper has a jigsaw, let him or her use that tool to make the cuts. If you have to use a coping saw, take your time. Cutting plywood is hard work!

3. Sand the edges of the figure so that you won't get splinters.

4. To help keep your garden art in place, make a stake for it by nailing a piece of scrap wood to its back; leave at least 12 inches of stake sticking out the bottom. (Skip this step if your design is one that you can hang up.)

5. Paint a coat of primer onto the figure, following the directions on the can. Let the primer dry thoroughly.

6. Use acrylic paints to brush on the colors and details.

7. When the paint is dry, brush on two coats of polyurethane as a protective coating. Be sure to let the first coat dry before you apply the second.

8. To set up hanging pieces, just hook them over a fence or gate. To set up standing pieces, dig a hole in the soil, put the stake in the hole, and firm the soil around the stake. For extra support, place a few rocks around the piece's base.

HYDRANGEA AND AUTUMN JOY WREATH

At the end of the growing season, bring the garden into the house by making this wreath. Autumn Joy (a late blooming sedum) and hydrangea flowers, which begin to change colors and look stunning as the weather gets colder, weave together beautifully. If you don't have either in your garden, ask for some from friends and neighbors who do. And don't forget to plant them both in next year's garden!

Many wreaths are made with flowers that have already been dried. This one, however, dries after it's assembled. Although it will fade, it will still look lovely.

What You'll Need

A metal wreath base
12 hydrangea cuttings
12 Autumn Joy cuttings
Flexible metal ties

Strawflowers, baby's breath, or statice
A spray fixative (optional)
Large paper clip

Tips

To prolong the wreath's life, you can spray it with a fixative, but you don't have to do this. Instead, when your wreath looks ready to retire, save the metal frame, give the flowers to the worms, and think about your next wreath-making project.

Wreath bases, spray fixatives, and a wide variety of dried flowers are available at many crafts-supply stores.

Autumn Joy is a hardy plant and is available at many garden stores and nurseries.

What to Do

1. Cut the fresh hydrangeas and Autumn Joy, leaving about 6 inches of stem on each one.

2. Thread the stems through the metal wreath base, and tie them to the base with flexible metal ties. Work around the frame, hiding the stems by overlapping flowers on top of them. Arrange the flowers in any design or pattern you like. Make sure to clump them very close together; as they dry, they'll shrink.

3. Add strawflowers, baby's breath, or statice as decoration.

4. To hang your wreath, bend a paper clip to make a hook. Slip one end of the hook into the wreath, and hang the other end from a nail or picture hanger.

MAKING COMPOST

I wonder if primitive cave people ever noticed the food that must have grown out of their garbage pits? Some households probably threw their rinds, pits, and leftovers into the woods or to the dogs. But I'll bet that at least one family preferred tidy piles of things. This family would have had a neat pile of wood for cooking, a pile of stones near the fire for warming their cave beds on cold nights, and a pile of hulls, spoiled fruits, and cooking scraps outside their cave. Healthy seedlings must have sprouted out of that pile. For awhile, the cave people might not have understood that this vigorous new growth came from old vegetation in the nutrient-rich pile. Then someone realized what was happening. The dawn of composting!

If your family throws kitchen scraps into the garbage, tell every family member that composting is fun, *PC* (politically correct), and productive. Not only will you be sending less garbage to the local landfill, you'll also be working on behalf of your household, the earthworms, and our planet.

Effective compost piles are more than heaps of garbage; they're built to meet certain requirements. The two projects here illustrate two different ways to make compost, by building an outdoor compost pile and by composting in a garbage-can bin that will work even if you only have a small patch of outdoor space. Both projects operate on the same basic principles. Provide air, water, and materials for the pile, turn it regularly, and you'll soon have tons of rich compost to add to your garden.

TRADITIONAL COMPOST PILE

What You'll Need

A pen
Drawing paper
A refrigerator magnet
A shovel
A covered, kitchen compost container
Branches or hedge clippings
Leaves
Grass clippings
Vegetable and fruit scraps
Egg shells
Hair
Animal manure (except dog and cat)
Soiled farm-animal bedding (old hay)
Bread and grains

What You Won't Need or Ever Put in Your Compost Pile

Black walnut husks
Meat
Fat
Sunflower shells
Coal
Dairy products
Dog and cat manure

Tip

Because compost piles usually take several weeks to decompose, you might want to build more than one. When you've built one pile, start another. As you add to the second, the first will be decomposing.

What to Do

1. Choose an outdoor spot that's on a slight slope, so that your compost pile drains properly. The closer this spot is to your garden, the better. To provide air circulation in the pile, make the first (bottom) layer out of coarse materials such as small branches or hedge clippings. This way, air will be able to move through the spaces under the pile.

2. With your pen, draw two columns on a sheet of paper. In one column, list all the materials that belong in your compost. In the other column, list the ones that shouldn't be included.

3. Display your chart for everyone to see by attaching it to the refrigerator with a magnet.

4. Place the compost container near the sink so that you can scrape plates right into it.

5. Collect outdoor materials, too. Rake up lawn clippings and leaves. Ask your neighbors for their yard waste!

6. If you've already collected a lot of materials, build the entire pile at one time by layering the different materials on top of each other. Add a shovelful of garden soil on top of each layer.

7. If you're collecting materials gradually, add them whenever you like. Everything in a compost pile will eventually decompose, but the smaller the bits of material and the more broken or bruised they are, the faster they'll break down. Before you toss in kitchen scraps, cut up big chunks such as broccoli stems, or run the scraps through an old blender. Another way to break up large scraps is to put them in a burlap bag, set the bag on a flat rock or tree stump outdoors, and pound the bag with a hammer.

8. Keep the pile as moist as a well-squeezed sponge so that the resident bacteria can do their work. Water the pile layer by layer as you build it, and whenever the pile begins to dry out. If water runs out the bottom of the pile, you're watering too much. Rainwater is the best water because it picks up oxygen, minerals, and nitrogen as it falls through the air. To help the pile catch rainwater, shape the top layer to look like a shallow dish.

9. Once in a while, punch air holes in the pile to provide for air circulation. Shove a big stick in and out of the pile in several places.

10. Turn the materials in your compost pile periodically to mix wet materials with dry ones and fresh materials with rotted ones. The temperature of the pile will help you figure out when to turn it. When organic matter decomposes, it heats up. This heat kills *pathogenic spores* (things that are capable of causing diseases in the plants and soil) and weed seeds. When compost piles have all the air, water, and finely chopped organic matter they need, they can heat up to 150°F (66°C) as often as once every three to four days! Measure the temperature with a thermometer, and whenever the temperature drops below 100°F (38°C), turn the pile. If you don't have a thermometer, turn the pile once a week or whenever it begins to smell bad or you see bluish-grey mold.

11. When the compost is finished, it will be dark and crumbly. It will also smell good, not a bit like garbage. Finished compost is full of nutrition for your garden plants.

GARBAGE-CAN COMPOST BIN

What You'll Need

A covered, kitchen compost container
An old plastic garbage can with lid
An adult helper with a sharp knife
Compost materials
A hammer
A large nail
A shovel

What to Do

1. Follow Steps 2 through 5 of the Traditional Compost Pile instructions.

2. Have your adult helper cut away the bottom from an old plastic garbage can.

3. With your hammer and nail, make holes in the sides of the garbage can. These will allow air to circulate. Make some holes in the lid, too. The lid will keep the rain from getting your compost too wet and will also provide shade to keep it from drying out.

4. Place the bottomless can over bare soil, preferably in or near your garden. Worms and microorganisms will quickly move in!

5. Once a day, empty the kitchen compost bucket into your garbage-can compost bin. Once a week during warm weather, throw in lawn clippings, leaves, and some soil. Keep the contents moist.

6. To turn the pile, turn the can over to tip out the compost. Then set the can upright again, and shovel the compost back in again.

7. Let the contents continue to compost until they're dark brown and crumbly. Then distribute the compost in your garden.

WORM CONDO

Many people know how to make outdoor compost piles, but *vermicomposting* (or composting with the help of worms) is another story—a shorter and more mysterious one. Almost overnight, banana peels, potato peelings, and other kitchen leftovers become rich, black earth.

This project—a condo for redworms—was one that we built after reading Mary Appelhof's wonderful book, *Worms Eat My Garbage: How to Set Up and Maintain a Worm Composting System* (Kalamazoo: Flower Press, 1982). Ms. Appelhof's second book on worms, written with Mary Frances Fenton and Barbara Loss Harris, is for kids and their teachers and is called *Worms Eat Our Garbage: Classroom Activities for a Better Environment* (Kalamazoo: Flower Press, 1993). If you're interested in worms, you'll want to read it, as it includes over 150 worm-related projects!

In warm weather, we keep our vermicomposter—a beautifully painted box that's cleverly disguised as a seat—on our front porch. There are no odors and very few bugs to give away the fact that inside this seat are hundreds and hundreds of worms. During cold weather, we move the box into the kitchen so that the worms won't freeze.

Inside their condo, the worms eat, reproduce, and excrete their valuable castings. It only takes these hungry creatures four months or so to digest all the scraps we throw into the condo and all the bedding that they started out with. What's left are worm castings, which offer more nutrients and vitality to plants than any other garden fertilizer available.

WHY BUILD A WORM CONDO?

—You like worms.

—You can keep worms even in places where "pets" aren't allowed.

—You like watching how quickly worm populations grow.

—You enjoy watching worms become aerobic gymnasts when you hold them.

—Worms produce the best fertilizer for your plants.

—It's convenient to be able to scrape the dinner plates right into the worm condo. You don't have to trudge out to the compost pile as often.

—Vermicomposting breaks down waste quickly and consistently

year round. Outdoor compost piles slow down in cold weather.

—You think you'd enjoy gift-wrapping a few hundred worms in a Chinese food take-out box and giving this gift to a gardening friend.

—Vermicomposting makes a great science project.

WHERE TO KEEP THE WORM CONDO

Try to set up the condo where you can feed its residents and follow their progress without having to hike too far. Some suitable places are:

—Under the sink, where it's cool and dark.

—In the basement, where it will stay cool during warm weather but where it won't freeze during the cold months of the year. Worm-phobic parents may be more comfortable about having worms in the basement.

—A garage that is well ventilated and cool but never freezing.

CONDO RESIDENTS

Night crawlers shouldn't live in condos because they don't do well in confined spaces. Redworms, on the other hand, thrive in condos, where they process large amounts of organic matter and reproduce quickly. Purchase a few redworms at a fishing or gardening store. They're sometimes called red wigglers, manure worms, red hybrids, or tiger worms.

HOW LARGE SHOULD THE CONDO BE?

The size of the condo will depend on how much waste you have to feed the worms. For a family of four to six people, build a "1-2-3" box, 12 inches deep, 24 inches wide, and 36 inches long. For a family of one to four, build a box that is 12 inches deep, 24 inches wide, and 15 inches long, or better yet, build the 1-2-3 box, and block off one half with a piece of scrap wood. This way, you can keep adding scraps to the half without worms, while your worms are busy digesting scraps in the other half.

Redworms are *surface feeders*. They like to do their eating close to the surface of the soil or bedding, so their condo should be relatively shallow.

HOW TO BUILD THE CONDO BOX

What You'll Need
3 3/4 by 11-1/4 x 34-1/2-inch pine boards (2 Sides; 1 Center)
2 3/4 by 11-1/4 by 24-inch pine boards (2 Ends)

1 24 by 36 inch piece of 1/2-inch-thick plywood

A tape measure

A pencil

A square

A crosscut handsaw

An electric drill and 1/2-inch bit

A 2-inch hole saw

An adult helper

1 pound of 2-1/2-inch galvanized ring-shank nails

A hammer

Tips

Before they start this project, beginning woodworkers should read "Woodworking Highlights" on page 132.

A hole saw fits into an electric drill in the same way a bit does. A circle of sharp teeth on the hole saw's end will cut a hole when you operate the drill. Be sure to get a 2-inch hole saw for this project.

Lumberyards carry 3/4 by 11-1/4-inch boards (known as 1 by 12s) in standard lengths. If the salesperson at the lumberyard won't cut these boards to the lengths you need, buy one 12-foot-long board and one 4-foot-long board. The instructions will tell you how to cut them apart.

What to Do

1. First, look at the photo that shows the condo standing on one 24-inch-long end piece. The two 34-1/2-inch-long side pieces stand straight up and down on the outside of the box, and the 34-1/2-inch center piece divides the box in half. Notice the holes in the center piece. These let the worms crawl back and forth from one half of the box to the other. The bottom piece also has small holes in it for drainage.

2. Before you cut the pieces from your long boards, you'll need to measure and mark cutting lines. Place the boards flat down on your work surface. Using your tape measure and pencil, mark the lengths for three 34-1/2-inch-long pieces and two 24-inch-long pieces. Then use your pencil and square to draw a line across the boards at each mark.

3. Have your adult helper hold the boards firmly in place. With your handsaw, cut along each cutting line. Use your pencil to label the five pieces after you cut them so that you'll know which piece is which. Two of the 34-1/2-long pieces are side pieces, and one 34-1/2-long piece is the center piece. Both 24-inch-long pieces are end pieces.

4. Have your adult helper use the electric drill and hole saw to bore holes in the center piece. These holes should be placed as shown in the photograph.

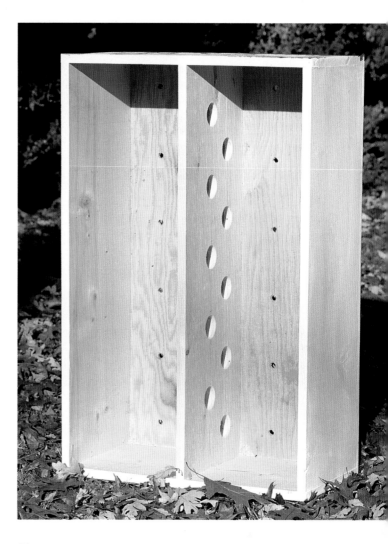

5. The bottom piece must have two rows of holes drilled in it so that moisture can drain out of the condo. To help you bore these holes in the right place, you'll need to draw two straight lines on the bottom piece. Place the piece flat on your work surface, with one short end facing you. At the bottom, measure 6 inches in from one long edge, and draw a straight line from that point all the way up to the top end of the board. Draw another line 6 inches in from the other long edge.

6. Have your adult helper hold the board steady while you use the drill and 1/2-inch bit to bore holes along each line. Space these holes about 6 inches apart.

7. To assemble the condo, use ring-shank nails to fasten the two end pieces to the ends of the two side pieces. Hammer in at least three nails at each corner.

8. Place the bottom piece on top of the frame that you've just nailed together. Use your square to make sure that each corner is 90 degrees, and then use ring-shank nails to fasten the plywood bottom to the edges of the frame.

9. Turn the box on one end, and slip the center piece in place, as shown in the photo. Drive nails through the end pieces to fasten the center piece in place. Flip the box over, and hammer a few nails through the bottom piece and into the edge of the center piece.

How to Furnish the Condo

What You'll Need
A large bucket or barrel
A shovel
Garden soil
Any combination of the materials listed in Step 1
Kitchen scraps
Redworms

What to Do
1. Outdoor redworms live in dense matted leaves and in manure piles, not in the soil. The bedding that you give them needs to be moist and dense with organic matter but loose and fluffy enough to allow the worms to burrow through it. It must also be safe for the worms to eat. Mix together any combination of the following materials:

—Shredded newspaper makes great bedding; worms love to devour current events. Stick to the black-and-white pages, though. Colored inks aren't good for worms.

—Shredded cardboard works well.

—Manure is a natural habitat for redworms. Mix aged manure with a few handfuls of soil, and moisten the mixture with water. Before you add your worms, let the

mixture heat up for a couple of days and then cool down again.

—Leaf mold is a wonderful medium. Maple leaves are less acidic than other leaves and break down more easily, too. Avoid leaves from trees close to heavy traffic. The lead from car exhaust builds up on these leaves, and you don't want to raise worms with low IQs.

—Egg shells, the calcium in which is alkaline, will sweeten acid bedding. Crush the shells before you add them to the bedding.

2. Moisten the bedding until it feels like a well-squeezed sponge.

3. Add a few handfuls of garden soil, which will introduce microorganisms to break down the compost and provide grit for the worms' digestive systems.

4. Layer the bedding and some kitchen scraps in the condo. Deep layers won't work; they'll compact and restrict oxygen, and if there's not enough oxygen in the condo, you'll know right away—it will smell!

5. Introduce the redworms to their new home by placing them on top of the bedding and giving them some time to burrow in.

How to Feed the Condo Residents

Redworms must be fed regularly. Gently mix your kitchen scraps into the bedding, or leave them on top of the bedding and cover them with a sprinkling of soil, leaf mold, or soaked and squeezed peat moss. Go easy on adding anything that contains meat, fat, or oil.

To keep the bedding moist, mist it thoroughly once a week or more often if necessary.

Different Ways to Harvest the Finished Soil

—Take 2/3 of the condo's contents (worms and all), and use it to side-dress your garden plants. The redworms may not survive in the garden, but their bodies will decompose and add more nutrients to the soil. Mix some new bedding with what remains in the condo. The worms that you didn't remove will quickly reproduce to fill the whole box.

—Gently shift the contents over to one side of the box, leaving the other side empty. Put some kitchen scraps and fresh bedding into the empty side. Let the old side finish decomposing undisturbed. Water the new side, but let the older stuff dry out. The worms will cross over to the new side as they seek food and moisture. Scoop out the finished soil from the old side, and let the new side spread out into the entire box again.

—Move the condo outdoors. Spread out an old sheet in the yard, and dump the condo's contents onto it. Make several cone-shaped piles out of the soil. After awhile, the worms will move down to the bottom of each pile. Scoop off the top of each pile for your garden, and return the rest—with the worms—to the condo.

WHAT TO DO WITH THE CASTINGS-RICH COMPOST

—Marvel at it. Be delighted by the results of your cooperative venture with worms.

—Bag it, and give it away.

—Add some to the soil next to your garden plants.

—Sprinkle some in the seed bed before planting.

—Place a handful in each hole when you set out transplants.

—Substitute 1/4 inch of castings for the top 1/4 inch of soil in houseplant containers.

—Look at it under a microscope. Look at other soil samples, and note the differences.

—Mix it in equal proportions with peat moss and garden soil to use as a fertilizer.

TROUBLE SHOOTING

—If fruit flies begin to linger around the condo, make a simple trap for them. Place about 1 inch of water in a jar, and mix in some bits of banana and a spoonful of sugar. Use a rubber band to secure a small plastic bag over the top of the jar. Poke a tiny hole in the bag. The flies will be trapped once they enter the bag. Fruit flies are sometimes persistent. If you can't control the flies and your condo is indoors, move it to the basement or outside where the flies won't bother you!

—There's no way to guarantee that bugs won't appear inside the condo, but they're not necessarily bad neighbors for your worms. Mixing in your kitchen scraps really well will help control their numbers. So will adjusting the moisture level; too much or too little invites bugs. Add peat moss to absorb extra moisture.

—If unpleasant odors develop, correct the bedding mixture to allow for more air flow.

WORM-CASTINGS EXPERIMENT

 Question: Is this stuff gold or a pile of dirt?
Answer: Both

What You'll Need

A handful of small rocks or gravel
Garden soil
Potting soil
Worm castings
2 terra-cotta pots, each 6 inches wide, with drip pans
2 container plants, same variety and size
Masking tape
A permanent-ink marker
A notebook
A pen or pencil

What to Do

1. Put several small rocks in the bottom of each pot. These will assist with drainage.

2. Fill one pot with a mixture of garden and potting soil. Fill the other pot with equal amounts of worm castings and potting soil.

3. Tape a label onto each pot so that you can tell which one has castings in it, and which one doesn't.

4. Transplant a plant into each pot.

5. Treat the two plants exactly the same. Water them at the same time, and give each one the same amount of care. Make sure they get the same amount of sun, too. Cheer them both on!

6. Record the results of your scientific experiment. While the plants are growing, keep track of their differences in your notebook or garden journal. Following are some questions to ask yourself as you conduct this experiment:

—How healthy does each plant look?

—Which plant is larger?

—Are the leaves on each plant the same color?

—If the plant is a flowering or fruiting variety, which one produced flowers or fruit first?

—Which plant produced larger flowers or fruit?

—Which plant had more problems with insects?

—What conclusions have you reached about the differences between the soil mixture and the worm castings?

We bought two ornamental kale plants for this experiment. Both were the same size and were purchased at the same time. The castings-fed kale plant now looks as if it's baby-sitting the other, much smaller plant.

COMPOST-PILE TARGET PRACTICE

This game is for gardeners who like to throw things. You get to play every time you've been weeding or gathering kitchen scraps! Make the target, set it up in front of the compost pile, and hurl the compost material in.

Give yourself two points when you get the compost in the little earthworm's mouth and one point when the big earthworm swallows it. Or just forget about scoring, and focus on aiming instead. There's no reason to limit yourself to this earthworm design. Make your target to look like something (or someone) else if you like.

What You'll Need

A pencil

An eraser

An adult helper, with or without a jigsaw

A sheet of exterior-grade plywood, at least 1/2 inch thick

2 1-1/2 by 1-1/2-inch stakes, at least 24 inches long

2 sawhorses or wooden boxes

A coping saw

An electric drill and 3/8-inch bit

Exterior latex primer and paint

Paintbrushes

100-grit sandpaper

What to Do

1. With your pencil, sketch your design on the plywood sheet. Make sure that the earthworms' mouths (or the interior cutouts on your own designs) are large enough to throw things into. Draw these cutouts fairly close to the outside edges of the design, or you won't be able to reach them with a coping saw.

2. Place the plywood across the sawhorses or wooden boxes, and have an adult helper help brace the plywood as you use your coping saw to cut along the outlines. You'll probably need to move the plywood once in awhile so that you can reach each section of the outline. If your grown-up helper has a jigsaw, let him or her use that tool to do the cutting. Take your time; cutting through plywood is hard work.

3. To cut out the mouth openings (or other interior cutouts), first use your drill and 3/8-inch bit to bore a hole just inside the sketched opening. Unfasten one end of your coping-saw blade from its frame, slip the loose end of the blade through the hole, and refasten the blade in the frame. Then use the saw to cut out the mouth shape.

4. Sand all the edges of the plywood so that you don't pick up any splinters.

5. Paint both sides of the cutout with primer, and when the primer is dry, apply two coats of paint. Follow the directions on the cans.

6. When the target is dry, carry it to the compost pile, and set it up at an angle by propping it up on the two stakes. Make sure that the stakes are set into the ground firmly so that your target won't tip over.

Tip

If you're someone who likes to take risks, here's a risk-taking game to play with your finished target. Before setting it up, staple or nail some very fine screen over the openings. Be sure the screen is firmly attached. Then sit behind the screen with your face showing through the opening. Let your friends stand at a challenging distance and throw water balloons at you. The screen will keep you from being hurt by the filled balloons, but if your friends aim well, the water will find its target—you!

APPLE LEATHER

If there are fruits you enjoy when they're in season and then miss for the rest of the year, enjoy them year round by making fruit leather. Contribute this tasty treat to your own school lunches and class snacks. Fruit leather might even qualify as a science project on preserving food. How thrilling to make a practical and delicious science project that you can eat, one that's just as good for you as it tastes!

What You'll Need

10 large apples, peeled, cored, and quartered
1 cup apple cider
Honey to taste, if the apples are tart
A blender
Cinnamon, to taste
A large stainless-steel pot with lid
A colander
A large bowl
A stirring spoon
2 or 3 cookie sheets
Oil for cookie sheets
Cheesecloth or plain brown paper
Cooling racks
Cornstarch or arrowroot
Wax paper or freezer paper

What to Do

1. Place the apples and cider in a large pot.

2. Cover the pot, and set it over low heat.

3. Cook the apples until they're soft, stirring them every few minutes to keep them from sticking. Add more cider (up to 1/2 cup) if the apples begin to stick to the bottom of the pot.

4. Separate the fruit from the juice by pouring the contents of the pot through a colander and into a large bowl. (Lift the fruit from the sides of the colander to let the juice run out.) The drier the fruit is, the easier it will be to turn it into fruit leather. Refrigerate the juice, and drink it when you're in the mood for a delicious treat.

5. Place the fruit in a blender. Blend, adding honey to taste. The mixture should be as thick as applesauce.

6. Oil your cookie sheets lightly.

7. Spread a 1/4-inch-thick layer of the apple mush onto each sheet. If the layer is too thick, it will take a very long time to dry.

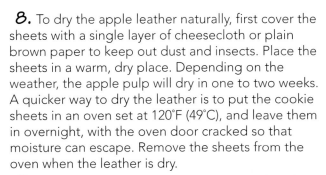

8. To dry the apple leather naturally, first cover the sheets with a single layer of cheesecloth or plain brown paper to keep out dust and insects. Place the sheets in a warm, dry place. Depending on the weather, the apple pulp will dry in one to two weeks. A quicker way to dry the leather is to put the cookie sheets in an oven set at 120°F (49°C), and leave them in overnight, with the oven door cracked so that moisture can escape. Remove the sheets from the oven when the leather is dry.

9. When the leather sheets are dry enough to be lifted up without tearing, gently pull them off the cookie sheets, and place them on cooling racks so that air will reach both sides. Cover them with cheesecloth or brown paper bags, and let them dry for another day or two.

10. When the sheets are no longer sticky, dust each one on both sides with cornstarch or arrowroot. Cover each leather sheet with freezer paper or wax paper, stack the layers, and store them in a cool, dry place.

Tip

Make leather cookies by using a sharp edged cookie cutter to cut the leather into shapes. If you have trouble pressing the cutter through the tough leather, use the cutter to press the pattern into the leather, and then cut along the pattern lines with a sharp knife. Be sure there's an adult nearby when you're using that knife!

Kids who are more comfortable working with metric measurements will find a metric conversion chart on page 142.

Herbs: From Head to Toe

Many of the things we use to take care of ourselves—hair rinses, mouthwashes, and body powders, for example—are easy to make, although you may feel like a mad but well-groomed scientist as you make them. If you don't have the herbal ingredients in your garden, buy them at your local health-food store.

Rose-Petal Bath Vinegar

Have you had a hard day? Is homework getting you down? Do you simply want a cozy treat? This rosy-red solution is a soothing and fragrant bath that will please and relax you. Make extra, pour some of the finished recipe into an attractive bottle, and give it to someone special.

What You'll Need

2 cups red rose petals
4 cups white vinegar
A saucepan
A large glass jar with lid
A measuring cup
A colander
A mixing bowl

What to Do

1. Place the rose petals in the glass jar.

2. In the saucepan, heat the vinegar, but don't let it boil.

3. Pour the hot vinegar over the rose petals.

4. Place the lid on the jar, and set the jar in a dark place. Let the petals steep in the vinegar for seven to ten days.

5. Strain the petals from the liquid by pouring the liquid through your colander and into a mixing bowl. Discard the petals.

6. Return the vinegar solution to the jar.

7. Run your bath. Before you hop in, add 1/2 cup of your Rose-Petal Bath Vinegar. Put the lid back on the jar, and store the vinegar in a cool, dark place.

Rosemary Hair Rinse

For this recipe, you'll need to make rosemary vinegar first and then dilute it with warm water. When you're finished, you should have plenty to give away!

What You'll Need

1/2 cup rosemary leaves, fresh or dried
Five quart-sized jars with lids
1 cup white vinegar
A saucepan
A measuring cup
A colander
A mixing bowl

Tip

Experiment with this recipe by substituting fresh or dried roses, sage, or basil for the rosemary.

What to Do

1. Place the rosemary in one of the jars.

2. In the saucepan, heat the vinegar, but don't let it boil.

3. Pour the vinegar over the rosemary.

4. Place the lid on the jar, and set the jar in a dark place. Let the rosemary steep in the vinegar for 7 to 10 days.

5. Strain the rosemary from the vinegar by pouring the liquid through a colander and into the mixing bowl. Discard the rosemary.

6. Place 1/4 cup of the vinegar into each of four jars. Then fill the jars with water. There you have it: Hair rinse that will remove all traces of soap and leave your hair shiny and sweet smelling! Don't be shocked by the strong vinegar smell. It fades out of your hair very quickly.

ROSE-AND-LAVENDER BODY POWDER

This is definitely a recipe to please your friends and family, so start looking for recycled, airtight containers to serve as gift boxes. Cover them with colorful paper to brighten them up.

What You'll Need

A blender or large mixing bowl
1 cup dried lavender buds and flowers
1 cup dried rose buds and petals
1 pound arrowroot powder
Patchouli or rose oil (optional)
An airtight container with lid
A powder puff or cotton balls

What to Do

1. In your blender or mixing bowl, blend the lavender and roses until they're powdery.

2. Add the arrowroot powder, and blend well.

3. For extra fragrance, add a few drops of patchouli or rose oil.

4. Store your powder in an airtight container, or its fragrance will fade. Dab the powder onto your body with a powder puff or cotton ball.

HERBAL TEA BAGS

To bring your garden indoors with you when the weather gets cold, make homemade tea bags, using your homegrown, dried herbs and flowers. If you haven't grown any this year, buy the herbs at a health-food store, and plan on growing some next year.

Cover an empty cardboard tea-bag box with colorful paper or cutouts, fill it with tea bags, make a fun, creative label to go on the outside, and you'll have a great gift for a teetotaler!

What You'll Need

Dried leaves and flowers suitable for tea
Seal-them-yourself tea bags
An iron, ironing board, and adult helper
A spoon

Tips

Borage, rosemary, sage, and peppermint leaves all make tasty teas. Mix them together to concoct your own "house" flavors.

Empty, do-it-yourself tea bags are available at many health-food stores. Be sure to read the instructions on the package; they may be different from the ones that follow.

Wrapping your completed tea bags in waxed paper will preserve their garden-fresh flavors.

What to Do

1. The tea bags often come in strips, with several bags attached to one another. Place a strip on your work surface so that the open end of each bag is facing up.

2. Use a spoon to loosely fill each bag with tea.

3. Carefully transfer the strip of bags to an ironing board, and turn the iron on low.

4. Along the open edge of the strip, you'll find an extra width of tea-bag material. Fold this over to cover the open edge, and make a crease along the fold line.

5. Carefully iron the strip down to seal the open edge. If you need to use one finger of your free hand to hold down the folded paper as you iron, be sure to keep that finger and hand out of the iron's path!

6. Separate the bags if you like, or leave them attached to one another until you're ready for a cup of tea.

7. Set a tea bag in a mug, and bring some water to a rolling boil. Pour the boiling water into the mug, let the tea steep for a few minutes, and then make a toast to the success of your project!

Zucchini Tea Cake

Sometimes, zucchini plants just won't stop producing. If you run out of friends and neighbors who are willing to accept any more zucchini as gifts, and you don't think you can face another zucchini salad yourself, try this cake recipe. Besides being delicious, this tea cake is a great way to keep the last of your huge zucchini harvest from going to waste.

What You'll Need

3 tablespoons sweet butter
3 eggs
1 cup oil
1 cup sugar
1 teaspoon vanilla extract
2 cups raw zucchini, grated
2 cups unbleached, all-purpose flour
2 teaspoons baking powder
1 teaspoon salt
1 teaspoon cinnamon
Edible flowers
Measuring spoons
Measuring cup
2 mixing bowls
Stirring spoon
1 baking pan, buttered

Tips

Any baking pan will do, as you can see by looking at the heart-shaped cake in the photo.

Turn to page 73 for a delicious icing recipe, or use one of your own favorites.

What to Do

1. Preheat the oven to 350°F (177°C).

2. Place the butter, eggs, oil, vanilla, and sugar in the mixing bowl, and beat them together well.

3. Mix in the grated zucchini.

4. In a separate bowl combine the flour, baking powder, salt, and cinnamon.

5. Add the wet ingredients to the dry ingredients. Blend them together, but avoid mixing them too much.

6. Pour the batter into your buttered pan.

7. Bake the cake in the center of the oven for about 1 hour and 15 minutes. To test the cake, insert a knife into its center. When the knife comes out clean, the cake is done.

8. Remove the cake from the pan, and let it cool.

9. Ice the cake, and don't forget to add the edible-flower decorations!

Kids who are more comfortable working with metric measurements will find a metric conversion chart on page 142.

SUNSHINE TEA PARTY

Have you ever read *Alice in Wonderland*? In this story, Alice wanders into a wonderfully odd tea party given by the Mad Hatter. In the days when Lewis Carroll wrote this story, people who made hats were exposed to all kinds of dangerous chemicals as they worked—chemicals that really made them crazy! That's where the expression "mad as a hatter" comes from.

Your tea party will probably turn out to be a more polite affair than the Mad Hatter's, and the treats you offer will be "madly" delicious. Eat your flowers! Brew your own herbs in the sun, and drink them! And what better setting for a tea party than your garden?

SOLAR TEA

What You'll Need

1 gallon jug, glass or plastic, with lid
Several tea bags or 2 to 3 handfuls of any of the
    following, either fresh or dried:
    Bee-balm leaves or flowers
    Calendula petals
    Catnip leaves
    Chamomile flowers
    Lemon-balm leaves
    Lemon-scented marigold petals
    Mint leaves, all kinds
Water
A sieve
Tea cups, mugs, or glasses
Honey to taste
An ice-cube tray (optional)
Borage flowers or rose petals (optional)

Tips

Dried herbs are available at many health food stores.

Mix the herbs if you like. We like a recipe that calls for a handful each of peppermint leaves, lemon-balm leaves, and bee-balm flowers and leaves.

Start your tea early in the morning on a sunny day.

For a special iced-tea treat, the night before you make your tea, place a borage flower or rose petal into each section of an empty ice-cube tray. Fill the tray with water, and freeze it. The next day, you'll have ice cubes with gorgeous edible flowers in their centers. Use them to make iced tea!

What to Do

1. If the tea leaves or flowers are dusty, rinse them gently.

2. Place them in the jug, and fill the jug with water. Put the lid on the jug, and set the jug outdoors in full sunlight for several hours. By late afternoon, *solar power* (or the power of the sun) will have heated up the water and released the flavor of the tea.

3. Pour the tea into individual cups or glasses, using a sieve to remove the leaves and flowers. To make iced tea, just pop in some ice cubes.

NASTURTIUM DELIGHTS

If there's one thing nasturtiums are, it's delightful. They're easy to grow, beautiful to look at, and absolutely delicious. Nasturtium plants are covered with buds and blooms throughout the season, and every one of their parts is edible. Prepare an appetizer with their blossoms that will surprise and impress everyone at the tea table—Nasturtium Delights. These amazing treats are made by serving beautiful, edible nasturtium flowers with a dollop of rich cream-cheese filling in each one.

What You'll Need

Nasturtium flowers, 4 per serving
4 ounces cream cheese
3 tablespoons fresh basil, chopped
3 tablespoons fresh parsley, chopped
8 or 9 walnuts, shelled and chopped
A mixing bowl
A fork
A serving plate
A knife

Tips 🥄

Fresh basil and parsley are available at many grocery stores.

Start this recipe about 15 minutes before you plan to serve it.

Pick the nasturtiums just before they reach full-bloom stage and just before you plan to use them.

What to Do

1. Rinse the basil and parsley with cold water.

2. Place the cream cheese, walnuts, basil, and parsley in a mixing bowl, and use a fork to blend them together.

3. Pick the nasturtiums, and spread them out on a serving plate.

4. Scoop up some of the cream-cheese mixture on the end of your knife, and press it gently into the center of a nasturtium blossom. Repeat to fill all the nasturtiums.

5. Serve immediately. Even in the refrigerator, Nasturtium Delights will wilt after an hour or two, so it's best to eat them right after you make them.

What You'll Need to Set Up for Your Tea Party

A table
A tablecloth
Silverware
Napkins
Chairs
Sunshine Tea
Nasturtium Delights
Hats, for a festive touch

What to Do

1. Invite your friends.

2. Set the table.

3. Eat, drink, and be merry.

Monster Pumpkin Figure

Would you like to grow a pumpkin that weighs four times more than you do? Producing pumpkins that are truly gigantic takes a few special steps, but it's not that difficult. A fairy godmother might want to turn your giant pumpkin into a mobile home, but if you harvest it before she does, think of what you can make with it. A floodlight for Halloween. The world's largest slug trap. A giant figure like the one in the photo.

What You'll Need

Pumpkin seeds (use large varieties only)

Indoor seed-starting containers

Potting soil or healthy garden soil mixed with some sand

Plastic wrap

A large bucket of manure, compost, and worm castings; or 1 cup organic fertilizer

1 cup lime

1 cup bone meal

Mulch (straw, hay, or black plastic)

Manure tea

Old clothes, slippers, socks, and scarf

Colored permanent-ink markers

Acrylic paints and paintbrushes

Rags and old sheets

Tips

Your household pets may take a shine to this pumpkin figure. Our cats spend a good bit of time napping on its lap!

You'll find that most garden catalogues sell the special varieties of seeds that yield giant pumpkins. Order one of these varieties, not one that yields average-sized pumpkins.

If your growing season is short, get a head start on it by planting your seeds indoors and transplanting them as soon as all danger of frost has passed. If your growing season is long, you won't need the seed-starting containers or potting-soil mixture. Just plant the seeds outdoors when the soil warms up.

The bottom portions of plastic milk jugs, empty coffee cans, or 6- to 8-inch-deep clay pots will make great seed-starting containers. Punch holes in the jugs or cans to provide for drainage.

What to Do

1. The night before you plant, soak the pumpkin seeds in water to make them sprout faster. (If you're planting the seeds outdoors, skip Steps 2 through 7.)

2. Fill your containers with potting soil.

3. Plant two seeds, about 1-inch-deep, in each container.

4. Cover the containers with plastic wrap, and set them in a warm, sunny spot indoors.

5. When the seedlings appear, remove the plastic, and pull up the weaker-looking seedling in each pair.

6. When the seedlings have two true leaves on them, move the containers outdoors. (Don't mistake these leaves for the two tiny leaves that came up with the sprout.)

7. New transplants need to get used to being outdoors before you put them in the soil. Your goal is to move them occasionally so that they get a little more sun each day. If you leave them out in full sunlight on the first day, they'll bake to death. This process of helping your plants accustom themselves to the great outdoors is called *hardening off*.

8. Decide exactly where you want to plant your pumpkins, keeping in mind that the plants will take a lot of space. They should be 8 to 12 feet away from each other and from any other plants and should also get as much sunlight as possible. Consider planting the pumpkins right next to or in the compost pile so that their roots can snack whenever they feel like it.

9. Build a planting hill (see page 37). Include plenty of high-powered pumpkin nutrition by digging in manure, compost, lime, bone meal, and fertilizer.

10. If you've started transplants, choose the two strongest looking ones, and plant them 8 inches apart in the hill. If you're planting seeds, this step doesn't apply! Just plant the seeds. When the seedlings are about 3 inches tall, pull up all but the two strongest.

11. After a week or so, pull up the weaker looking plant, and toss it in the compost. If both plants do well, give one away to a friend, and leave one to continue growing in your garden.

12. Before the foliage spreads, spread mulch around the plant; extend it 8 feet in all directions.

13. When the blossoms appear, pluck off all but three or four of them, so that your giant pumpkin doesn't have to share nutrients with too many friends! Water your pumpkin plant at least once a week, and offer it plenty of nitrogen-rich fertilizer once the pumpkins start growing. Turn them once in awhile, so they'll ripen on all sides. If the ground is especially damp, set the small pumpkins up on concrete blocks to keep them from rotting.

14. When the pumpkins turn orange, they're ripe. Cut their stems with a sharp knife, leaving a few inches of stem on each one.

15. As you create your giant pumpkin figure, you'll realize that its head is too heavy to attach to the body! Find a table or bench. You'll balance the pumpkin head on its edge, and then prop the body underneath and in front of it. As you can see in the photo, we placed our pumpkin on the edge of a bench.

16. Use your markers and paint to create a face on the pumpkin. When the paints are dry, get some help lifting the pumpkin onto its support.

17. Fill the socks with rags, and place them in the shoes.

18. Stuff the pants with rags, and position the legs over the socks.

19. Stuff the blouse, and rest it between the head and the pants. Your pumpkin figure is done!

FAMILY TREES

When people talk about their families, they sometimes refer to their *family trees*. A family tree is actually a diagram that shows all the members of the past and present family and is one way to root our relationships together into a single unit. The diagram often looks like an upside-down drawing of a real tree, complete with roots, stems, and branches.

My family charts itself by planting real trees. When a new family member is born, or when someone in the family marries or celebrates a birthday or anniversary, we plant a tree. By now, we must be responsible for at least a forest's worth of trees. You don't need a special occasion to plant a tree, but trees do make great landmarks for the memorable events in your life.

When we moved from the city to the country, we celebrated by planting a blue-spruce sapling that couldn't have been more than five feet tall. The tree is now so huge that we can't reach the Christmas lights that we left on it when we could still reach the top. It reminds us of how long we've been away from the city.

Tip

Trees for planting are sold in several different ways. You'll find different sets of instructions here for three of them. If your tree comes in a container full of soil, dig a hole that's a little wider and deeper than the container. Gently remove the tree from the container, keeping as much soil as possible around its roots, and set it into the hole. Then fill in the hole, and follows Steps 7 and 8 in the first set of instructions.

What You'll Need for Balled-and-Burlapped Trees

A tree   A trowel
A shovel   Soil amendments (optional)

What to Do

1. When you buy these trees from a nursery, their roots are wrapped up in burlap. Don't expose the roots to the air; leave the wrapping on.

2. Dig a hole twice the width of the root ball and 6 inches deeper than the root ball is long. If your soil is heavy clay, dig a shovelful of organic matter into every three shovelfuls of garden soil that you take out of the hole. If the root ball contains soil very much like the soil in your garden, don't add any amendments.

3. Return some of the soil mixture to the bottom of the hole, and make a small, cone-shaped mound with it.

4. Place the tree on the mound.

5. Fill in some of the soil around the root ball.

6. Loosen and peel back the top of the burlap, and then finish filling the hole. The burlap will be buried when you're done. Don't worry; it will rot away.

7. Use your trowel to make a shallow moat in the soil around the tree. This will act as a watering basin. Then water the tree thoroughly.

8. Place a circle of mulch around the tree, but don't cover the 2 inches of soil right around the trunk.

What You'll Need for Bare-Root Trees

A tree
A shovel
A trowel
A big bucket

What to Do

1. These trees come from the nursery with completely bare roots. Soak the roots overnight in a big bucket of water.

2. Dig a hole two to three times as large as the root mass.

3. Return some of the soil to the hole, and make a small, cone-shaped mound with it.

4. Spread the roots out over the mound so that they trail down its sides.

5. Cover the roots lightly with some of the soil, and water the tree well.

6. Fill the hole with the remaining soil, and step on the soil lightly to press out any large air pockets.

7. Follow Steps 7 and 8 in the instructions for balled-and-burlapped trees.

What You'll Need to Plant Dwarf Trees in Containers

A tree
A trowel
A large container, 24 to 36 inches wide and deep
Small stones or pieces of a broken terra-cotta flower pot
Potting soil
Compost, aged manure, or worm castings

What to Do

1. In the bottom of the container, place a layer of stones or broken pieces of terra-cotta. These will help the soil to drain properly.

2. Fill 1/3 of the tub with potting soil.

3. Make a cone-shaped mound in the center of the soil, and spread the sapling's roots over it. If the roots are tangled, separate them from one another first.

4. Fill another 1/3 of the tub with soil.

5. Water the soil in the container to settle the soil and roots.

6. Add more soil until the container is filled to within 3 inches of its top.

7. Firm the soil, and water thoroughly once again.

8. Apply about 2 inches of compost or aged manure as a mulch, leaving the area just around the trunk uncovered.

What You'll Need

2 sheets of pulp paper or blotting paper
2 heavy books
Blank cards or note paper and envelopes to match
Extra blank cards or note paper
Scissors
All-purpose glue
Clear self-adhesive plastic shelf paper
Parts of your garden: Leaves, seeds, flowers, stems, weeds, and grasses

Tips

Look for blank cards and envelopes at photocopy shops and stationery stores.

If you have envelopes but can't find blank cards, get some high-quality construction paper, and cut it so that when you fold the cut pieces in half, they'll fit inside your envelopes.

What to Do

1. Wait for a sunny day to harvest the materials that you want to dry. Flowers should be almost, but not quite, in full bloom. Cut the stems about 1 inch below the flowers.

2. Arrange your harvest on one piece of blotting paper, setting the flowers face down. Leave at least 1/4 inch between each flower or leaf.

3. Place the other piece of blotting paper on top of the plant materials, and put a couple of heavy books on top of the paper. Leave the pressed materials alone for about two weeks. No peeking!

4. Remove the books and the top sheet of paper, and you'll find that the perfectly shaped, flat flowers are still colorful.

5. With a colored marker or paint, draw a rectangle or the outline of a picture on the front of your card.

6. From your extra note paper, cut a piece that's a little smaller than the rectangle or picture outline that you drew in Step 5. To check that the piece is the right size, set it inside the lines you drew. You should be able to see the colored "frame" of ink or paint around it.

7. Put a little glue on the back of each dried flower, and press it down onto the cut piece of extra note paper. Arrange the flowers any way you like. (Your dried materials can also be glued directly onto the card instead of onto this piece of cut paper.)

PRESSED-FLOWER CARDS

Sending beautiful store-bought cards is a thoughtful way to express your love for someone, but handmade cards are more likely to be treasured by the people who get them.

Our friend, Gertrude Laravie, showed us how to create these stunning homemade cards. We assembled some right away from small flowers, weeds, grasses, and leaves from our garden. Now it's your turn to put a part of your garden into handmade stationery.

8. When the glue has dried, turn the rectangle over, and put a little bit of glue on its back, all around the edges.

9. Press the rectangle down onto the front of the card so that it's surrounded by the colored frame.

10. Cut a piece of clear self-adhesive paper, making it a tiny bit smaller than the front of the card. Carefully press it in place over your dried-flower arrangement. Trim away any messy edges with your scissors.

11. Write your message inside the card, and don't worry if you're not the world's best writer. The outside of your card will send two strong, clear messages: You care enough to send the very best, and you have a great imagination!

12. Sign your work of art before you send it.

PRODUCE STAND

Do you feel like doing something creative and productive? Would you like to make some money? Have you grown more than you can use? If your answer to these questions is "yes," open up your very own business, and sell your homegrown, vitamin-laden, locally grown, vine-ripened harvests!

GUIDELINES FOR SUCCESS

Specialize

Set yourself apart from other produce stands by selling tasty and fresh produce that people will go out of their way to buy. Offer the unique, the unusual, and the organic! Items on the list below are bound to attract customers:

Edible flowers

Purple, yellow, and green beans

Fresh basil

Little yellow pear tomatoes

Homemade scarecrows

Vermicomposters with start-up worms and bedding

Garden art

Flower bouquets, cut to order

Cold, fresh-squeezed lemonade with borage flowers floating in it

Pressed-flower note cards

Clothes poofs

Be Visible

Build your stand close to the garden so that you can work in it when you're not busy and pick fresh produce from it for your customers. If your stand can't be seen from the road, let people know where you are by advertising at grocery and health-food stores.

Word of mouth will also bring in the customers, so try to satisfy every one who drops by.

Make a Special Sign

If your garden is located by a road, a bold, attractive sign will let people know exactly what you're doing. Find an old sheet, and turn it into an inviting sign. As you can see in the photo, part of the sheet will shade you, and the other part will flop down to announce your presence.

Be Consistent

People need to know when you'll be open for business. If you advertise that you're open at certain times, be there at those times, or have a friend fill in for you.

Keep Prices Fair

The next time you're in a supermarket, write down the prices of the vegetables that you'll offer at your stand. If you don't have transportation, call a few stores, and try to find a patient produce manager who will tell you the prices that you'd like to know. Then put a comparable price on your own produce. Of course, not many people sell edible flowers and scarecrows, so you may have to come up with your own fair and priced-to-sell figures for these items!

Find out how many vegetables (carrots, for example) come in each grocery-store package. This way, if you don't own a scale, you'll get some idea of how much to charge for how many carrots.

SUCCESS!

Adults are so eager to see kids working and using their imaginations, they'll generally support any enterprise that you put your heart into. If you've designed a great sign and stocked your stand with sturdy scarecrows, bunches of flowers, and high-quality produce for sale, you'll have so many eager and curious shoppers that you may have a parking problem.

What You'll Need

A shovel
4 tall saplings or wooden posts
4 smaller saplings or narrow boards
A hammer
Nails
An adult helper
An old sheet
A ladder
Colored, permanent-ink markers
Poster board
Change
A pencil
Paper
A calculator or good math skills
A table
A tablecloth
Chairs
Baskets
Recycled bags
Produce and projects to sell

Tip

Although it will provide shade for you and your produce, the framing and roof aren't absolutely necessary. If you're short on adults to help build the framing, just skip the framing steps, and hang your sign from the front edge of your table.

What to Do

1. With help or permission from an adult, cut the saplings. The four large ones will be the posts that support your "roof."

2. Dig four holes for the saplings or posts, making each one at least 18 inches deep. Space the holes so that your sheet will stretch across the saplings' top ends with room to spare.

3. Set the saplings into the holes, and fill the holes with soil, packing it tightly to keep the saplings in place.

4. With your hammer and nails and help from an adult friend, attach the smaller saplings or boards across the upright saplings to make a sturdy frame.

5. Use a ladder to climb up and place the sheet on top of the framing. Check to see how much of the sheet will drape down in front.

6. Remove the sheet, and use your colored markers to make a sign on the part that will be visible once the sheet is in place.

7. Raise the roof again! Nail its corners to the posts so that it won't blow away.

8. Set up a table and chairs. A clean tablecloth can make even an ancient card table, an old door, or ugly boxes look attractive.

9. On the poster board, make a price list, and display it where your customers can see it easily. If you're willing to bargain or barter, say so on your sign!

10. Display your produce and projects in eye-catching ways.

11. Have a megaphone on hand, and announce specials in the produce department!

Woodworking Highlights

Beginning woodworkers need to know a few basic woodworking terms and techniques.

Squares

Squares come in many sizes, but they all share the same main jobs—to help you draw straight lines across boards and to help you check that corners are 90 degrees. The blade of a square is held at a right angle to its handle, usually by screws.

When you need to draw a cutting line across a board, first measure the required length with your tape measure, and make a mark on the board. Then hold the flat inner edge of the square's handle against the edge of the board. Line up the metal handle, which will lie flat across the board, with the mark you made, and use the blade as a ruler to draw your pencil line across the board. If the blade is too short to stretch all the way across the board, first draw as far as you can. To continue the line, pick up the square, and reposition it on the other edge of the board.

Drills and Bits

Drills don't cut holes—bits do. The drill provides the power, and the sharp edges of the bit cut the wood. Be sure you have permission to use an electric drill before you start any of the projects that require one!

Have you ever tried to drive a screw in with a screwdriver, only to have the screwdriver slip because you didn't have the strength to force the screw in? A drill and bit can come in handy here. When you predrill a starter hole for each screw, you don't have to exert as much pressure on the screwdriver. The bit you use to bore these **pilot holes**, as they're called, should be a little bit narrower than the threaded part of the screw. This way, the sharp threads on the screws will have a little wood to bite into as they enter the pilot holes.

Crosscut Handsaws

Crosscut saws are used to cut across boards. **Ripsaws,** which you won't need for any of these projects, are used to cut along their lengths.

To start a cut, first make sure that you clamp the board to your work surface, or have an adult hold the board steady. Rest the teeth of the saw on the line that you drew, at the edge of the board that's farthest from you. Set your free hand next to the saw blade, with your thumb against the blade's side, just above the teeth. Holding the saw at an angle, draw the teeth back towards you while you use your thumb to keep the blade on the line. Lift the saw up, reposition

it, and draw it back towards you again. Keep doing this until the saw has cut a groove at the marked line. Then saw back and forth, with the blade in the groove, exerting pressure on the downward stroke.

Coping Saws

The coping saw is made up of a very narrow flexible blade and a U-shaped frame with a handle. The removable blade is held tightly between the tips of the U-shaped frame.

This saw is especially useful for cutting curved shapes and for making interior cutouts. If you want to cut the hole out of a wooden doughnut, for example, you use a coping saw. How? First, sketch the doughnut on your lumber. Then use a drill and bit to bore a small hole inside the doughnut hole. Unfasten one end of the coping-saw blade from the saw frame, slip it through the drilled hole, and fasten it back onto the frame again. The coping-saw blade will now be inside the drilled hole, but the frame and handle will stay outside the doughnut, where you can hold the handle as you cut out the doughnut hole.

Cutting

Whenever you use a saw to cut wood, be sure that the wood is held firmly. Either clamp it to your work surface, or have an adult helper hold it in place for you.

Nail Sets

A nail set is just a solid tube of strong metal that's narrower at one end than it is at the other. By putting the narrow end of the nail set on the head of a nail and hitting the other end with your hammer, you can sink a nail below the surface of the wood.

Finishes

Four kinds of finishes are used in this book: acrylic paint, exterior-grade latex primer and paint, rust-preventive primer for metal, and polyurethane.

Acrylic paints are water-based and are easy to use, but for projects that will be used outdoors, protect acrylic finishes with a coat of polyurethane. When you use polyurethane, always work outdoors, and avoid inhaling the fumes! To clean up your brushes (and your body), follow the directions on the cans. The same advice applies when you're using metal primers. The fumes they give off are not good for you.

Primers seal all the pores in wood or metal; they help paint to stay on instead of peeling off. Use an exterior-grade latex primer on outdoor wooden projects before you paint them with latex paints. Latex primers and paints are water-based, so soap and water will remove them from paintbrushes and your skin.

Beans, Green

Annual

Height: Bush beans, 12 to 14 inches
Pole beans, 5 feet or more

Spread: 8 inches

pH Preference: 6.0 to 8.0

How Many Plants Per Person: 18 to 20 pole beans; 16 to 18 bush beans

For Container Planting: Use large containers, 6 to 12 inches (or more) wide by 10 inches (or more) deep.

Planting: Beans like a lot of sun and plenty of humus-rich soil. Bush beans don't require a support system, but pole beans do. Start planting in early summer, and plant more seeds once every 2 weeks until midsummer. To keep pole beans from shading shorter plants, plant them on the north side of the garden, along a fence or on poles. Sow bush-bean seeds 2 inches deep and 4 to 5 inches apart. Sow 6 to 8 pole-bean seeds, 2 inches deep, around each pole.

Care: Don't handle or pick beans when the plants are wet, or you may encourage plant diseases. Keep the area free of weeds, especially early in the growing season. Beans are shallow rooted, so weeding them later might injure them.

Nutrition: Beans are high in minerals, including iron and zinc. They're also a fat- and cholesterol-free source of protein.

Carrots

Biennial: If you sow the seeds one year and leave some of the carrots in the garden, they'll mature and produce more seeds. These seeds will drop into the garden soil and produce another year's worth of carrots.

Height: 7 to 12 inches

Spread: 8 inches

pH Preference: 6.5 to 8.0

How Many Plants Per Person: 30. Plant more if you plan to juice them.

For Container Planting: Use containers 12 inches wide by 10 inches deep.

Planting: Although they can tolerate shade, carrots like sun, cool weather (they're frost hardy), and deep, loose, sandy soil. If your soil is heavy, either choose a short carrot variety instead of a long one (the short carrots won't have as far to push down into heavy soil), or add sand to your garden bed. In hot weather, carrots turn "woody."

Carrots need small amounts of nitrogen, moderate amounts of phosphorus, and large amounts of potassium (wood ashes, greensand, or composted leaves). If too much manure is added, the carrots will be hairy, and their shapes will be odd.

Sow the seeds thinly, about 1/2 inch deep and at least 3/4 inch apart. Try a toilet-paper seed tape; carrot seeds are small.

Care: When the young plants start to look crowded, thin them to 3/4 inch apart. Eat the tiny carrot thinnings. Mulch carrots to keep moisture in the soil.

Nutrition: Almost every known mineral and vitamin is packed into root crops. Carrots lead the pack in vitamin A. They're also rich in magnesium, calcium, and vitamin B-6.

CORN

Annual

Height: 5 to 6 feet; as high as an elephant's eye

Spread: 5 inches

pH Preference: 6.0 to 6.8

How Many Plants Per Person: If you love corn, plant an acre, and rent freezer space for the extras! Actually, 20 plants per person will give you 20 corn-on-the-cob servings. If you want corn every other night, do some math and plant accordingly.

For Container Planting: Corn is not a good choice for container planting.

Planting: Corn likes well-drained, warm, humus-rich soil but will adapt to many soil types. It needs large amounts of nitrogen and phosphorus and moderate amounts of potassium.

Sow the seeds in blocks or circles, not in single, narrow rows. Corn is pollinated by the wind, so planting it in groups gives it a better chance to cross-pollinate. Plant the seeds 2 inches deep and 4 to 5 inches apart, and sow only one variety of corn at a time. Two weeks later, plant another variety. This will keep one variety from cross-pollinating with another.

Care: To keep bugs out of the corn silk, put a few drops of mineral oil or a pinch of cayenne pepper into the silk as soon as the silk shows. Corn benefits from mulch and must be watered when the plants begin to tassel. Side-dress with organic fertilizer at this time. Don't pull off the tiny corn suckers that often grow next to the big ears of corn; they'll produce small ears.

Nutrition: Corn rates high in vitamin B-6 and potassium. If it's grown in rich soil, it will also be a source of selenium.

CUCUMBERS

Annual

Height: Trailing plants, 7 inches
Vining plants, 4 to 6 feet
Bush plants, 12 inches

Spread: Trailing plants, 3 feet
Vining plants, 6 to 8 feet
Bush plants, 4 feet

pH Preference: 5.5 to 6.8

How Many Plants Per Person: 1 vining plant or 2 bush plants. Plant more if you intend to pickle your harvest.

For Container Planting: Use containers 12 inches wide by 8 inches deep.

Planting: Cucumbers like warm soil, full sun, and plenty of room to climb or trail. Make nutrient-rich planting hills by adding compost and/or manure. Cucumbers can be allowed to trail on the ground, but to keep them from rotting, it's best to build a tepee or trellis for them.

After all danger of frost has passed, sow 2 or 3 seeds per hill, placing them 1/2 inch deep. Set out transplants if you prefer.

Care: These heavy feeders need moderate amounts of nitrogen and potassium and high amounts of phosphorus. Cucumbers get thirsty and need plenty of water, especially during flowering and fruit development stages.

Nutrition: Cucumbers are high in magnesium, potassium, and folacin.

LETTUCE

Annual

Height: 12 inches

Spread: 12 inches

pH Preference: 6.0 to 6.8

How Many Plants Per Person: 12 plants every 3 weeks

For Container Planting: Use containers 18 inches (or more) wide by 8 inches deep.

Planting: Lettuce likes rich, well-drained soil, cool weather, and partial shade. Plant the seeds 6 weeks before the last spring frost date. A few varieties do well in warm weather, but most lettuces need to be started early. Lettuce is a hungry plant and likes moderate amounts of nitrogen and potassium.

Plant lettuce in a patch all by itself or between plants that mature more slowly, such as beets or in the protective shade of leafy beans or tall corn, where the little lettuce heads will stay cool. Don't worry if you live in the city; just harvest your lettuce from window boxes.

Toilet-paper seed tapes work well with tiny lettuce seeds. Mixing the seeds with a handful of dry sand and then dribbling the mixture into the garden soil will also work. Pelleted seeds (seeds that have been placed in pellets large enough to count and handle) are another alternative.

Moisten the area to be seeded. Space the seeds or pellets 2 or 3 inches apart, or roll out your homemade seed strip. Then cover the seeds with a fine dusting of soil. Once every 3 weeks, plant a few more seeds, so that you'll have young, tender lettuce over a period of time. Stop planting when the weather starts to warm up.

When the plants are 2 inches tall, thin them to 3 to 4 inches apart by picking out the weakest looking ones and putting them on your sandwiches or in your compost pile.

Care: Lettuce is shallow-rooted and likes watering, so cover the soil with a straw or hay mulch. Don't use pine straw, pine needles, bark, or sawdust, though; they're too acidic.

Serve manure tea for a quick pick-me-up or when leaves begin to look yellow. Blood meal is a good source of nitrogen also.

Nutrition: Loose-leaf lettuce is one of the most nutritious foods you can grow. It's rich in calcium, magnesium, potassium, iron, folacin, zinc, and vitamins A, B-6, and C.

PEAS

Annual

Height: 18 to 24 inches

Spread: 4 inches

pH Preference: 6.0 to 7.5

How Many Plants Per Person: 23 to 30 plants

For Container Planting: Use containers 12 inches wide by 8 inches deep.

Planting: Peas like cool weather and can tolerate frost, so plant the seeds as soon as the soil can be worked (or from 6 weeks before to 2 weeks after the average last frost date). Some gardeners sow their pea seeds when the weather gets chilly and let them lie in the frozen soil so that they'll sprout as soon as the ground thaws. Planting the seeds late in the growing season for a harvest that season won't work. The mature plants don't like nippy weather as much as young plants do. To spread their nitrogen-fixing benefits, plant these legumes in a different spot each year.

Peas prefer partial shade and a well-drained, fertile, sandy loam but will adapt to all but heavy, poorly drained soils. These legumes need only low amounts of phosphorus and moderate amounts of potassium. Sow the seeds 1 inch deep and 2 to 2-1/2 inches apart, in double rows 24 inches apart, and don't forget that peas need support.

Warning: Some companies add a pink coating to the outside of pea seeds. This substance prevents fungal diseases on plants. Don't get this chemical anywhere near your mouth, and wash your hands well after planting!

Care: Peas don't usually require much feeding during the growing season, but do apply a mulch, and water well, especially during flowering and pod-development stages. Don't pick or work around peas when they're wet and receptive to diseases.

Nutrition: Green peas are especially rich in iron, magnesium, and zinc. They're a great source of protein, have almost no fat or cholesterol, and provide fiber to keep our digestive systems healthy.

POTATOES

Annual

Height: 30 inches or more

Spread: 30 inches or more

pH Preference: 5.0 to 6.5

How Many Plants Per Person: 7 to 10 plants. Potatoes store well!

For Container Planting: Use a container at least 12 inches wide, or plant in stacks of old tires (see page 62).

Planting: Potatoes like sun and cool weather, so plant them about 4 weeks before the last frost date for your area. Continue to plant more once every few weeks, right through early summer. Choose a midseason variety if you want to grow potatoes in warmer weather.

Potatoes tend to rot in heavy, clay soil, so add plenty of well-rotted organic matter. Peat moss will also loosen the soil and will help it drain properly.

To plant potatoes right in your garden bed, dig a trench 6 to 8 inches deep. Place the seed-potato pieces in the trench, 12 inches apart. Cover them up with 4 inches of soil.

Care: As the plants start to grow above ground, add soil around them, gradually making a hill around each plant. This will give the potatoes more underground room in which to grow and will protect them from sunlight, which will turn them green and make them unfit to eat. Mulch, and water thoroughly when the weather is dry. Stake potato vines to encourage good air circulation and to keep the soil cooler.

Nutrition: During a terrible famine in the 1800s, many thousands of Irish people lived on nothing but potatoes, so you can imagine how nutritious they are. Don't peel your homegrown potatoes; much of what makes them so good for you is in the skin and just under it.

PUMPKINS

Annual

Height: 3 feet

Spread: 6 feet

pH Preference: 6.0 to 7.0

How Many Plants Per Person: 1

For Container Planting: Pumpkins aren't a good container choice unless you have a broken pickup truck and can fill its bed with rotted manure!

Planting: If you plan to eat your pumpkins, be sure to get a variety that's recommended for its taste and not just for its size! Pumpkins need warm, sunny, fertile hills. If you live in an area with a short growing season, buy established plants, or start the seeds indoors, 6 weeks before the last frost date, and transplant them after all danger of frost has passed. Plant 4 to 6 seeds (or transplants) in each hill, placing each seed about 1 inch deep. Provide moderate amounts of nitrogen, large amounts of phosphorus, and plenty of food.

Care: When the plants are established, mulch them well. Turn the growing pumpkins from time to time to keep them round and evenly ripened. Prop them up on blocks to keep them off the damp ground.

Nutrition: Pumpkins contain a lot of calcium and Vitamin A. They have more vitamins and less calories than winter squash. Sugar pumpkins can be substituted for squash in recipes.

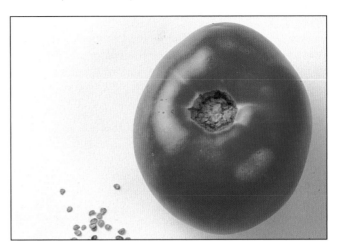

TOMATOES

Annual

Height: Depends on variety; 2 to 5 feet

Spread: Depends on variety, 2 to 10 feet

pH Preference: 6.0 to 7.0

How Many Plants Per Person: Unless you're growing tomatoes for sale, 1 cherry tomato plant and 2 slicing tomato plants will do. If you plan to make tomato sauce, add 2 roma tomato plants.

For Container Planting: Use containers 8 to 10 inches wide and at least 8 inches deep. Cherry tomatoes grow well in containers such as hanging baskets, boots, or coffee pots.

Planting: Tomatoes love sun, hate frost, and won't do at all well in cool weather, so don't set out your plants until you're sure that Jack Frost won't show up. Choose a sunny spot, one where tomatoes haven't grown for a while. Tomatoes like nitrogen, so plant them in different spots each year, or they'll eat up all the available nutrients.

To start transplants, begin about 4 weeks before the last spring frost date. Sow the seeds 1/2 inch deep in old egg cartons, or use regular planting trays, and sow the seeds 1/2 inch deep and 3/4 inch apart. Transplant the indoor-grown seedlings or transplants when all danger of frost has passed, placing them about 12 inches apart. (Buy transplants if you like.)

Plant your tomatoes 1 foot apart in each direction. Dig a hole for each one, and add well-rotted manure and a handful of bone meal. To make the soil more acidic, add some peat moss, too. Gently strip off all the leaves on each plant, except for a few at the top. Place the plant's stripped stem into the hole, positioning it at a slant, with about 6 inches of stem above ground level. The plant will still grow straight above the soil. Then cover the stem with soil. New roots will develop on the buried stem, producing a really strong root system.

Care: If tomatoes are allowed to ramble along the soil, they'll sometimes rot where they touch the ground, so spread a mulch of dry hay around each plant. Staking or caging your plants will not only keep the tomatoes away from the damp earth, but will also allow you to plant them closer together. While the fruits are growing, apply manure tea and side-dress with compost once a week.

Nutrition: Tomatoes are high in vitamin C, vitamin A, magnesium, and copper.

ZUCCHINI

Annual

Height: Trailing plants, 12 inches
Bush plants, 24 inches

Spread: Trailing plants, 3 to 6-1/2 feet
Bush plants, 3 feet

pH Preference: 6.0 to 7.0

How Many Plants Per Person: 1

For Container Planting: Use containers at least 14 inches wide by 12 inches deep. Try planting zucchini in a bathtub or sink outdoors.

Planting: Zucchini like sun, warm soil, and a lot of room. They do well growing on tepees or trellises, which keep the fruit off the ground. The plants need moderate amounts of nitrogen and high amounts of phosphorus.

Sow 2 or 3 seeds, 3/4 inch deep, in a hill. Give the plants plenty of room by spacing the hills 3 to 6 feet apart.

Care: Fertilize every other week with a side-dressing of compost and a sprinkling of colloidal or soft rock phosphate. Manure tea is a treat, but zucchini grows so well and so easily by itself that you may want to let it alone.

Nutrition: Zucchini have more calcium, magnesium, and zinc than any other summer squash.

BEE BALM

Perennial

Height: 3 to 5 feet

Spread: Eventually, the world. Bee balm, once planted, pops up everywhere and will continue to spread underground by sending out runners. If you want to confine it, plant it in a container. If you'd like a lawn full of bee balm, plant it in the garden soil!

pH Preference: 5.5 to 7.5

For Container Planting: Plant in large containers such as old bathtubs. Alyssum and nasturtiums make attractive companions.

Planting: Bee balm is hardy and dependable. It likes rich moist soil and sun or partial shade. If you like, start your own plants from seeds sown indoors in flats (or planting trays). Bee balm flowers in purple, red, and white spikes on tall stems. Once every year or two, late in the growing season, dig out the extra plants, and share them with friends.

Care: Bee balm needs no special attention.

Nutrition: Bee balm is very rich in vitamin C.

BORAGE

Biennial: If left to go to seed, borage plants will return for one more year.

Height: 4 to 5 feet

Spread: 3 feet

pH Preference: 6.0 to 7.0

For Container Planting: Plant in any well-drained, large container.

Planting: Sow the seeds 1/2 inch deep and 6 inches apart, in a dry, sunny location, right after the last frost date. The blue flowers stay fresh longer than many other flowers, and the plant itself is a great trap for Japanese beetles. The bugs love the leaves and don't bother the flowers.

Care: Yet another care-free, flowering, edible plant!

Nutrition: Borage is rich in vitamin C, calcium, and potassium. It stimulates adrenalin production in our bodies, which helps us to adjust to stressful situations. Centuries ago, people thought that borage brought courage and good cheer.

NASTURTIUMS

Annual

Height: Short ones, 12 inches
Climbers, 6 feet

Spread: 8 inches

pH Preference: 5.5 to 8.0

For Container Planting: Nasturtiums love containers and will thrive in coffee pots, worn-out boots, blenders, flower pots, and large cans. Be creative! Anything that drains and is at least 4 inches deep will work.

Planting: Nasturtiums like full sun (though they'll tolerate light shade) and dry, sandy, infertile soil. Sow the seeds thinly, 1/2 inch deep and about 6 inches apart. When the soil is too nitrogen-rich, the plants will produce more leaves but fewer blossoms.

Care: Nasturtiums require almost no care.

Nutrition: Nasturtiums are rich in vitamin C and minerals.

SUNFLOWERS

Annual

Height: Standard varieties, 6 to 12 feet
Dwarf varieties, 2 to 5 feet

Spread: 4 feet

pH Preference: 5.5 to 7.0

For Container Planting: Use containers at least 12 inches deep. Try an old umbrella holder!

Planting: Sunflowers like warmth, sun, and fertile soil. Plant the seeds along the northern edge of the garden so that they won't shade the shorter plants. Sow the seeds after all danger of frost, placing them 3/4 inch deep and 3 feet apart.

Care: Sunflowers may need staking. To help them grow tall and strong, side-dress them with compost, and offer them weekly drinks of manure tea.

Nutrition: Like many seeds and nuts, sunflowers are a wonderful source of protein and dietary fiber. Although their fat content is also high, most of this fat is unsaturated.

ZINNIAS

(Are Not for Eating!)

Annual

Height: Standard, 3 feet
Dwarf, 6 inches

Spread: Zinnias don't really spread. They look like rockets!

pH Preference: 5.8 to 6.5

For Container Planting: Yes! Plant dwarf zinnias in small containers such as kids' boots or flower pots. Larger zinnias look great in tubs, large pots, and adults' boots.

Planting: Plant zinnia seeds indoors about 4 weeks before the last frost, and set out the small plants in rich, moist soil, 8 to 18 inches apart, depending on the variety. Zinnias like sun but can tolerate shade. To avoid mildew problems, give the plants plenty of space.

Care: Water your zinnias during very dry weather. Their leaves are sensitive to mildew, so when you do water, try not to get the leaves and flowers wet.

Nutrition: Zinnias are for beauty and bouquets, not for eating.

CHART THREE:
COMPANION PLANTS

Beans, Bush: Beets, cabbage, carrots, chives, corn, cucumbers, lettuce, nasturtiums, peas, potatoes, radishes (Avoid onions)

Beans, Pole: Carrots, corn, cucumbers, lettuce, peas, radishes (Avoid beets, onions, and sunflowers)

Carrots: Bush and pole beans, chives, lettuce, onions, peas, radishes, tomatoes (Avoid dill)

Corn: Bush and pole beans, cucumbers, peas, potatoes, pumpkins, zucchini, and other squashes (Avoid tomatoes)

Cucumbers: Bush and pole beans, corn, lettuce, onions, nasturtiums, peas, radishes, sunflowers (Avoid potatoes and strong-smelling herbs)

Lettuce: Bush and pole beans, carrots, cucumbers, onions, radishes

Peas: Bush and pole beans, carrots, corn, cucumbers, radishes (Avoid onions and potatoes)

Potatoes: Beans, borage, corn, cabbage, marigolds. (Avoid pumpkins, zucchini and other squashes, cucumbers, sunflowers, and tomatoes)

Pumpkins: Corn (Avoid potatoes)

Tomatoes: Basil, borage, cabbage, carrots, chives, marigolds, nasturtiums, onions, parsley (Avoid corn, cabbage, and potatoes)

Zucchini: Borage, corn, nasturtiums, onions, radishes

CHART FOUR:
METRIC CONVERSION

Inches	CM	Inches	CM
1/8	0.3	20	50.8
1/4	0.6	21	53.3
3/8	1.0	22	55.9
1/2	1.3	23	58.4
5/8	1.6	24	61.0
3/4	1.9	25	63.5
7/8	2.2	26	66.0
1	2.5	27	68.6
1-1/4	3.2	28	71.1
1-1/2	3.8	29	73.7
1-3/4	4.4	30	76.2
2	5.1	31	78.7
2-1/2	6.4	32	81.3
3	7.6	33	83.8
3-1/2	8.9	34	86.4
4	10.2	35	88.9
4-1/2	11.4	36	91.4
5	12.7	37	94.0
6	15.2	38	96.5
7	17.8	39	99.1
8	20.3	40	101.6
9	22.9	41	104.1
10	25.4	42	106.7
11	27.9	43	109.2
12	30.5	44	111.8
13	33.0	45	114.3
14	35.6	46	116.8
15	38.1	47	119.4
16	40.6	48	121.9
17	43.2	49	124.5
18	45.7	50	127.0
19	48.3		

Volumes

1 fluid ounce	29.6 ml
1 pint	473 ml
1 quart	946 ml
1 gallon (128 fl. oz.)	3.785 l

Weights

0.035 ounces	1 gram
1 ounce	28.35 grams
1 pound	453.6 grams

ACKNOWLEDGEMENTS

As this book takes shape, my gratitude and delight grow. I want to declare a holiday honoring earthworms, gardeners, and all good land stewards. My thanks go to:

—My husband, Alan, and daughter, Casey, for the fun, peace, patience, and craziness we had working together—with the cast of thousands in our garden. For all the dinners, laundry, and homework that went on while I was camped out in the garden and in front of the computer, I give you both my love and thanks. Special thanks to Alan for helping with all the projects that involved wood and math.

—My mother, Mildred Rhoades, for sewing clothes poofs and making hanging hearts; my father, Benjamin Rhoades, for building rustic trellises and drawing lizards; and both my parents for inspiring me to believe that work is fun.

—My brothers and sisters—Carolyn, John, Donald, and Chris—for the basic magic in growing. Thanks especially to you, Chris, for inspiring our bathtub planter, designing the watering can, and for moving to Hendersonville to play with us and to keep us company in the garden.

—Mary Appelhof, author of *Worms Eat My Garbage: How to Set Up and Maintain a Worm Composting System* and (with Mary Frances Fenton and Barbara Loss Harris) *Worms Eat Our Garbage: Classroom Activities for a Better Environment* (Kalamazoo: Flower Press, 1982 and 1993). The Worm Condo project would not have been possible without Ms. Appelhof's expertise, good humor, and amazingly generous spirit.

—Photographer Evan Bracken, for the beautiful work. My special gratitude to Evan for having kept an even tone of voice throughout the months of rain, shade, kids, and collision-course deadlines.

—Suzette Cloutier, for allowing us to photograph her flower bed.

—Art director Kathy Holmes, for the book's beautiful layout and design and for her artistic contributions.

—Lawrence Hill, of Citizens Home Center in Asheville, North Carolina; Steve Holladay, of Holladay Paint & Wallpaper in Asheville, North Carolina; and Dr. Charles Janes, of the University of North Carolina at Asheville, North Carolina, for their expert advice.

—Gertrude B. Laravie, of Vero Beach, Florida, for her pressed-flower note cards.

—Louise Lauk, for her forest honey.

—Andy and Heidi Morgan, for the red claw-foot bathtub in our garden.

—Louisa Nelson, who receives the World's Most Enthusiastic Gopher and Scarecrow Maker of 1994 and the Most Likely to Bring a Cup of Hot Tea with a Huge Smile Awards.

—The late Jane Palmer for her "cone" sculptures (the earthworm mannequins in our garden). I am so glad to acknowledge Jane's accomplishments. Thanks, too, to Jane's mother, Madge, for her generosity in allowing the sculptures to live in my garden during this time, and for grace and mobility.

—Chris Rich, my editor, for doing all the worrying for me, for conjugating with intent, and for giving me plenty of freedom to enjoy the making of this book.

—George Sroda, Amherst Junction, Wisconsin, for so generously sharing his worm expertise. The photo on page 28 depicts Mr. Sroda and his worm, Herman.

—Charles Taylor, of Hendersonville High School in North Carolina, for his help with the onion experiment.

—Susan Weed, for the pH-test violet solution project.

—Carolyn Wengerd at the Secret Garden in Flat Rock, North Carolina, for her help with projects and location photography.

—Jay Westin, for inspiring me to plant potatoes in tires.

—Joen Zinni-Lask, for her help with location photography.

—All the kids who kept me company in the garden, digging, planting, and delighting in bugs and discoveries. Their photos appear throughout this book.

The Kids

Chelsea Cloutier	Carissa Parks
Eliana Cloutier	Casey Rhoades
Stephen Hartsell	Brenna Rosenstein
Abigail Hendrix	Sarah Rosenstein
Donald Hendrix	Brit Skeele
Jamin Hendrix	Dallas Skeele
Jeffrey Hendrix	Monica Sweeney
Ryan Hendrix	Jessamyn Weis
Timothy Hendrix	Karla Weis
Jennie Nelson	Alima Wieselman

Actions speak louder than words, and that brings me to the great role models I have in this mountain community, where my friends tread lightly and take delight in gardening, hiking, being outdoors…being! You know who you are—our own local talking heads. Thank you!

And finally, thanks for the still, small voice in each one of us that speaks and listens to and appreciates the possibilities in a garden.

INDEX TO SUBJECTS

INDEX TO PROJECTS

CULTURES
IN
COLLISION

The Boxer Rebellion

———•———

WILLIAM J. DUIKER

PRESIDIO PRESS
SAN RAFAEL, CALIFORNIA
LONDON, ENGLAND

Published by Presidio Press of San Rafael, California,
and London, England, with editorial offices at
1114 Irwin Street, San Rafael, California

Library of Congress Cataloging in Publication Data

Duiker, William J   1932-
  Cultures in collision.

  Bigliography: p.
  Includes index.
  1. Boxers.   2. Nationalism — China.   3. China —
History — 1900.   I. Title.
DS771.D84   951'.03   77-73550
ISBN 0-89141-028-7

Cover illustration by Karl O. Lichtenstein

Printed in the United States of America

To my favorite daughters,
Laura and Claire

Contents

Contents

Illustrations

Maps

Acknowledgements

In the course of writing this book I received assistance and encouragement from a number of sources. To Joyce Eakin and Richard Sommers of the Military History Archives at the Army War College, I would like to express my appreciation for introducing me to the files on the Boxer Rebellion contained in the Spanish-American Survey. I am also indebted to the staffs of the Orientalia Division at the Library of Congress and at the Archives in the Ministry of Foreign Affairs in Paris, and to Mr. Li Nien-hsüan at the Academia Sinica at Nankang, Taiwan, for helping me to locate useful archival sources.

Thanks are also due to Leon Stout of the Penn State Room in Pattee Library at The Pennsylvania State University for assisting me in selecting the photographs used in this book, and to Mrs. Karen Zwigart for her typing and editorial assistance.

Finally, I would like to thank the Institute for the Arts and Humanistic Studies, and the College Fund for Research of the College of Liberal Arts at The Pennsylvania State University for providing financial assistance in bringing this project to fruition.

As always, my deepest gratitude goes to my wife, Yvonne, for making our home such a pleasant place in which to live and work.

Introduction

For three-quarters of a century the Boxer Rebellion has captured the imaginations of readers throughout the world. To a certain extent this fascination simply reflects an enduring interest in the behavior of human beings under stress: the Boxer uprising led to one of the most horrifying news stories of modern times — the murder of dozens of Christian missionaries and the siege of the foreign diplomatic community in Peking. In the years immediately following the revolt, literally dozens of books and stories — diaries and memoirs of participants and popular accounts by journalists — appeared in Western languages, making the siege and its consequences one of the most thoroughly reported events of its day.

In recent years the impact of the Boxer Rebellion and the siege at Peking has faded as modern man finds new ways to test the endurance of his fellow creatures. A number of scholarly accounts on the origins of the crisis have appeared, and popular histories of the siege itself have been published at irregular intervals. Curiously, however, few attempts have been made in recent years to write a balanced account of the war for the general reader searching for its causes and its consequences for China and its rela-xvi *Introduction*

tions with the West. This is unfortunate, because there is much more to the Boxer Rebellion than the siege at Peking and its effects on the lives of the individuals involved. The conflict represents a period of history that has an importance all its own. It is the story of two cultures on a collision course: an expanding West, vigorous, vital, and self-confident, clashing with an introverted China, tradition-bound, arrogant in its self-sufficiency, and anxious above all to be left alone. The Boxer Rebellion was not simply a struggle of arms and of governments but of contending civilizations, of two contradictory views of the world and the nature of man. The consequences were tragic. Misunderstanding escalated into hatred and bloodshed, resulting in a confrontation between China and virtually the whole Western world.

For Americans, the Boxer Rebellion is particularly noteworthy, for it marks a significant stage in the rise to prominence of the United States in Asia. The uprising led to America's first land war in Asia and its first military action taken in conjunction with other Western powers. As such, the conflict was a brief forecast of things to come. Like the period after World War II when the United States attempted to play a decisive role in the affairs of China, it demonstrated some of the inherent contradictions in America's foreign policy in Asia—contradictions which still exist in our own day. In a very real sense, then, the Boxer Rebellion marks the beginning of the present revolutionary century in Asia.

Yet the modern reader, learning today about the causes of the Boxer Rebellion, is likely to conclude that the world has come a long way since 1900. China is now master of its own fate and a central political and military force in East Asia. Foreign nations no longer possess massive territorial concessions on the China mainland, Christian missionaries no longer dream of converting millions of Chinese, and the myth of the China market is no longer an active enticement to the Western businessman. In short, today the behavior of the Western powers during the crisis seems petty and almost incomprehensible.

Before we become too arrogant in our condescending view of our ancestors, it is worth reflecting on our own experience. The cultural misunderstanding which led to the Boxer Rebellion has not dissipated in our own time and is a major factor in creating the gap that still exists between the West and China. The Boxer uprising was the first truly spontaneous reaction of the Chinese people to the growing Western presence in China, and the intense hostility of the rebels stunned Western observers there, most of whom were almost totally unaware of the resentment their activities had aroused. Now, over half a century later, China has again rejected the West, and again we have not yet fully understood why.

The repetition of the pattern carries a sobering message with dangerous implications for the future. Today, as in 1900, we are paying a price for our failure to understand the Chinese people and the causes of the deep resentments they have held against the West. Hopefully, reexamining the Boxer Rebellion — seemingly so distant now in time — will help to shed light on the relationship between these two great cultures.

Chapter One

Worlds in Collision

For nearly two thousand years the dominant position of China in East Asia was unquestioned. Centrally located on the highly populated eastern rim of the Eurasian land mass, the Chinese empire emerged in history in the final centuries of the pre-Christian era and gradually assumed a major role in the international affairs of the Western Pacific. Two of China's great dynasties, the Han and the T'ang, concentrated on land expansion and spread southward into Southeast Asia, westward into Central Asia (with expeditions going as far as the Caspian Sea), and northward to the southern edge of the vast Gobi Desert in Outer Mongolia.

Over the centuries the force of Chinese expansion was irresistible, and by the rise of the Ming dynasty in the fourteenth century the Chinese empire extended from the Red River delta in the south to Manchuria in the north, and from the borders of Tibet and Turkestan in the west to the China Sea in the east. Under the Ming (1369-1644), China for a time even entertained thoughts of becoming a sea power. In the early fifteenth century the imperial court dispatched naval expeditions to the Indianized states of Southeast

1

Asia, the Indian subcontinent, and as far as the Red Sea
and the eastern coast of Africa. The primary motive for
the voyages was apparently trade, rather than political
domination, but they marked the growing influence of the
Chinese empire in the southern seas as well as along its
western and northern frontiers. Generally, China's interest
in neighboring countries lay in political influence and border security, rather than outright military conquest or extension of territory. For this reason, China was normally
satisfied to establish a tributary relationship with its smaller
neighbors, guaranteeing peace and security in a mutually
amicable relationship. Except for Vietnam, which for a
thousand years was treated as a military province of China,
the imperial court rarely ventured militarily beyond the
southern border with Southeast Asia, except to avenge an
insult or to protect the patrimony of a friendly ruler.

Chinese power was not always invincible. Occasionally
the empire was attacked and even conquered — by the
Mongols in the thirteenth century and by the Manchus four
hundred years later. Foreign conquest did not necessarily
disrupt the traditional pattern, for the new rulers normally
adopted existing institutions and customs and were gradually absorbed into Chinese society. In any event, the pri-
macy of China in Asia was not questioned — certainly not
by the Chinese themselves, whose very name for China
(Chung Kuo, or the Central Kingdom) strongly implied a
central position in human affairs. For the most part,
China's neighbors acknowledged its suzerainty in return
for trading privileges, the Chinese emperor's recognition of
the legitimacy of a fellow ruler, and occasionally Chinese
protection against internal or external enemies. If the tri-
bute system, by which all of its neighbors were linked to
China through ties of fealty and allegiance, was an advantage to China, it provided benefits for neighboring countries
as well.[1]

In the sixteenth century this Sinocentric cultural uni-
verse was shaken by arrivals from the West. Early Western
visitors to China — for the most part traders or missionaries —

wanted to establish trading relations with the Chinese empire or preach the Christian religion to the "heathen Chinee." Limited by their numbers and by the vastness of the empire, they had a realistic idea of the obstacles involved and apparently did not aspire to carry out their operations on a large scale. The missionaries, usually Jesuits, Franciscans, or Dominicans, undoubtedly hoped to change Chinese religious practices and those social habits which were considered incompatible with Christianity, but they had no desire to overthrow the empire or to change Chinese political and social institutions as a whole. Early Western visitors either were indifferent to the culture or actually admired Chinese ways—the courtesy and intelligence of the leaders, and the industry and peacefulness of the people.

Western involvement in China was thus limited, and the feeling was mutual. China itself had no particular interest in things Western. Aside from a passing fascination with the scientific gadgetry proudly displayed by early Jesuit missionaries, the Chinese saw few benefits from connections with the West. Eventually they began to view Western ideas as a threat to their culture: Western commerce eroded Chinese self-sufficiency and depleted local currency; Western religion, avowing that there was only one God and that his viceroy was in Rome, diminished the status of the Confucian ruler. When Catholic missionaries began to criticize the Chinese practice of ancestor worship as idolatrous, Chinese officials feared Christianity would weaken their people's morals. It is difficult for a Westerner today—and perhaps was virtually impossible for the Westerner of the seventeenth century — to understand that many Chinese saw Christianity as a serious threat to their way of life much as a modern American might view communism. In general, the Jesuits attempted to minimize the disturbance of established ritual. However, such attempts were undermined by rival Catholic orders and were eventually denounced by the Vatican. By then the Chinese court had already taken steps to limit its relations with the West. Catholic missionaries were compelled to leave China, and

Western traders were restricted to one port, Canton, far from the major population centers.

Until early in the nineteenth century, then, contact between China and the West was curtailed by distance and by Chinese indifference to the outside world. For a long time, preoccupied by problems and interests elsewhere, Europe acquiesced and allowed its relations with China to stagnate. By the early years of the nineteenth century, however, new circumstances altered Europe's perception of its interests in Asia. The Industrial Revolution simultaneously created new needs and new opportunities—a rising demand for raw materials which European nations could not themselves supply, and competition for consumer markets which could absorb the increasing output of European factories. To meet the challenge of a growing commercial economy, Western merchants began once again to look to Asia and its wealth of oil, tin, rubber and other natural resources, and particularly to China with its 400 million potential customers.

Great Britain was the leader in the struggle to open China to Western trade. For a century the British had suffered a trade imbalance with China as the Chinese had refused to buy English goods in return for the export of Chinese tea to England. By the end of the eighteenth century the British had found a commodity to recoup currency losses to China: opium. Grown in northern India and shipped to south China by the East India Company, opium became so popular in China that by the first quarter of the new century the currency flow had reversed. The Chinese government attempted to stop the importation of opium, claiming, with some justification, that it had a deleterious effect on the health and morale of the Chinese peasant. In a famous letter to the young Queen Victoria, a Chinese official, Lin Tse-hsü, wrote:

Let us ask, where is your conscience? I have heard that the smoking of opium is very strictly forbidden by your country; that is because the harm caused by opium is clearly understood. Since it is not per-

mitted to do harm to your own country, then even less should you
let it be passed on to the harm of other countries—how much less to
China! Of all that China exports to foreign countries, there is not a
single thing which is not beneficial to people; they are of benefit
when eaten, or of benefit when used, or of benefit when resold; all
are beneficial. Is there a single article from China which has done
any harm to foreign countries?[2]

England, however, was not persuaded. In the view of
British officials in London and of merchants in Birmingham,
Glasgow, and Manchester, the issue was not opium but
freedom of trade. If the Chinese would open their doors to
Western commerce and permit Western firms to sell their
wares without hindrance throughout the empire, there
would be no need for shippers to sell opium in China, and
the problem would resolve itself.

The imperial court, however, was determined to suppress the opium trade. This position led in 1839 to war with
Britain, a humiliating military setback, and the resulting
peace treaty of 1842 compelled the Chinese to open selected
coastal ports to Western trade. The Opium War decisively
changed the course of Asian history. In succeeding decades
the Western presence increased as China was gradually
forced to open its villages and towns to foreign commercial
activities, not only in so-called treaty ports, but in the interior as well.

Where Western merchants trod, missionaries were not
far behind. The great missionary explosion of the sixteenth
and seventeenth centuries had come primarily from the
Catholic countries — France, Italy, and Spain. During the
nineteenth century, when a revival of religious fervor swept
Great Britain and the United States, the Protestant nations
began to take the lead. Missionary groups throughout the
Western world focused their attention on the benighted
Chinese peasant, and, as the merchant called for oil to light
the lamps of China, the missionary called for spiritual sus-
tenance for Chinese souls.

In the Western mind, missionary activity provided an
ethical counterpoint to commercial activities in China.

If Western commerce raised the material level of Chinese civilization, then Christianity would provide spiritual uplift and justify the white man's presence in Asia. It is easy to see the Westerner as hypocritically rationalizing commercial greed with a superficial morality. Yet in the nineteenth century, interference in underdeveloped societies in Asia and Africa was considered not only inevitable but ultimately beneficial. By the last quarter of the century, Charles Darwin's theory of natural selection, of "survival of the fittest," was being applied to human societies. Thus, in the evolution of mankind, those civilizations which failed to respond to the challenges of external forces would lose the struggle for survival and would be driven off the crowded ladder of civilization. The process was relentless, and through it the species evolved.

The theory of evolution gave support to Western colonization, making it a matter of enlightened self-interest as well as cultural beneficence. Western imperialist nations felt they needed colonies in order to maintain their status as great powers. At the same time they could justify their colonial activities by considering them altruistic attempts to provide the natives with the secrets necessary to succeed in the brutal struggle for survival.

Western expansion in China, then, was motivated by a variety of factors: a commercial interest in natural resources and consumer markets; an evangelical urge to spread the gospel and the wonders of Western civilization; and a general belief that national greatness required colonies in far-flung corners of the globe. With the defeat of the Chinese by Great Britain in 1842, the waves of imperialism began to lap at the outer bulwarks of the Chinese empire. From the north and the northwest, tsarist Russia used the pretext of trade to expand into Outer Mongolia and Chinese Turkestan. In the southwest, the British gradually advanced northward from Burma and India to Tibet, where they collided with an outpost of St. Petersburg. The French, ever concerned that they might fall behind the British in the race for colonies, reacted to the British move into Burma

A typical scene inside the Tartar city, Peking (*Leslie's Weekly*, July 14, 1900, cover)

by seizing Vietnam, Laos, and Cambodia and creating a French "balcony on the Pacific." Even China's Asian neighbor Japan was anxious to share the spoils. In the mid-1870s Japan staked a claim to the Ryukyu Islands, traditionally a Chinese tributary area. A decade later Tokyo began making gestures aimed at detaching Korea from the Chinese empire.

In themselves, these advances did not directly threaten the independence of China. The areas occupied or coveted by the imperialist nations were not integral parts of the Chinese empire, nor were their populations Chinese in race or culture, although Korea and Vietnam had modeled their own civilizations after the Chinese. These areas, in fact, were the outer defenses of the Chinese state and had been viewed as such by the Chinese for hundreds of years. Still, stripped of the protective covering which the tributary system had historically afforded, China would feel increasingly vulnerable to foreign conquest.

Western advances into China during the last third of the nineteenth century were in some respects misleading indications of the degree of Western success in opening Chinese society to outside influence. The volume of trade generated with China was undoubtedly disappointing to enthusiastic believers in the China dream. The myth of the China market never materialized — nor has it developed to this day. However, Western commercial interests in China continued in other promising areas: mining, banking, and railroad construction. By the 1880s a new type of imperialist device had evolved, known now as the sphere of influence. When political and social problems at midcentury started to weaken the centralized authority of the court, provincial governments began exerting an increasing degree of independence. Western companies that had penetrated into the interior of China began (sometimes with the aid of their governments) to make special arrangements with provincial authorities whereby they would gain monopolies over construction and mineral rights. By the middle of the 1890s such spheres of influence, each dominated by a single foreign power, had become commonplace in China: the British in the Yangtse Valley; the French in Yunnan and Kwangsi in the south; the Russians in Manchuria; and the Japanese in coastal Fukien. While Western governments had not yet overtly attempted to usurp administrative powers in such areas, foreign interference in Chinese affairs was on the rise and the court in Peking was increasingly powerless to stop it.

THE CHINESE RESPONSE

China was slow to respond to the growing challenge from the West. Long convinced of the innate superiority of its own institutions, China did not find it easy to accept the new vulnerability. A few intellectuals, concerned at China's defeat in the Opium War, recommended changes in the administration in Peking, but the court, now entering a long period of decline which would last beyond the end of the century, failed to see the necessity for urgent action. Even after a second defeat by Western powers in the late 1850s, the dynasty resisted change. By the 1870s progressive elements had finally and reluctantly come to the conclusion that reform was necessary. A gradual period of modernization in the military, commerce, industry, transport, and communications was initiated. A few young Chinese were sent abroad to study.

These hesitant efforts to modernize, however, could not halt the paralysis that was gradually affecting the empire. Beyond the cities, village China was virtually untouched by reform. Even the most progressive Chinese hoped that Western technology could be grafted onto the Chinese system without irreparably damaging sacred institutions and that industry and commerce could be developed without altering the country's traditional agrarian character. The attempt at restricting cultural reform primarily to economic spheres was often advantageous to the individual businessman. Ambitious Chinese made their fortunes in trade and then used their new wealth to buy land or to obtain a position in the bureaucracy. For many, Western ways were simply a tool to achieve status in the traditional sectors of society. For a generation after 1875, China hesitated between old and new, reluctant to advance but afraid to retreat.

China's failure to halt the gradual intrusion of Western culture inevitably caused a growing split over how to handle the problem. Some Chinese, exposed to Western civilization through travel abroad, contacts with missionaries and merchants, or translations of Western books, began to conclude that only major reforms, including a willingness to borrow ideas from the West, could save China from political and cultural annihilation. Such attitudes were common in the big coastal cities, but the people of the great Chinese heartland by and large resisted the idea that China must Westernize or perish. To them, China's way of life and venerated institutions must be preserved, even at the cost of continued military defeat — a Chinese equivalent of the "better dead than red" argument in Cold War America. These contrasting views were reflected at the court in Peking, where moderate reformist Chinese ministers argued for change against the stubborn resistance of conservative Manchu nobles.

This bitter controversy raging in the capital and the treaty ports along the coast had no counterpart in the towns and villages where the great mass of the Chinese population lived. Congenitally indifferent to the outside world, for a long time village China was only dimly aware of the growing cultural confrontation between China and the West. For the average Chinese, the West was represented by an occasional traveller or by those few merchants or missionaries who lived in the vicinity. Often the villager, peaceable and tolerant by nature, simply ignored the foreigner or considered him a mild curiosity. Sometimes, however, it was difficult to maintain such an attitude of easy tolerance. As the century wore on and the Western presence in China gradually increased, the effects on the daily lives of Chinese became more marked. Increased imports of Western goods, facilitated by a Western-imposed standard tariff of only five percent *ad valorem* on all imports, cut into Chinese manufactures, especially cloth goods. A large proportion of the traditional clothing of China had been provided by home handicraft producers. While cheap and sturdy, such local products had difficulty competing with the machine-made products of the West.

Another area affected by the Western presence was transport. Western consortia built railroads from Peking to Tientsin, along the Yangtse Valley, and from north China to the Yangtse River cities of Shanghai and Hankow, gradually curtailing the river junk trade which had long functioned as the major means of transporting goods. Thus, slowly but inexorably, Western commerce was beginning to disrupt the social and economic structures of Chinese civilization. As it did so, the Chinese came to see the West not as a curiosity but as a menace.

It was the missionaries, however, whose presence was most resented in China. In the last half of the nineteenth century there was a sharp rise in missionary activity in China. Until midcentury China had been almost entirely a Catholic preserve. Catholic proselytizing had begun with the arrival of Franciscans and Jesuits in the sixteenth century, while the first Protestant missionary did not arrive until almost three hundred years later. As a result of treaty agreements in 1858, however, Western Christian missionaries were allowed to travel freely and preach throughout China, and Protestant groups began to carry the gospel to the Chinese. In 1858 there were eighty-one Protestant missionaries in China, all in the southern and coastal areas. By 1889 there were over thirteen hundred scattered throughout virtually every province in China. Over fifty percent of these missionaries were from Great Britain; the bulk of the remainder came from the United States and Germany. Their activities had been rewarded with some success —an estimated fifty-five thousand Protestant converts in China.

The Catholics were still strong contenders in the competition for Chinese souls, however. By the mid-1890s

there were about 750 Catholic priests in China, mostly
French, with a few Italians. Because the Catholics had
been active longer than the Protestants, they had achieved
greater success — approximately half a million converts
throughout China. The competition climaxed in the final
decade of the century. By 1900 there were over 2,800
missionaries in China. They worked in every Chinese province except for the traditionally xenophobic Hunan and
claimed nearly a million converts. The Catholics still pre-
dominated with 720,000 followers; the various Protestant
denominations totaled over 130,000.

In retrospect, it seems obvious that such a mass of
foreigners, with their alien customs and doctrines, would
invite the hostility of simple farmer and suspicious scholar-
gentry alike. Few of the newly arrived missionaries spoke
Chinese, unlike the first Catholic arrivals, who had attempted not only to master the language but also to understand the inner nature of Chinese culture. With no know-
ledge of the language and little interest in Chinese civilization, the late-nineteenth-century missionaries operated
under their old prejudices. Many, if not most, were con-
temptuous of Asian civilization and communicated their
arrogance and condescension in their dealings with the
Chinese. Often the missionaries themselves came from small
towns and had little cosmopolitan interest in other civilizations. On arrival in China, they would install themselves
in a mission compound, preserving their own way of life
and isolating themselves from the native population. Often
the missionaries were women, and their activities particularly excited suspicion and contempt, for the place of
women in China was exclusively in the home.

The new arrivals often exacerbated the situation by
their open interference in the traditional way of life. Con-
temptuous of local mores and justice, many went out of
their way to protect their converts from legal charges levied
by village authorities. To the missionary, it appeared that the
non-Christian authorities deliberately harassed those who
had accepted Jesus. To the local authorities and the non-

Christian population in general, it appeared (with some justice) that many bad elements in the village became Christians
simply to escape punishment. These "rice Christians" —
Chinese who converted to Christianity solely for its material
benefits — were scorned and ridiculed by their neighbors.

Missionaries were almost always oblivious to the consequences of their interference with the legal process. They
commonly appealed over the heads of local authorities to
the district magistrate and threatened foreign intervention.
Such disruptive behavior often embarrassed the European
governments and their official representatives in China,
but nevertheless the local consulate or the legation in
Peking frequently intervened in favor of the missionaries.
Usually the local authorities would submit to such pressure
and conceal their bitter resentment.

Inevitably, then, the missionaries became the object
of suspicion and dislike among the Chinese. Churches, like
railroads, were suspected of annoying local spirits, *feng-
shui,* and thus causing harm to the villagers. Rumors circulated that strange and despicable behavior occurred behind
the walls of the mission compounds. The Westerners
running orphanages, who frequently did engage in questionable practices in locating children to be raised in a
Christian environment, were suspected of murdering their
young charges and boiling their eyeballs during secret
rituals.

For the most part the missionaries shrugged off these
reactions as the superstitions of simple and credulous peasants. But the dislike of the missionaries and their activities increased among the educated — local officials, success-
ful and aspiring candidates for the Confucian civil service
examinations, local landed gentry — and the reactions of
these people, as opposed to the peasants, were of more
concern to the foreigners. This informal local aristocracy
had a great stake in the traditional system, and Western
ways represented a very real threat. The peasant would not
attack the foreigners on his own initiative, but if he came
to feel his hostility had the support and encouragement,

Chapter Two

The Climax of Imperialism in China

I t is one of the ironies of history that throughout the last hundred years many international crises have arisen in areas of relatively limited political or economic importance to the parties involved. At the end of the nineteenth century the European powers several times came close to war over a few hundred square miles of African wasteland or over areas in Asia thousands of miles from their own borders. World War I itself was precipitated by rivalries in the Balkans, a region of minor international importance. More recently, the United States squandered its resources and its reputation in a prolonged war in a southeast Asian country few Americans had even heard of before the Geneva Conference of 1954.

The explanation, of course, lies in the international system which in recent decades has governed relations between the great powers. Since the nineteenth century the world system has been based on a balance of power between competing states. With several great powers jealously guarding their own interests, even a slight shift in the spread across north China toward the Sea of Japan, Tokyo grew watchful and bided its time.

CLIMAX IN SHANTUNG

In 1897 events took place which were to bring the imperialist wave to a crest. Germany, a latecomer to the China land-grab, coveted a position in the Pacific. Since Bismarck's successors did not share his distaste for Asian adventures, by 1895 Germany's commercial interests in China had become second only to those of Great Britain. German military strategists had kept a sharp lookout for prospective locations for a sphere of influence or a naval coaling station. They finally settled on two possibilities: Chusan Island, off the China coast near the mouth of the Yangtse River, and the island of Formosa, long attractive to several European powers. Formosa lost its appeal when it was seized by Japan after that country defeated China in the war of 1894-1895. Since Chusan Island was techni- cally in the general area of Britain's sphere of interest in the Yangtse Valley, China rebuffed Germany's advances, claiming that it had promised the British not to allot the strategic island to another foreign power. Germany would have to look elsewhere for its outpost in the Pacific.

By the late 1890s German attention began to focus on the Shantung Peninsula, which jutted into the North China Sea. Rocky and inhospitable, Shantung had relatively little to recommend it from a commercial point of view, but it was strategically located and its Chiao Chow Bay was an excellent location for a naval base. A further in- ducement was the fact that for nearly twenty years German missionaries had been operating in the interior of Shantung Province and entreating Berlin to protect their interests.

The Germans feared that the dismemberment of China could leave them without a share. Consequently, in 1895, immediately following the defeat of China by Japan, they opened talks with Peking on the possible cession of land in Shantung Province for a German naval base. Unfor-

tunately for the Germans, the Chinese government was itself becoming interested in building a naval base in Chiao
Chow Bay. Encouraged perhaps by the Russians who were
also mildly interested in the area, the Chinese refused the
German request.

The negotiations, however, had whetted the Germans'
appetite, and they were determined to find a pretext to
seize what they could not obtain by diplomatic means.
In November of 1897 the pretext presented itself when
rioting Chinese peasants murdered two German missionaries
in the interior of Shantung Province. Kaiser Wilhelm checked
briefly with Tsar Nicholas to make sure that Russia would
take no counteraction (Nicholas simply noted in the margin
of the message from the German monarch that he could
not "approve or disapprove"). The kaiser then gave his
enthusiastic assent and the Germans moved in. They occupied the area around Chiao Chow Bay and demanded
leasing rights to construct railways and mines elsewhere
in the province. With German efficiency, they soon began
to build up the area, planting trees and constructing roads,
a bathing beach, a new hotel, and even an underground
sewer system. Local Chinese suspected that the latter was
intended as an escape route for when the Chinese drove
the Germans into the sea.

In Peking several court officials who had witnessed
with growing anger the rapacity of the great powers were
inclined to strike back, regardless of the costs. Others,
however, feared that, unless China could obtain help from
other world powers — notably Russia, who had somewhat
hypocritically posed as China's friend against the other
European powers — Chinese resistance would simply spark
a land-grab that would complete the dismemberment of the
empire. The proponents of appeasement were temporarily
victorious, and agreement was reached with Germany,
primarily on the latter's terms, by January 1898.

In world capitals reaction to the German advance
into Shantung was mixed. The Russians, who had seriously
contemplated seizing Chiao Chow Bay for themselves, were

missionaries in China had nearly doubled during the 1890s, to more than a thousand by the end of the century.

The tension in America due to its China policy was evident in its behavior as the situation rose to a crisis. The McKinley administration, as well as the man in the street, was repelled by the rapacious seizure of Chinese territory by the imperialist powers. In 1898 the American minister to China, Charles Denby, recommended to Washington that the United States officially protest the dismemberment of the Chinese empire. Yet there were signs of support for American imperialism. Spokesmen for commercial interests advocated a foreign policy that would actively protect Yankee business concerns in China. Missionary groups clamored for official protection by American diplomatic representatives. And the strains of *realpolitik* had begun to be heard in the United States. With American commercial interests on the rise, the United States gradually became involved in the balance-of-power game, and those with a financial stake in the policy came to accept its rules. American participation in the exploitation of China was extolled as natural and inevitable. Some justified an activist policy by claiming that the United States was simply bearing the "white man's burden." Others considered imperialism to be its own justification. Illustrative is an article entitled "Expansion Unavoidable" in *Harper's Weekly*:

If history teaches anything, it is that conservatism when it prevails habitually indicates national decay. As stagnant water breeds the microbe of death, so nature itself preaches action, and in national life action is synonymous with progress. The people of the United States, known for their restless energy, which possesses the boy not yet out of his teens equally with the man who has reached or passed the allotted threescore years and ten, are expanding constantly. It is by this innate spirit of expansion that the marvellous wealth of our time was created.

Since, then, our trade with China has even now assumed such gigantic proportions as to call for a written guarantee of non-interference, the United States must be prepared to defend its vested rights on the other side of the Pacific. In order to be able to do so, territorial acquisition, or territorial expansion, is a necessity. There is no other alternative; it is either, Renounce expansion of commerce, or Be prepared to defend it. Only a naturally weak nation or one strong but unprepared is likely to be attacked. Physical strength always imposes respect, with individuals as well as with nations. The old adage, In time of peace prepare for war, is as true now as it ever was. [1]

Concrete evidence of the growing imperialist trend in American foreign policy appeared in 1898. Taking advantage of the war with Spain, American forces seized the Philippines and, despite the fact that rebellious Filipino forces had already declared the islands a republic, transformed them into an American colony. His decision, President William McKinley explained, had been motivated by moral concern. More realistically, perhaps, the Philippines were attractive for their economic value. To the new American minister-designate to China, Edwin Conger, the Philippines were a stepping-stone to the China market. Ironically, two years later there were those who advocated an activist American foreign policy in China as a means of protecting our investment in the Philippines.

THE OPEN DOOR NOTES

American foreign policy at the turn of the century thus reflected the conflicting attitudes of two centuries: traditional anticolonialism versus economic imperialism, a natural sympathy for the underdog versus a belief in the white man's burden. This mixture of sentiments was reflected in the attitude of U.S. Secretary of State John Hay. Like many of his countrymen, Hay was unhappy at the land seizures which had been launched in late 1897. On the other hand, he was pressured by commercial and missionary interests to undertake an active role in the China crisis. When American naval interests voiced their desire to obtain a coaling station on the coast of Fukien Province, Secretary Hay was mildly favorable to the request, protesting only its timing. Nor did he dispute the contention that commerce was America's main interest in China.

Though some elements in American society called for greater involvement in China, the nature of American interests there diverged in important respects from those of such powers as France, Russia, and Germany. Whereas the needs of the latter seemed to lie in the establishment of commercial and economic monopolies in a given area, thus limiting their interest to clearly defined spheres of influence, American commercial groups seemed more anxious to open all of China to free trade conditions. For this reason, and because of America's moral sympathy for China, Secretary Hay issued the now famous Open Door Notes of September 1899. Although advised by some to accept the spheres of influence as an "established fact," Hay was finally persuaded to state the general principles of American foreign policy in China and ask the great powers for their adherence. The first note called for a gentleman's agreement among the powers to preserve the territorial integrity of China. It did not require the imperialist powers to abandon their spheres of influence but asked them to make a distinction between freedom of trade, under which all nations would have equal rights throughout China, regardless of individual spheres of influence, and special interests for mining and investment. The spheres of influence were thus acknowledged, but their scope was to be carefully circumscribed.

Responses from the powers showed a variety of attitudes. The British feared the consequences of a divided China, and their interests, like those of the United States, lay in maximizing trading opportunities; they were delighted. The French and Germans responded carefully, stating in effect that they would concur if others did also. The Russians, against whose activities in Manchuria the notes seemed primarily directed, sent the most ambiguous reply, declaring that their previous actions had adequately demonstrated their adherence to a policy of "open door." (To many observers, this was a dubious statement.) More significantly, the Russian reply totally ignored a major point in Hay's note: that the powers agree not to charge discriminatory rates against the goods of other foreign powers on rail lines in its sphere of influence. This point was a specific expression of the Open Door policy; by ignoring it St. Petersburg essentially rejected the note's principles.

The Russian rejection, according to a sympathetic observer, was dictated primarily by economic motives. Andrew Malozemoff, whose *Russian Far Eastern Policy, 1881-1904* is one of the standard works in the field, claims that, since Russia was the only power which had begun to construct railways in China on a large scale, the principle of nondiscriminatory rates itself amounted to a form of discrimination and could be considered hostile to Russia. In his view the Russians had sound reasons for applying discriminatory rates on their Manchurian rail system since, unlike their Western rivals, all of their commerce came by land, rather than by sea. According to Malozemoff, Russian acceptance of Hay's note "would have been disastrous to Russian financial and economic interests in Manchuria. The doctrine as applied to Russia in the Far East was much too one-sided."[2]

It was the Russian finance minister, Sergius Witte, who pointed out to Foreign Minister Nikolai Muraviev the implications of the Open Door Note, and it was presumably at his instigation that the reference to discriminatory rates was deliberately left out of the Russian reply. Malozemoff points out that, since several of the powers agreed to respect the principles in Hay's circular only if all the other powers did likewise, the note was in effect rejected by them when the Russians refused to comply. Secretary Hay, however, took the disparate responses as a general agreement and declared in a second note in March 1900 that the Open Door was now accepted as "final and definitive."

For decades the Open Door Notes were viewed as the cornerstone of American foreign policy in East Asia. To succeeding generations of Americans they appeared to be a perfect synthesis of American morality and economic self-interest — directed at protecting the basic rights of the Chinese people, while at the same time coaxing the empire gently into the mainstream of the modern world. At the time they reflected the twofold nature of American interests in China, but they did not clarify the ambiguity in American policy as evidenced by the administration's response to the request for a coaling station. President McKinley approved the request, and Secretary Hay himself appeared mildly favorable but noted, in an understatement, that the moment was inopportune for America to start land-grabbing. Hay's compunctions notwithstanding, the major obstacle to the station turned out to be Japan, which maintained that Fukien lay in Japan's sphere of influence. The project was dropped.

THE CHINESE RESPONSE

The events touched off by the German seizure of Chiao Chow Bay in late 1897 led to a re-examination of foreign policy strategy at the Manchu court in Peking. After Western pressure on China intensified during the middle years of the century, the Chinese government had begun to experiment with various ways of coping with the foreigners. They had tried ignoring them, promoting internal reform along traditional lines, maintaining a policy of compromise and conciliation, resisting forcefully, and playing off one power against another. Generally, none of these policies had worked very well, and this must have been painfully evident to the Chinese policy-makers. By the last quarter of the century, however, once the pattern of Western pressure had been established, Peking was stressing the conciliatory approach, while attempting to maximize its advantages by balancing one jealous rival against the others. Simultaneously, half-hearted efforts were made to modernize China's military services in the hope that at some future date it could confront an aggressive imperialist power. The conciliatory approach was used in a variety of circumstances — land seizures, foreign requests for mining and railway rights, and issues raised by the presence of Western missionaries in the interior of China.

Occasionally, elements at court or in the provinces had advocated a more militant response to Western encroachments, even at the risk of war. Proponents of this aggressive approach sometimes supported rapid modernization as well, but more often they contended that all forms of Western influence should be rejected as harmful to traditional institutions and values. This policy of militant traditionalism was seldom put into practice for the simple reason that it was not an effective means of dealing with the well-armed foreigners. However, as the conciliatory method itself showed signs of wear and tear, the militant conservatives were heartened to try again.

The conflict between alternatives, of course, reflected the split at court between those who felt that at least some changes would be necessary if China were to survive and those who felt that traditional institutions and customs were to be defended at all costs, even in the face of military defeat. Until the events of 1897 and 1898, the advocates of gradual reform had for long had the upper hand at the court in Peking. But the humiliating concessions made in those two years demonstrated to some the bankruptcy of the policy of moderation and compromise. More insistently, voices began to call for basic changes in Chinese foreign policy. Some officials reacted to the German demands by seeking help from Germany's traditional rivals, England and Russia, but their efforts were undermined by those countries' own demands for territorial compensation. When the German military attacks occurred, the Manchu court reluctantly began to react to the growing internal criticism of foreign encroachment. Governor Yü Hsien of Shantung was instructed to prepare local military forces for possible armed action against the Germans, and Yü Lu, the governor of Chihli Province, was ordered to station troops at Tientsin for a possible defense of the capital area. The hardening attitude in Peking, though not yet trans-

lated into action, was an indication that a number of the
more militant figures in China were gaining power. These
included Jung Lu, commander of all military forces in
north China; the Manchu nobles K'ang Yi and Prince Tuan;
General Tung Fu-hsiang, commander of the Kansu army;
and Li Ping-heng, ex-governor of Shantung and a man
noted for his antiforeign attitudes (Li was governor at the
time of the murder of the two German missionaries, and
Berlin felt he had been sympathetic to the antiforeign
outburst. At the German government's demand, the court
had declared him henceforth ineligible for high office. By
1899, however, he was a popular figure at court). Generally,
Chinese officials tended to be more moderate, the Manchu
nobles more militant.

The antiforeign militants were not the only advocates
of change in Chinese policy. For several years reformists
among low-level bureaucrats and young scholar-gentry had
begun to contend that only comprehensive institutional
reform could save the country. Until the final years of the
century they had held little sway among the policy-makers
in Peking. But in the spring of 1898, using the events of
the preceding year as yet another example of the failure
of gradual reform, the reformists renewed their efforts at
persuading the court to introduce aspects of Western culture into Chinese society. Leader of this faction was
K'ang Yu-wei, a young Confucian scholar from Kwangtung
Province in south China. Convinced of the need to start
at the top, K'ang addressed several petitions to the young
emperor, Kuang Hsü, urging major reforms in order to preserve the independence of China.

For a time it appeared that K'ang Yu-wei's attempt to
enlist the emperor's support might succeed. Kuang Hsü,
who was twenty-three years old in 1898, had only recently
come to power. Progressive, well-meaning, and open to
outside ideas, Kuang Hsü had been distressed at the course
of international events. He was attracted to K'ang's pro-
posals and invited the young reformist to visit the imperial
palace to discuss his ideas. K'ang was evidently even more

persuasive in person, for in the summer of 1898 he helped the young emperor to prepare a series of wide-ranging edicts designed to reform the vast and antiquated bureaucracy. During the course of several weeks, decrees were issued that ordered drastic fundamental changes in such areas as education, administration, and justice.

There was a major flaw in the reformers' tactics, however. The real power in Peking lay not in the emperor's hands but in those of the aging empress dowager, Tz'u Hsi. Born to the family of an impoverished Manchu noble in 1835, the young Tz'u Hsi had been selected as a concubine for the emperor Hsien Feng. Tough-minded and astute, she had quickly learned how to protect her interests at court. After Hsien Feng's death in 1872 she was named regent for her son T'ung Chih. When he died in 1875, she retained her influence under his successor and was named empress dowager for the new emperor, her three-year-old nephew Kuang Hsü. On reaching his maturity Kuang Hsü took power, but Tz'u Hsi's influence remained crucial.

When Kuang Hsü came under the influence of K'ang Yu-wei's reformism, Tz'u Hsi resented being passed over and quickly turned hostile to the new faction. Kuang Hsü gradually became aware that forces in the capital were scheming to scuttle his reform program and turned to the commander of the Peiyang Army at Tientsin, General Yüan Shih-k'ai, to remove Tz'u Hsi from power. Yüan, an effective administrator as well as the creator of China's first modernized army, was reputed to be moderately progressive in his views toward reform and toward the foreign powers. Yüan was also a realist, however, and he quickly noted the weakness of the reformers' position. While ostensibly agreeing to help Kuang Hsü, Yüan instead informed Tz'u Hsi's confidant, Jung Lu, of the emperor's plans. When word reached Tz'u Hsi, she mustered her own forces and drove the progressives from their positions of influence. Six reformers were executed, although K'ang Yu-wei himself managed to flee to Japan. The young

Prince Tuan, Manchu reactionary (*Leslie's Weekly,* July 28, 1900, p. 64)

emperor, Kuang Hsü, was imprisoned on an island in the palace grounds. With Tz'u Hsi again firmly in control, rumors circulated that Kuang Hsü was terminally ill and about to abdicate.

Thus the conservative faction had managed to restore its power at court. Jung Lu, who had briefly held the post of viceroy of Chihli, was now named grand secretary in Peking, while retaining his command of all Chinese military forces in north China. In Shantung Province the moderate governor Chang Ju-mei was replaced by the militant Manchu xenophobe, Yü Hsien, who had been a justice in the province under the previous governor, Li Ping-heng.

It did not take long for the militants to strike at the top. Kuang Hsü's apostasy in supporting the progressives and plotting against the empress dowager could not be forgiven, and the conservatives now attempted to force his abdication. They intended to replace him with young P'u Chün, the son of the reactionary Manchu Prince Tuan. The plot failed, however, due to protests from foreign diplomats and influential Chinese officials in the provinces, including Liu K'un-yi, viceroy of Nanking. As compensation, Prince Tuan was able to have his son declared heir apparent early in 1900, as Kuang Hsü's "illness" continued.

The new conservative trend immediately surfaced in the arena of foreign policy. Angered at the Italian government's request for a naval station at San Men Bay, the court decided to refuse further concessions. The Italian demand was rejected. Viceroy Liu K'un-yi was directed to repel any Italian military advances and was given a free hand to take whatever action was necessary. Faced with this surprisingly tough Chinese response, the Italians abandoned their claim.

This new toughness at court reflected a rising wave of antiforeign sentiment in the country as a whole. Throughout the spring and summer of 1898 riots against foreigners occurred in several provinces, usually beginning as attacks on railways or missionary compounds. The discontent was centered in Shantung Province, scene of the recent German takeover. For months Western missionaries in the southern districts of the province had been seeking official protection against anti-Christian agitation, sparking resentment among local officials and villagers. Other factors soon made the situation explosive. The Germans took a heavy-handed approach to obtaining land rights along the railroad right-of-way from Tsingtao, in the newly leased Chiao Chow area, to Tsinan, capital of the province. Attacks on construction sites along the railway therefore rose in number and intensity. Then, to add to the problems, bad weather resulted in crop failure for the already impoverished peasants in the province.

According to some observers, the antiforeign unrest in the countryside was not totally spontaneous but reflected the attitudes of those in power in Peking and authorities in the districts and provinces. Whether or not this was the case, antimissionary agitation was certainly on the rise as 1899 drew to a close, particularly in Shantung Province, where Governor Yü Hsien appeared increasingly reluctant to suppress anti-Christian riots. Signs of a major confrontation between China and the West were surfacing with ominous frequency.

Chapter Three

The Rise of the Boxers

A s the century drew to a close, the convergence of several factors was leading inexorably to a crisis in China's relationship with the West. The rapid disintegration of power in China had not only whetted the appetites of the great powers, but also had increased their fears that their rivals would profit from a dismemberment of the empire. On a local level, Western residents in China—missionaries in the provinces, merchants in the treaty ports, diplomats in Peking—had reacted to the land-grab with increased contempt for the Chinese people and their institutions. Their demands for special privileges were a local counterpoint to the large-scale land seizures by the great powers on the national level.

The Chinese are traditionally a tolerant and peace-loving people, accustomed to hardship, oppression, and even foreign conquest. Rarely had they given vent to their feelings in physical action. Suspicion of foreigners had always been common in Chinese villages, but antiforeign incidents had been surprisingly rare, considering the ever-growing presence of missionaries in the countryside. Now, however, Western insensitivity inevitably was having its effects and a sense of desperation was beginning to grow. The latest land seizures by the Western powers not only increased the Chinese sense of humiliation, but also made the collapse of the Chinese empire and the destruction of Chinese civilization real possibilities. Rumors circulated among Chinese as well as foreigners that the partition of the country among the various powers was only a matter of time. In late 1898 China responded at the national level by creating a new leadership determined to resist any further foreign encroachments. At the local level, villagers retaliated with increasing attacks on missionaries and other symbols of the foreign presence.

Had another factor not intervened, this wave of anti-foreign sentiment might have passed without a major crisis. The great powers, as evidenced by their reaction to John Hay's Open Door Note of 1899, had no particular desire to divide China among themselves. Indeed, many statesmen in world capitals were reluctant to take actions that might trigger the final collapse of the Chinese empire. If the court at Peking had been able to restore its territorial integrity and internal sovereignty without significantly affecting foreign trade, building, and missionary activity, most of the powers would probably have acquiesced with a considerable degree of relief.

The new militancy in Peking, then, was not by itself sufficient cause for the rising crisis in relations between China and the outside world. The catalytic force that plummeted China into the throes of war came from the villages of north China, where thousands of angry peasants unleashed the fury of their frustrations in an attack on Westerners that was unprecedented in its fierceness. Never in China's three centuries of acquaintance with the West had such an incident occurred. Rising anti-Western sentiment alone did not adequately account for the ferocity of the outburst. In the last years of the century disastrous climatic conditions had created unusual hardship for farmers throughout the empire, and particularly in central and north China. Since 1898 bad weather had seriously affected the grain harvest in the lower provinces of the Yangtse Valley, and floods throughout the area had made thousands, perhaps millions, homeless. In the north, the Yellow River had burst its banks every year since 1896. Finally, in the spring of 1900 a severe drought in the flatland area stretching from the Gulf of Chihli to the provinces of Shansi and Honan threatened crop failure in the breadbasket area of north China. For millions of Chinese peasants, hunger and starvation became tragic realities.

Historically, bad weather conditions in the rural areas of China had been followed by revolts against the established order, and the year 1900 was no exception. What was unique, however, was the conjunction of economic crisis and an active campaign against the Western invader. In the minds of superstitious peasants, the two factors became inextricably linked. Foreigners, who had angered local spirits by disrupting graveyards to build railroads and churches, were blamed for the bad weather that afflicted China. As one broadside put it,

The arrival of calamities is because of the foreign devils. They have come to China to propagate their teachings, to build telegraph lines and to construct railways. They do not believe in spirits and they desecrate the gods. It is the desire of the gods to cut up the telegraph lines, to rip up the railroads, and to cut off the heads of the foreign devils.[1]

A popular rumor in north China predicted that rain would fall if the Chinese cut off the heads of the foreign devils. Thus two problems were to be solved at one swoop.

Out of a gripping economic crisis, then, arose the specter of a vast and sacred war against the foreigner, of armies of refugees roaming the countryside, searching for food and seeking scapegoats for their afflictions. The peasantry of north China threatened to become a desperate, primitive force, bent on ridding the nation of its oppressors.

The exact origins of the Boxer movement, that vast antiforeign offensive which suddenly sprang up in villages and towns throughout north China in late 1899 and 1900, have long been disputed. Some scholars argue that the Boxers — named, apparently, for the Chinese boxing ritual performed by the adherents in preparation for action — emerged from the countless secret societies which for centuries had proliferated among poor and illiterate peasants. The origins of these secret societies — the White Lotus, the Triads, the Eight Trigrams, the Elder Brother Society, the Big Knife Society — are shrouded in legend. Most were composed of local peasants who banded together for security against bandits, rapacious landlords, and corrupt officials. Sometimes the societies were tolerated by the local authorities, but not infrequently they had an antidynastic coloration and were suppressed. Several were primitive nationalistic cliques formed to drive out the foreign rulers — the Mongols in the thirteenth century, the Manchus in the modern period. Ideologically, the secret societies were usually fairly primitive. Often the members shared a belief in local spirits and practiced secret rituals and incantations, such as the ritualized boxing (similar to the contemporary *T'ai-chi-ch'uan*), to knit together the group and guarantee themselves long life or immortality.

Secret societies had existed in Shantung Province in north China for centuries and had caused considerable difficulty to the Manchu dynasty throughout much of the nineteenth century. Organizations practicing ritual boxing had been common in the area since the 1700s, but no major society going by the name of Boxers (in Chinese, *I-ho-ch'uan,* "righteous harmonious fists") had appeared in the area until 1899. At that time local peasant groups calling themselves Boxers seemed to spring up spontaneously throughout the province. A local Chinese magistrate, Lao Nai-hsüan, published a study of the movement, claiming that it originated in the antidynastic societies which had long existed throughout the area. By extension, therefore, the movement could be considered not only anti-Western, but also anti-Manchu.

Those who locate the origins of the Boxers in the

antidynastic secret societies do not believe that the court was directly responsible for the events leading to the antiforeign movement at the turn of the century. However, many foreigners living in China during the period of the Boxer revolt felt that the court, and the empress dowager herself, had actively connived to promote the Boxer agitation. In 1927 *China and the Occident,* a serious study of the Boxer revolt by George N. Steiger, carried this assumption to its logical conclusion. Steiger contended that the Boxers did not develop out of anti-Manchu secret societies, but were a volunteer militia deliberately created by the court to resist the foreigners.[2] He argued that the name "Boxers" (*I-ho-ch'uan*) was simply a popular play on the actual name *I-ho-t'uan* ("righteous harmonious militia") and referred to the adherents' use of Boxer-like rituals. These ritual drills, Steiger claimed, were actually a Chinese adaptation of Western military drills.

Recent evidence, however, clearly shows that the Boxers were not, as Steiger claimed, simply a village militia formed at the behest of the court in Peking. The government did call for the formation of local militia at about the time the Boxers were beginning to appear, but there is no indication that the two groups were related. Indeed, the aim of the militia was to suppress local disorder, not to exacerbate it.[3] While the court can be charged with using the Boxers for its own purposes at a later stage, it cannot legitimately be accused of creating the movement.

It is probable, though not definitely established, that the Boxers were, in fact, a type of secret society formed in reaction to missionary activity, imperialist expansion, and the starvation and discontent rampant in the countryside. The movement may have originally been antidynastic in tone, but, as it grew, the court began to discern its utility in focusing antiforeign sentiment. At that point the throne attempted to shape the Boxers into militia-type organizations and to assimilate them (usually without success) into the established military framework.

Whatever its specific origins, it is clear that the Boxer

movement was both a product of antiforeign or anti-
Christian feeling and a response to economic conditions.
The two were related since the Boxers often seemed to
believe that, if the foreigners could be driven from China,
conditions would improve. In the beginning the movement
was probably local and spontaneous, without centralized
leadership, erupting in the villages and spreading rapidly
among poor peasants, merchants, unemployed soldiers,
and Buddhist monks. According to some reports, most
active Boxers were adolescents, but there is evidence that,
particularly as conservatives came to power in Peking,
some local officials and scholar-gentry began to offer their
support and encouragement.

Organizationally, local Boxer units (called *t'uan* in
rural areas and *t'an* in the cities) had from twenty-five to
a hundred members and usually made their headquarters
in the village temple. As might be expected of local peasant
organizations, a wealth of superstition and supernaturalism
was connected with the movement. Charms, incantations,
and ritualized dancing, usually performed on the village
"boxing ground," were thought to provide protection
against injury and death in battle. The Boxers made much
of the legends and myths of rural China, as well as poems
and historical plays such as *Monkey, All Men Are Brothers,*
and *The Romance of the Three Kingdoms.* A favorite
hero was the famous medieval Chinese diplomat-leader
Chu-ko-liang, whose trickery and astuteness had enchanted
readers of *The Romance of the Three Kingdoms* for centuries.

Until the early months of 1899 the Boxer movement
was simply an expression of local discontent in certain
villages in Shantung Province and along the border between
Shantung and Chihli. When antiforeign incidents had first
erupted here in May 1898, the court had ordered the
governors of the two provinces to investigate and take the
necessary action. Governor Yü Lu of Chihli had suppressed
the activity on the Chihli side of the border. Governor
Chang Ju-mei of Shantung was not particularly sympa-

thetic to the Boxer movement, but apparently he did not take it very seriously and was reluctant to use force to suppress it. In March 1899, however, Chang was replaced by Yü Hsien. Yü Hsien had been a judge in the administration of the anti-Western Li Ping-heng and was notoriously hostile to foreigners, particularly missionaries. With the province under his control, Boxer activities rapidly spread, and their actions became more violent.

Under the leadership of a peasant with the colorful pseudonym of Red Lantern Chu (Chu Hung-teng), the Boxers of Shantung began to loot and burn missionary compounds, railway stations, and the areas where Chinese Christian converts lived. When a local magistrate attempted to end riots at P'ing Yüan, killing a number of Boxers and dispersing the rest, Governor Yü Hsien angrily dismissed him. The message was loud and clear: the authorities, at least in Shantung Province, would condone anti-Western activities. A number of Boxer groups with several hundreds of members each, sensing official sympathy for their cause, began to circulate throughout Shantung Province, encountering no opposition from Governor Yü Hsien. In the opinion of many contemporary observers, Yü Hsien's dismissal of the magistrate marked the beginning of the Boxers' rise to national prominence.

In Peking the court vacillated between sympathy for the Boxers and reluctance to irritate the foreigners. When Chang Ju-mei, the moderate governor of Shantung Province who preceded Yü Hsien, had reported the rise of anti-foreign activities in his area, the Grand Council in Peking had ordered him to suppress the agitation. But by late 1899 the court had apparently developed a pro-Boxer position. It appeared anxious to turn the movement from an antidynastic to a prodynastic, anti-Western force. The court apparently even had some success in assimilating the Boxers into the local militia. As 1899 drew to a close, local Boxer groups began carrying four-character posters inscribed with the slogan, "Support the Ch'ing, Destroy the Foreigners."

When Yü Hsien removed the magistrate for suppressing Boxer riots at P'ing Yüan, Western diplomatic circles in Peking were outraged, and Edwin Conger, the American minister to China, demanded that the court dismiss Yü Hsien. In Conger's words, "If this governor will not or cannot control the rioters and protect these people, he should be removed at once and someone put in his place who can and will."[4] For a brief period the court resisted, but finally it acquiesced, and on December 6, 1899, Yü Hsien was recalled and replaced by Yüan Shih-k'ai. When Yüan left Hsiao Chan for Tsinan, the capital of Shantung Province, he took his Peiyang Army with him. Yüan, always the realist, was known to feel that the Boxers were a dangerous antidynastic movement which could easily turn against the court, and he was opposed to using a force which might unnecessarily incur foreign wrath against the Chinese government. On assuming his new duties, he quickly made it clear that, unlike his predecessor, he would not look benignly on Boxer activity in Shantung Province. Furthermore, he informed his subordinates that any local authorities permitting Boxer activities would be severely punished. He struck quickly at the rioters and executed Red Lantern Chu. When several Boxers volunteered to go before his firing squad to prove their invulnerability to bullets, he obliged. They were wrong.

Yüan Shih-k'ai's crackdown dramatically reduced the unrest in Shantung Province. It seemed clear that, although the court and the local authorities did not directly control the movement, official attitudes had much to do with the rise and decline of Boxer activities in north China. Yüan's own forceful repression of the Boxers did not totally end trouble in the region, however. Harassed by Yüan's forces, Boxer groups simply moved north into Chihli Province or into borderland areas where they could retreat to the opposite side when pursued by provincial military forces.

As the Boxers spread throughout the lowland areas near the capital, they evidently gained support from many elements in the local population, including the scholar-gentry, who began to view the movement as a righteous force cleansing China of its foreign enemies. Not all local officials sympathized with the movement, however. Magistrate Lao Nai-hsüan, author of the first serious study of the origins and nature of the movement, was convinced that the new prodynastic orientation of the Boxer leadership was a ruse and that the true nature of the movement was lawless and self-serving. As rioting increased in nearby districts in Chihli Province, Lao Nao-hsüan convened a meeting of his fellow magistrates in the vicinity and, with their concurrence, drew up a six-point program to suppress the movement. The program was sent to Governor Yü Lu, but he was apparently under pressure from antiforeign forces in nearby Peking and made no attempt to implement it.

In Peking the government was now clearly leaning toward the Boxers. Yü Hsien, who had been recalled from his post in Shantung "for an audience," found considerable support for his hard-line position at court. He was rewarded for his behavior in Shantung with the governorship of Shansi Province, a move that would have tragic consequences for hundreds of Christians in that area of north China. Acting Governor Yüan Shih-k'ai in Shantung was admonished by the court not to be too severe in his treatment of local Boxer groups and to make a careful distinction between loyalists and simple brigands.

By early spring of 1900 Boxer groups were moving north and west and were beginning to appear in the capital area. Youngsters were seen practicing Boxer drills within the city, and placards began to appear on city walls, predicting the burning of Peking and the destruction of the foreign legation quarters. The situation appeared even more ominous south of the capital along the Peking-Hankow railroad, where a number of missionary groups had extensive compounds. Roaming crowds of Boxers cut rail lines around the transportation hub of Pao Ting Fu and burned railway stations all along the line. More seriously, in Lai Shui district, they attacked an area inhabited by

Christian converts, killing sixty-eight and wounding many more. Boxers and government troops clashed in the area several times, but Governor Yü Lu, undoubtedly influenced by the situation at court, was reluctant to take strong action.

Opinion at the court in Peking was sharply divided. Moderates claimed that the Boxers were simply rebels who would harm China's relations with foreign powers and ultimately turn against the dynasty itself. If China cannot defeat Japan, they asked, how can it hope to defend itself against all the foreign powers at once? But the conservatives at court were becoming bold in expressing their resentment of Western activities. They tended to blame the foreigners, not only for the land-grab of 1898, but for K'ang Yu-wei's constitutional reform movement of the same year (K'ang had received considerable support from the British legation in Peking). Led by such Manchu nobles as K'ang Yi and Prince Tuan, the conservatives called for war and the destruction of the legations. Two middle-level officials presented to the court a proposal stating that there were only three options: to make peace; to abrogate the existing treaties and demand that the Westerners leave China; or to make war.

Throughout this frenzied period Tz'u Hsi kept her own counsel. Occasionally, she expressed exasperation at the Boxers, and one skeptic at court observed that they were "ripe for the cabbage market" (the site of executions in Peking). On the other hand, she apparently sincerely believed that the Boxers had magical powers, and moderates who dared to criticize them aroused her instant anger. A few moderates were executed, inspiring the reactionary Hsü T'ung to note with satisfaction, "The more of this kind of running dogs we kill the better." The militants were clearly in control, and China was moving inexorably toward war.

Chapter Four

The Escalating Crisis

T he first mention of the Boxers by name, according to one student of the period, occurred in the *North China Daily News* on October 2, 1899. Until the first months of 1900, observers in world capitals and the legation quarter in Peking did not take the Boxers very seriously. Over the years the West had held a deep-rooted skepticism of the capacity of the Chinese to unite and resist the foreign challenge. Even by 1899, when the situation had grown serious, cries of alarm from missionaries in inland areas tended to be taken lightly by observers in Peking.

The legations, however, were capable of rapid action when trouble arose near the capital. In 1898, when the Muslim troops of General Tung Fu-hsiang had threatened Europeans in the Peking area, the ministers demanded that 130 European soldiers be dispatched to the capital to guard the foreign population. Despite official protests from the Chinese court, these troops remained in Peking until the following spring.

Incidents had been occurring sporadically in rural areas for years, but Western observers had received somewhat skeptically cries of alarm from the interior. Now, however, in the latter months of 1899 it appeared that the

end of the century the Russians were advancing gradually but persistently, not only into Outer Mongolia and Chinese Turkestan, but also in the area northeast of the Great Wall. They had negotiated an agreement with Peking to build a rail line directly across the heart of Manchuria to the port of Vladivostok on the Pacific coast. In 1900 St. Petersburg did not have any immediate aims for further territorial expansion in the area. Russia was content to assimilate its new sphere of influence in the Liaotung Peninsula and to develop commercial activities throughout the three provinces of Manchuria. But Russia's long-term plans, epitomized by the far-seeing strategy of Minister of Finance Count Witte, included a desire to bring all of north China under full Russian domination.

In their concern over Russian advances in East Asia, the British had a potential ally in Japan, who, having recently strengthened its position in Korea in the war of 1894-1895, was determined to forestall possible Russian expansion in southern Manchuria and in the Korean peninsula, an expansion that was already well underway.

If the British were concerned at Russian successes in the north, the latter returned the hostility in full measure. To St. Petersburg, Russian advances in Asia were simply a process of manifest destiny, an extension of the Russian empire's centuries-old eastward expansion beyond the Urals and across the frozen wastes of Siberia. Since the middle of the nineteenth century Russia's greatest rival in this process had been Great Britain. London had countered Russian advances east of the Caspian Sea by moving into Afghanistan and had reacted to growing Russian influence in Turkestan by attempting to solidify a position in isolated Tibet. The Boxer crisis simply added a new dimension to the worldwide Russo-British rivalry.

The Russians felt that it was unfair to portray their policy toward China in purely selfish terms. In the view of the tsarist court, Russia was the only true friend of China among the European powers. Convinced that its geographical position carried with it a unique sympathy for the needs and aspirations of the Chinese, the government at St. Petersburg saw itself as the true protector of the Chinese against the rapacity of the other imperialist powers. In 1860 Russia had stepped in to mediate a settlement at the end of the Lorcha Arrow Wars (and in the process had managed to detach several thousand square miles of Chinese territory as compensation) and in 1896 had signed a secret treaty of friendship with Peking in conjunction with the agreement permitting Russia to build railroads in Manchuria. As the Boxer crisis developed, Russian policy was persistently distinguished by ambivalence—a wish to help Peking against the other powers, and a desire to profit from China's troubles by solidifying Russian influence in north China.

The United States, the other major power in China, also took an ambivalent position toward the court's reaction to the Boxers. It had participated in the commercial and missionary activities in China during the previous half century and had a general concern for the interests and safety of American residents there. Its commercial interests in particular had increased rapidly during the 1890s, and the United States was on the verge of developing major economic and political needs in the Western Pacific. Yet America's long-standing anticolonial tradition and its lingering distrust of alliances with other powers had led it to a deliberately independent position in China as the crisis deepened. Maintaining a balance between isolation and collaboration with the other Westerners in China would prove to be increasingly difficult. The suspicion in world capitals regarding the court's intentions was reflected in the diplomatic community in Peking. As might be expected in the case of a small and virtually self-contained community, the personalities of the ministers themselves frequently came into play. The *dramatis personae* in Peking were an interesting lot, but their diverse characteristics led to misunderstanding and a mutual lack of respect which would result in considerable difficulty as the crisis unfolded.[4]

Sir Claude MacDonald, the
British minister in Peking
(*Leslie's Weekly*, August 18,
1900, p. 119)

Edwin Conger, the American
minister in Peking (*Leslie's
Weekly*, July 28, 1900, p.64)

Stephen Pichon, the French
minister in Peking (*Leslie's
Weekly*, July 28, 1900, p.64)

Baron Klemens von Ketteler,
the German minister in Peking
(*Leslie's Weekly* July 28, 1900,
p. 64)

British Minister Sir Claude MacDonald was the acknowledged head of the diplomatic community in Peking. An ex-military officer with the Scot's Greys, MacDonald was a steady but unspectacular performer who had not earned high plaudits during the early years of his tour in Peking. The German minister, Baron Klemens von Ketteler, was almost his direct opposite. Like MacDonald, he had a military background, having served in Peking as military attaché during the 1880s. This assignment had gained him a reputation as one of the few "China hands" among the foreign ministers in Peking. Von Ketteler, who allegedly possessed in generous measure the arrogance often associated with Prussian aristocrats, was as flamboyant as MacDonald was stolid, and, although he was married to an attractive American wife, rumors circulated that he was involved in several love affairs in the Peking diplomatic community.

Stephen Pichon, MacDonald's counterpart in the French legation, possessed a generous sense of *amour-propre* and a lively suspicion of all his colleagues. In his dispatches (now available at the Quai d'Orsay in Paris) Pichon emerges as somewhat pompous and petty. Unlike most of his colleagues, he began to voice his concern about the Boxers when most foreigners were inclined to scoff at the danger. Pichon's persistent references to the activities of "les Boxeurs" caused considerable merriment within the diplomatic community until reports from the countryside began to prove that his warnings were not exaggerated. Pichon had an advantage over his colleagues. He was receiving periodic reports on Boxer activities in the provinces from the French bishop of Peking, Monsignor Favier, who in turn received appeals for help from French missionaries scattered throughout China.

The Russian minister was the fairly colorless M. N. de Giers. Edwin Conger, the representative from the United States, was a political appointee from the Midwest with little experience in foreign affairs. A commoner in an aristocratic profession and an amateur at the art of diplomacy, Conger was generally considered a lightweight in the councils of the ministers in Peking. Moreover, there are indications that his own superior, Secretary John Hay, had serious reservations about his capabilities.

The call by the ministers for naval demonstrations in the waters off north China did not meet with strong support from most of the home governments. In London, Foreign Secretary Salisbury was reluctant to take such a drastic step, considering it "not without danger" and premature under the circumstances. Lord Salisbury's attitude reflected a trend in British policy toward caution and against active involvement in Chinese affairs. Washington evinced a similar attitude. Although Conger in Peking had endorsed the request, Secretary Hay refused to participate and informed the British ambassador that Washington did not feel it could join in a naval demonstration which it felt was "contrary to its traditions." Actually, Hay was feeling his way cautiously in the crisis. As he later conceded to a friend, he had been badly informed on the situation and was anxious to avoid taking a provocative stand, since imperialism and executive authority were likely to be major issues in the upcoming presidential campaign. To protect his diplomatic flank, he telegraphed Conger on June 10 instructing him:

We have no policy in China except to protect with energy American interests, and especially American citizens and the legation. There must be nothing done which would commit us to future action inconsistent with your standing instructions. There must be no alliances[5]

Domestically, the purpose of the telegram was obvious since it was immediately given out to the press.

The French, too, felt that a naval demonstration was premature and decided to hold off temporarily, but the Ministry of the Marine was instructed to hold the Pacific Fleet in readiness. The Russians, with only two hundred and fifty citizens residing in China, also wanted to maintain an independent position and refused to get involved in a possible joint action. The Germans were less reluctant,

55555555555555

and Berlin proceeded to dispatch warships to Chinese coastal waters. In response, Salisbury ordered two British ships to the area, "a simple measure of precaution," he said, "destined to satisfy English citizens and to awaken the government of China to the perils of a policy of hostility with regard to strangers." Washington, while still denying the need for a joint naval demonstration, also reacted to Berlin's move, and at the end of March ordered an American vessel, the *Wheeler,* to proceed from Manila Bay to the waters off north China. Secretary Hay was obviously nervous and told French Minister Jules Cambon that he believed Minister Conger in Peking to be "excessively zealous." If Conger threatened the Chinese with landing American military troops, said the secretary, he would be disavowed in Washington.

THE GROWING CRISIS

For a brief period it looked as though the situation in China might improve. In early April, with the Boxers increasing their activities in Chihli Province and rapidly approaching the capital, the Tsungli Yamen published in the *Peking Gazette* a report by Viceroy Yü Lu of Chihli containing the text of the decree that the ministers had earlier demanded be published. In response to this apparent about-face in the official attitude toward the Boxers, Chihli officials were temporarily inclined to put down disorder with severity. The shift in attitude, however, was more apparent than real. By late April Boxer groups were congregating along the north-south Peking-Hankow railway line, and on April 24 two thousand Boxers attacked a Catholic village at Chiang Chia Chuang near the rail hub of Pao Ting Fu. The Chinese Christians in the area had been prepared for the attack and defended themselves with courage. As a result, the Boxer forces were defeated and the defenders suffered only light losses. Elsewhere, however, Boxers began to appear openly in the Chinese sections of Peking and Tientsin, and anxiety increased in the legation quarter. Besieged by appeals from French missionary groups in Chihli Province, Minister Pichon began pressing his colleagues for energetic action to compel the court to maintain order. For a time, Conger and MacDonald refrained from putting pressure on the Chinese, fearing that to do so might lead to a collapse of the government and the onset of anarchy.

By late May, however, it became clear that Pichon's warnings had to be taken seriously. The news of the attack on the Chinese Christian village south of Pao Ting Fu was supplemented by rumors of an impending massacre of all foreigners in China. Early in May Pichon received an urgent message from the doughty bishop of Peking, Monsignor Favier, reporting that sixty of his Chinese converts had been burned alive during a Boxer attack. Rumors circulated that the Boxers were surrounding the capital and lighting fires in the heart of Peking. Placards appeared announcing the imminent annihilation of missionaries and a general uprising against all foreigners. Favier relayed a report received from an informant that the Boxers planned to enter Peking *en masse* at a signal, and added that he needed a minimum of forty to fifty French sailors to protect the Peitang Catholic Cathedral in the heart of the city. On May 20 the ministers accepted Pichon's proposal to send a message to the Tsungli Yamen demanding that the government take immediate measures to restore secure conditions. The ministers unanimously agreed that, if the situation did not improve, they would formally request a naval demonstration and the dispatch of troops from the ships stationed off the coastal waters near Taku. In response to appeals for help from citizens in the provinces, they advised all missionaries living in outlying areas to send their dependents to more secure areas in the center, where they were considered safe under the protection of viceroys Chang Chih-tung and Liu K'un-yi.

Official Chinese opinion continued to vacillate. In the first few days of May the court discussed the possibility of assimilating the Boxer groups into the militia and asked Yü Lu and Yüan Shih-k'ai to concur. By May 16 both governors had responded in the negative. Yü Lu's reply was to the point. He said that most Boxers were only roving troublemakers who tried to seduce the people and make private profit. As a rule, they lacked military talent, and it would be difficult to assimilate and control them. For the moment the court withheld action on the matter.

As massacres of Christians continued during the final days of May, and the Tsungli Yamen resisted giving total satisfaction, the powers began to consider further action. Pichon called the French ship *Descartes* to Shantung, and the Russians ordered two ships from Port Arthur. These measures did nothing to alleviate the crisis. On May 28 the legations received news of further attacks by Boxer units at Pao Ting Fu — railway stations and bridges had been burned and a number of foreigners killed. The survivors, mostly railroad engineers and their families, had managed to escape on foot and fled toward the foreign concession area at Tientsin. Several were killed en route in scattered Boxer attacks; the remainder were rescued by a troop of Russian Cossacks sent from Tientsin.

Reports of the attacks at Pao Ting Fu galvanized the legations into action. The ministers decided unanimously to request a call-up of military forces from the warships off the coast near Taku. The Tsungli Yamen was informed of the decision and asked to make trains ready at Taku to bring the foreign troops to the capital. The court, apparently warned that open confrontation with the foreigners might occur, immediately responded that it was taking action and asked the ministers to postpone their decision. At the same time it issued a decree calling on local authorities to arrest Boxer leaders and disperse their followers. As before, the decree drew a delicate distinction between vagabonds and troublemakers and loyal elements. The ambiguity was sufficient to negate at the local level the potential effects of the decree on behalf of the foreigners.

The ministers refused the request of the Tsungli

Yamen to postpone this call-up of forces. Indeed, Pichon had already instructed French forces to get underway, and British Minister MacDonald informed the Tsungli Yamen that troops would be sent, with or without Chinese permission. If transport was not provided by the government, the joint force would be sent on foot and come in augmented numbers. On May 31 the resistance of the Chinese government collapsed, and the foreigners were given permission to move their troops, provided the number of guards was limited to no more than thirty for each legation. The decision had not been an easy one for the court to make, and, according to one student of the period, it was the troop call-up that precipitated the eventual outbreak of conflict. There was serious discussion within the court of the possibility of stopping the Western troops by force. K'ang Yi, one of the more determined members of the antiforeign faction, proposed to resist them at the gates of Peking. The moderates, led by Jung Lu and Prince Ch'ing, were able to reject the suggestion only with considerable difficulty.

On May 30 Russian and French troops had begun to leave their ships off the coast at Taku. Chinese troops in the vicinity menaced them and threatened to fire, so they immediately reembarked and waited for further instructions. After permission had been received from Peking on May 31, debarkation resumed. The contingent sent to Peking consisted of 340 men — 75 Russians, 75 British, 75 French, 50 Americans, 40 Italians, and 25 Japanese. Despite the Chinese stipulation that only 30 men per country be deployed, they met no opposition and arrived at the capital in the early morning of June 2. An additional contingent of 52 Germans and 37 Austrians followed soon afterward. The majority of the troops available to the powers remained on shipboard off the coast.

The dispatch of the legation guards from Taku to the capital exacerbated the crisis at court. Moderates such as Jung Lu wanted the Boxers suppressed. Although not particularly motivated by sympathy for the foreigners, they were convinced that war with the barbarians would lead to disaster for China. Although they were able to win approval for the troop movement, they were overruled on other issues by the war party. At one meeting, when the militants argued that the Boxers were patriots and should be treated as supporters of the dynasty, the empress dowager significantly kept silent.

The actions of the court were more eloquent than words. When forces under General Nieh Shih-ch'eng clashed with Boxers who had burned railway stations on the Tientsin-Peking line and killed hundreds of innocent Chinese, he was reproved by the court. It was evident that the empress dowager was leaning toward the reactionaries. On June 6 the Grand Council made a half-hearted decision to disband the Boxers, but a mission sent by the court to see the Boxer leaders near Peking failed to achieve results. The members of the mission were unable to see the rebel leaders and, according to one account, simply posted proclamations in the Boxer camp. However, they returned to the capital, with demands from the Boxer leaders: withdraw the military troops of Nieh Shih-ch'eng from the vicinity of the capital; punish all magistrates who had taken hostile actions against Boxer elements; and permit the Moslem troops under General Tung Fu-hsiang to attack the foreigners. The third suggestion was rejected, but the first two were soon to be implemented. Once again, the court issued a decree which drew a distinction between the Boxers, who were considered to have formed legitimately for "self-defense purposes," and bandits who were interested simply in stirring up social disorder. Significantly, the decree was also critical of "bad elements" within the Chinese Christian community. The Chinese court was moving inexorably closer to a confrontation with the foreigners.[6]

The strengthening of the antiforeign attitude at court, combined with the growing boldness of Boxer attacks in Chihli Province, worried the legations. On June 6 rioters cut the rail links between the capital and Tientsin, halfway to the coast. The ministers, facing the possibility of complete isolation in Peking, sent a joint telegram asking their governments to instruct the naval authorities at Taku "to take concerted measures for our relief." Some proposed even harsher measures. The German minister, Baron von Ketteler, wanted to march on the summer palace and overthrow the empress dowager.

Reaction in world capitals to the new developments in China was mixed. British Foreign Secretary Salisbury was inclined to trust his man-on-the-spot and informed MacDonald and Admiral Edward Seymour, British naval commander at Taku, to take whatever action they deemed necessary. Several British warships—the *Centurion,* the *Endymion,* the *Whiting,* and the *Fame*—had just arrived off Taku to strengthen Seymour's flotilla. The French government decided to dispatch a fleet of ships to China under Admiral Cournejelles to be held at Minister Pichon's disposition. The Russian admiral at Port Arthur declared himself ready to send five thousand Russian troops if needed, and Minister Giers in Peking was authorized by St. Petersburg to call on these forces if he deemed it necessary.

Washington continued to hold back, however, despite Conger's plea for joint action. Secretary Hay feared that the United States would be drawn into an anti-Chinese alliance. He told the French ambassador in Washington that American actions in China would necessarily be limited, since the nation's forces in Asia were currently being used to suppress the guerrilla insurrection led by nationalist general Aguinaldo in the Philippines. Hay did agree to dispatch a token force of marines whose duties would be limited to protecting the American legation. They would not be permitted, he said, to join in a collective action against China.

Despite Hay's position, there were signs that the United States was being gradually drawn into an anti-Chinese coalition. Certain representatives of the American press were incensed at Boxer attacks on Christian missionaries and called on the McKinley administration to show some backbone in protecting American and Christian interests in China. The French ambassador to Washington, Jules Cambon, noted that the United States, "which had always affected not to talk of Chinese affairs," had "suddenly changed its attitude." Possibly as a trial balloon, a dispatch by Minister Conger describing the alarming situation in north China was given to the press, along with a report by Admiral Louis Kempff, commander of American forces at Taku.

Hay sent ambiguous instructions to his minister in Peking, advising him to "act independently in protection of American interests where practicable, and concurrently with representatives of other powers if necessity arise." Hay was obviously in a difficult position. He explained to the French ambassador that the American troops already in China were there only to protect the American legation, but when Cambon pressed him on American actions in the event of war, he agreed that it might be necessary to place American forces in China under joint allied command. As Hay explained the situation, the United States would agree to "concordance" but not "accord" with the actions of the powers. Presumably, the secretary was attempting to distinguish between informal cooperation and formal agreement. This subtle distinction would prove difficult, if not impossible, to maintain in practice.

Within China the situation was rapidly deteriorating. On June 4 the telegraph lines from Peking were cut. Except for the imperial telegraph line, all telecommunications with the coast were severed. Two days later news arrived that the Boxers intended to burn the Peitang cathedral, which was promptly placed under guard. On June 7 the Boxers set fire to the thatch roof of a police hut adjacent to the legation quarter; European volunteers from a neighboring building put out the blaze while the police at the post apparently still slept inside the hut. Word then began circulating that the Boxers intended to burn not only the legation quarter, but also the nearby Tsungli Yamen, the symbol of China's humiliation at the hands of the West. When he heard of the plan, British Minister MacDonald was prompted to comment with some irony, "In that case I hope a favorable wind will carry the fire toward the palace." On June 8 Russian Orthodox missions just outside the walls of the city were burned. On the following day, as usual, the train left Machiapu, at the south entrance to the capital, for the coast. Because of Boxer attacks in the area to the east of Peking, it would be the last train to leave the capital for the sea until the end of the crisis.

The diplomatic corps promptly asked the Chinese government for permission to request additional troops, but the request was refused. At court antiforeign elements were now in complete command. Ominously, a shift of personnel took place at the Tsungli Yamen which, under the presidency of Prince Ch'ing had long been a source of moderate attitudes within the Chinese government. On June 9 Prince Ch'ing was replaced by Prince Tuan, a diehard of the antiforeign bloc. Three other Manchu reactionaries—Ch'i Hsiu, Na T'ung, and P'u Hsing—were also appointed to the group. For the first time the Tsungli Yamen became an instrument of the pro-war faction. Minister Conger, on hearing the news, called these appointments "extremely unfortunate" for the safety of the foreigners in Peking.

The menacing situation around Peking soon—and perhaps inevitably—erupted into violence. Until now foreign residents in Peking had not been personally harassed or threatened. On June 9, however, a contingent of Boxers burned the grandstand at the International Race Course just beyond the south gates of the city. Incinerated in the conflagration were a number of Chinese Christian converts who had apparently been brought there expressly for that purpose. A group of young British diplomats out for a ride on horseback came upon the scene by accident and had to flee for their lives.

This incident prompted British Minister MacDonald,

on his own initiative, to send a telegram to Admiral Seymour:

Situation extremely grave, unless arrangements are made for immediate advance to Peking it will be too late.

(At the time someone unkindly remarked that MacDonald was more worried about his horses than about the human lives involved.) Then on June 10 the summer homes of several British legation families, located on a hill to the west of Peking, were looted and burned. Only with difficulty were the British dependents—women and children—rescued and brought to the legation quarter. The next day the chancellor of the Japanese legation, Akira Sugiyama, left the quarter to find out whether additional detachments of foreign troops had arrived. Nearing the Yung Ting gate, he was murdered by some of the Kansu troops of General Tung Fu-hsiang. Sugiyama was the first member of the legation staffs to be harmed by the antiforeign element. The murder was a harsh demonstration that the diplomatic corps was not exempt from attack.

The crisis seemed to intensify daily. On June 11 the telegraph line to Russia (through Kalgan and Kiakhta), the last tie to Europe, was severed (although it was briefly re-established the next day, it was permanently cut on the thirteenth). By that evening, the entire area to the northeast of the legation quarter in Peking was in flames, including several Western missions and churches. With Boxer attacks rapidly approaching the very doorstep of the legation quarter, the people inside were finally persuaded to try to protect themselves. On June 13 Boxers began to enter the quarter, and the ministers took their first actions to isolate themselves from the contagion in the city. That afternoon temporary barricades were erected at both ends of Legation Street and at the northern and southern termini of Customs Street on the eastern border of the quarter. Patrols were set up in the area to drive Boxers

from the streets and to shoot those who appeared. Foreigners and Chinese Christians living in the city who could
not find protection elsewhere began gathering in the legation quarter, Favier's Peitang Cathedral, the Nan T'ang
Cathedral in the Chinese city, and at the American
Methodist Mission to the east. At the mission several hundred converts were guarded by a small contingent of U.S.
Marines. At the Peitang Cathedral Favier called urgently
for assistance, and a party of forty-three French and
Italian marines was dispatched in response.

Obviously, the Boxers had become a serious threat.
That evening large crowds of Boxers gathered at the
Imperial Bank just east of the quarter on Ch'ang An
Street. Attempting to set fire to the bank, they were
driven back by Austrian troops nearby, but they soon
turned on the foreign defenses. A foreign member of the
Imperial Maritime Customs in the area at the time des-
cribed the sight:

Everything had been quiet after the first ten minutes, when a few
volleys scattered the half-hearted Boxers, who had attempted to set
fire to the Imperial Bank of China (so ardent is the patriotism of
these Boxers that they destroy indiscriminately Government railways and the Government banks!), but about 10:30 lights were seen
approaching.
    These increased in number, and soon the Austrians felt sure that
a mob of several thousands was approaching with torches to fire
their Legation and the Customs. They waited until the lights came
within a hundred yards, and then bang, bang, bang went their guns,
and volley after volley rang out, and it seemed that nothing could
live under that hail of bullets . . . . At the first volley the centre of
the line of torches was simply wiped out, and after the fourth there
were only a few lights to be seen. But what I can't understand is that
not one sound, not one moan, was heard.[7]

That same night the Boxers attacked and set fire to
the Nan T'ang Cathedral, built in 1622. Trapped inside and
burned to death were several hundred Chinese Christians,
inhabitants of the area who had sought safety in the
cathedral. A patrol sent out from the legation quarter ar-

rived too late. They found the church in ashes and several hundred corpses smoldering in the ruins.

The following few days saw a continuation of the violence. On the night of the fourteenth all foreign premises outside of the guarded area were burned, including fifty-four Protestant dwellings, eighteen chapels, twenty-seven schools, and nineteen dispensaries and hospitals. Not all the destruction was aimed specifically at the foreigner. On the evening of June 16 Boxers set fire to several shops which catered to foreigners in the commercial sector of the Chinese city, not far from the south wall. According to Richard O'Connor, author of *The Spirit Soldiers: A Narrative of the Boxer Rebellion,* the Boxer leader responsible had intended to destroy only certain selected shops and had believed that his magical powers would prevent the spread of the conflagration. He had overestimated the force of his persuasions, however, and before the fire burned out, it had destroyed several blocks of shops as well as the tower of the famous Ch'ien Men, the imperial entrance along the south wall of the Tartar city.[8]

As the situation rapidly deteriorated, the legations attempted to strike back. Troop patrols were sent out on actual raids; on June 16 one group located over fifty Boxers looting a Chinese temple and killed them all in cold blood. Some of the legation troops at the barricades began to fire at the soldiers of Tung Fu-hsiang's army, who by this time had joined the Boxers in the growing siege surrounding the quarter.

Similar conditions existed in Tientsin. On June 2 Boxers raced through the foreign concession area setting buildings afire. On the fourteenth Boxer elements entered the native city in force, evoking no response from the local administration. More buildings were burned in the foreign concession area, and mobs destroyed chapels and the famous French Catholic Cathedral in the heart of the city.

During this week of semi-siege, Boxers circulated freely throughout both cities but made no concentrated attacks on foreign-held areas. They seemed to be waiting for a word from authority. As for the Chinese government, it seemed to be either powerless or unwilling to take any action to quiet the situation. It was clear to all that the worst was yet to come. The attacks had shown the foreigners a side of the Chinese temperament that they had not known existed. One foreign observer described an exchange of fire with Boxer groups near the legation quarter:

An hour afterwards we heard the most terrible and awful sound that we had ever imagined. The sky was rent with yells of "Sha, sha" [kill, kill], and the whole city seemed to be battering at the gates and thirsting for our blood. It was the yell of wild beasts; no pen could describe it; and our blood simply froze in our veins.

It was not the fear of what they could do—most of them, in fact, almost all, were only armed with swords; but it was our first dreadful peep into the depths of a Chinaman's heart, and we saw there the deadly, undying wild beast hate of the foreigner that we had barely guessed at before.[9]

Chapter Five

The International
Detachments

On the evening of June 9 Admiral Edward
Seymour, commander of the British naval forces
in north China waters and the senior officer
among the allied commanders in the area, received a telegram from Sir Claude MacDonald asking
urgently for assistance. Seymour immediately wired back
that a relief force under his command was just leaving the
coast and heading for Peking. Seymour's reply was the last
message received by the legations before all communication with the outside world was cut off.

MacDonald had sent his hasty telegram after the
burning of the Peking International Race Course, and the
wire had finally spurred to action the military forces off
the north China coast. The decision to act had not been
easy for the Western military commanders. Warships had
been congregating off the China coast at the port city of
Taku since late in May. By early June fifteen warships of
various nationalities were already anchored near the mouth
of the Pei Ho, and more were expected shortly. Through
communications from the legation quarter in Peking the

allied commanders were aware that the situation in north China had become critical, but they had not received specific orders from their home governments. In the absence of such instructions they had the power to take such actions as they saw fit to protect the lives and property of their nationals in China.

The original contingent of guards had been sent to Peking by rail on May 31 in response to the request of the legations. On June 4, after hearing of the attacks at Pao Ting Fu and the murder of several Europeans by marauding bands of Boxers, the commanders sent an additional mixed force by rail to the capital. The next day Admiral Seymour called a joint conference to arrange for coordinated action among the powers in case hostilities broke out. At a subsequent meeting it was agreed that, if the legations were physically cut off from communication with the coast, the commanders would dispatch a relief force to Peking.

On receiving MacDonald's urgent appeal on June 9, Seymour acted quickly. He immediately ordered the debarkation of troops from British warships off Taku and at six o'clock the following morning left with them by train for Tientsin, some thirty miles inland. Seymour's action was considered by some to be unduly precipitous, especially since he had not informed the other allied commanders personally of his decision. Instead, he left messages suggesting that they follow his action at their earliest opportunity. Seymour's troops arrived in Tientsin after an uneventful trip. By the end of the day most of the other Western commanders had followed his lead, and a relief force of about two thousand men of various nationalities (915 British, 450 Germans, 358 French, 312 Russians, 112 Americans, 54 Japanese, 40 Italians, and 25 Austrians) had gathered for an advance to Peking.

At the time Seymour's apparent aim was to transport his troops all the way to Peking by rail. Since much of the Tientsin-Peking line had been destroyed by Boxer attacks, he planned to take with him material for repairs along the way. On his arrival at Tientsin Seymour had requested per-

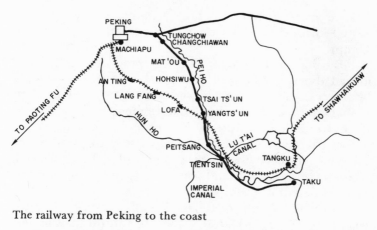

The railway from Peking to the coast

mission from local authorities to requisition railroad cars to transport his troops to Peking. Governor-General Yü Lu was somewhat reluctant, but at 9:30 A.M. on June 11 he gave his permission. The relief force of slightly over two thousand men, with three days' provisions, left immediately for Peking. Seymour hoped to arrive at the capital later the same day. But between Tientsin and Peking were uncounted numbers of Boxers and the imperial military forces of Nieh Shih-ch'eng.

With the approach of Admiral Seymour's mixed force, the Chinese government faced a crucial question. Did the Chinese army have the ability to protect the capital and resist the Western forces? Since the middle of the nineteenth century periodic military confrontations with Western powers had consistently resulted in defeat and humiliation. In fact, the main cause for China's failure to stem Western aggression was the poor quality of its military forces. Under the Manchus, the Chinese army had traditionally been divided into two main forces—the Manchu bannermen, two hundred thousand strong, and the so-called Green Standard Army, a force of five hundred thousand native Chinese troops under Chinese command. The Green Standard forces were poorly trained and had proven useless in combat. Their officers regularly claimed to have more men under their command than actually existed in order to claim their salaries, and were generally corrupt.

During the Taiping rebellion at midcentury, the hard-pressed dynasty had been unable to resist the rebels with the forces under central command. Thus, it had been compelled to agree to the establishment of local forces which would defend the provinces and fight the rebels. In the aftermath of the rebellion these provincial forces had grown into cumbersome armies under the control of governors and viceroys and were totally divorced from the control of central authorities.

In the last decade of the nineteenth century the court began to make some halting efforts to reform the Chinese military establishment, particularly after the defeat by Japan.[1] A few progressive officials had suggested that the province-based Green Standard armies be disbanded and replaced by new modern armies of several hundred thousand well-trained troops. Others advocated the establishment of modern military schools, the hiring of foreign military advisers, and a complete reorganization of the empire's entire defense system. In the waning years of the century a few attempts were made by the dynasty to implement these suggestions. Foreign officers were hired to provide modern training in weapons and tactics, arsenals were built, and a few modern weapons were purchased. Most important, two modern armies were organized and put under the command of two of the more influential Chinese civil officials in the empire. The so-called Self-strengthening Army of Chang Chih-tung, viceroy of Wuchang, was established in the central provinces of the Yangtse Valley. The second was the New, or Peiyang, Army, set up by Yüan Shih-k'ai in the northern area near the capital. These two forces were to be formulated along Western lines, with separate units for infantry, cavalry, and artillery. They were to be armed with modern weapons and trained by foreign advisers. The two armies were to form the nucleus of a modernized defense force that could protect China against outside attack. Both Chang and Yüan believed that the key to an efficient army was the quality of the officers and men. Their officers were to be well trained and incorruptible, the troops literate and well paid. With support from central revenues, the new modern armies were able to recruit the best among the Green Standard Army, and both forces totaled several thousand men as the century came to a close.

The reform of China's outmoded defense establishment would require a lot more than two crack modern armies. The entire system was corrupt, the soldier was held in low esteem in Chinese society, and there were no modern weapons or training personnel. Finally, there was no central control over the remaining Green Standard forces. These factors combined to make the modernization of China's armies almost impossible.

In 1898, desperate to find a means of resisting the encroachments of Western powers, the court agreed to a plan calling for the formation of a Chinese militia. The idea had originally been proposed by K'ang Yu-wei and implemented during the hundred days of reform in the summer of 1898. When Tz'u Hsi was restored to power in September, she agreed to continue with the plan. The function of the proposed militia was not clear; according to one source, they were to be used internally for protection against bandits. Their training and weaponry would almost certainly prove inadequate for combat against foreigners. These vague aspects of the militia plan created confusion in the minds of foreign observers, and some contended that the militia was the basis for the Boxer movement itself. The evidence shows, however, that the Boxers were not fundamentally a creation of the dynasty.

In 1899 the court made one final major attempt to prepare for a possible confrontation with the foreign powers. To strengthen Manchu control over forces in the capital area, it appointed Jung Lu, grand councilor and ex-viceroy of Chihli, as commander of all Chinese forces in the Peking area. These troops formed a new Guards Army (often called the Grand Army in the West) under the control of the central government. Jung Lu immediately reorganized them into five divisions (actually armies) representing left, right, front, rear, and center. The Front Army, under General Nieh Shih-ch'eng, one of China's finest soldiers, consisted of some thirteen thousand troops to be placed at Lu T'ai, directly north of Taku near the coast. The Left Army, with ten thousand men under General Sung Ch'ing, was to be located at Shanhaikuan, on the northern coast, and would be responsible for protecting the eastern entrance at the Great Wall. Troops for both forces would be recruited from the old Anhui provincial army formed by Li Hung-chang several years earlier, and both would be reorganized along modern lines.

The Rear Army, under the ex-brigand Muslim general Tung Fu-hsiang, was to be located at Tungchow, directly east of the capital. Tung Fu-hsiang's ten thousand men, previously known as the Kansu Army, had the reputation of being ill-disciplined, but good fighters. The Right Army, the Peiyang Army of Yüan Shih-k'ai, was to be based at Hsiao Chan, near Tientsin. At Nan Yüan, just south of Peking, Jung Lu himself would command the Center Army, which consisted primarily of Manchu bannermen. This force would number fewer than ten thousand men. Headquarters for the five armies, which totaled approximately sixty thousand men, was to be located in Peking. Additional troops, most of them under the command of the new Chihli viceroy, Yü Lu, would make the total forces in the metropolitan area approximately ninety thousand.

The formation of the new Guards Army was a major step in the modernization of Chinese military forces. There were already signs, however, that it might not be adequate for the occasion. Foreign military officers who inspected the Chinese troops in the capital area commented on a variety of continuing problems: poor leadership, lack of training, the wide variety of weapons (Ralph Powell, author of *The Rise of Chinese Military Power, 1895-*

1912, says that one unit had fourteen different types of rifles), and those persistent evils, corruption and inadequate pay.

The court also made halting efforts to modernize the military forces elsewhere in China, particularly in those areas considered vital to the defense of the empire — Manchuria, the Yangtse Valley, and the area of the Huai River near Hsüchow. Local autonomy and lack of funding were major obstacles and not much was achieved. In a war against the foreigner, Jung Lu's forces in the metropolitan areas would have to bear the burden of the fighting.

CONDITIONS IN THE CENTER

A decision to resist the foreigner would create an additional and perhaps more serious problem for the court. Peking's belligerent reactions to the activities of the great powers were not echoed with the same intensity in official circles elsewhere in China. To the contrary, many top officials in the central and southern provinces were aghast at the possibility that China would go to war against all the Western powers at the same time. This was certainly the attitude of the two Chinese viceroys in the Yangtse Valley area — Chang Chih-tung, viceroy of Hunan and Hupei, and Liu K'un-yi, viceroy of Kiangsi, Kiangsu, and Anhui; and of Li Hung-chang, viceroy of Kwangtung and Kwangsi provinces in south China. Unlike many of the Manchu noblemen in the north, who had relatively little acquaintance with the West and held a deep-seated suspicion of all things foreign, the Chinese viceroys who ruled the central and southern provinces with considerable autonomy were sophisticated and worldly. They had dealt with the Western nations for several decades and had long believed that, in order for China to survive, it must gain time in which to modernize. To do so China would have to learn to conciliate.[2]

For years Chinese viceroys such as these had held the Manchu empire together. Chang, a native of Chihli, was born in an official family in 1837. He was a bright classical scholar in his youth. At the age of twenty-six he began to show a tendency toward unorthodoxy by concentrating on contemporary problems in the metropolitan examinations for a bureaucratic career. Entering government service in 1867, Chang earned a reputation as a moderate convinced of the need for China to reform in order to compete in the modern world. In 1882 he received his first gubernatorial appointment and quickly showed himself to be a major force for moderate change in China, building arsenals, advocating reform of commerce and industry, and forming the new Self-strengthening Army. Although Chang Chih-tung was more progressive than most of the Manchu aristocrats at court in Peking, he was a cautious man in a crisis, and his loyalty to the dynasty was unquestioned. If he opposed the Boxers, it was because he saw them as a danger to the dynasty, creating an excuse for Western powers to intervene in China to protect the lives of their citizens.[3]

At the time of the crisis, Liu K'un-yi, a Hunanese with thirty-five years of service to the dynasty, was nearing the end of a long and distinguished career. In earlier years he had often been active in diplomatic negotiations and was generally identified with a policy of conciliation. While governor-general of Kiangsi and Kiangsu in the early 1890s, he had severely suppressed antimissionary riots led by secret societies. Earlier considered a conservative on social matters, he had gradually become a cautious supporter of reform.

The final member of the triumvirate, Li Hung-chang, was the most prominent statesman in China during the last quarter of the nineteenth century. From an official family in Anhui Province, he had risen to the vital position of viceroy of Chihli in the 1870s and 1880s. After nearly a half-century of service to the dynasty, he was considered to be one of China's most astute diplomats. While his probity was sometimes questioned, Li was generally thought to be a man with whom Western governments way station en route to facilitate the shipment of new supplies up the line.

Seymour hoped to continue on to Peking the next morning, June 13, but reconnaissance units reported that they were unable to penetrate beyond the village of An Ting, only a few miles west of Lang Fang, because of Boxer acitivity. Short of food and water and in need of additional material to repair the rail line, Seymour called a halt and sent back for supplies. Now, however, his troubles began to multiply. Supply trains attempting to return to Tientsin for provisions were forced to turn back because of new destruction on the rail line. Unable to advance toward Peking, and cut off from the rear, Seymour's forces were trapped.

In Peking, reports of the approach of the allied expeditionary force had caused consternation in court circles. The Tsungli Yamen, now controlled by reactionary elements, pleaded with Sir Claude MacDonald to halt Seymour's advance. On the morning of June 13, while Seymour was debating whether to move on toward the capital or to retreat, the court told the legations that the thousand guards already in Peking were more than adequate to guard the diplomatic community and demanded that Seymour's force return to Tientsin. When the ministers refused, the Chinese government realized that open hostilities were inevitable. At a meeting of the Grand Council it was decided that imperial troops would be used to resist the further advance of the allied expeditionary force. Viceroy Yü Lu was ordered to instruct General Nieh Shih-ch'eng to place his troops along the railroad line to guard against any attempt on the part of the Western troops to threaten the capital. At Taku, General Lo Jung-kuang was ordered to be on the alert for any surprise moves by the Western naval forces off the coast. To protect Peking, which now had about five thousand troops under Tung Fu-hsiang and Prince Tuan, the court ordered General Yüan Shih-k'ai to rush his troops to the city.

At Lang Fang, the situation was perilous. Seymour

could negotiate. In 1899, at the age of seventy-six, he was appointed viceroy of the southern provinces of Kwangtung and Kwangsi.

In response to the trouble in the north the court had instructed civil authorities throughout China to put their military forces on a war footing and to resist any attempt at the landing of foreign forces in China. In May 1899 K'ang Yi, antiforeign Manchu nobleman and head of the War Ministry, was sent to central China. His mission was to inspect the defensive conditions in the Yangtse Valley area and to garner financial and political support for the central government from Viceroy Liu K'un-yi. Like Chang Chih-tung and Li Hung-chang, Liu had survived in the bureaucracy by learning how to conciliate influential persons at the court, and he graciously consented to provide funds for the imperial treasury. His opinions on the crisis were another matter, but for the moment he kept them to himself.

Liu K'un-yi might have been willing to make a token gesture to the court in its hour of need, but he and his fellow viceroys were concerned by the drift toward war in the north and they began to consider actions to prevent the spread of the crisis elsewhere in China. As the trouble grew, they attempted to isolate the areas under their control from the antiforeign rioting and to exterminate every manifestation of the Boxer movement throughout central and south China. A few scattered signs of unrest had appeared in these areas, but they could usually be attributed to starvation conditions rather than hostility against foreigners. Once it became evident that the antiforeign contagion had infected the court in Peking, the viceroys began to consider the feasibility of mutual alliances in order to protect themselves from the madness in the north.

THE SEYMOUR EXPEDITION MOVES OUT

Admiral Edward Seymour had the choice of two

Bird's-eye view of the north China plain from the coast to Peking
(*Leslie's Weekly,* July 28, 1900, p. 92)

possible routes to cover the sixty-odd miles between
Tientsin and Peking. One route followed the bank of the
Pei Ho, directly northwest of Tientsin, through the commercial city of Tungchow and thence up to the eastern
gates of the capital. The other and more southerly route
followed the Tientsin-Peking railroad. North of Tientsin

the rail line followed the east bank of the riv[er]
Yangts'un, where a railroad bridge carried the line
to the opposite bank. From there the railroad w[ent]
west-northwesterly direction considerably south [of the]
river and eventually connected with the Peking-[Han?]
line just south of Peking.

Admiral Seymour was aware that the flatlan[ds be-]
tween Tientsin and the capital were infested with [Boxers]
who had ripped up much of the rail line to Peki[ng. He]
planned to repair the line en route, thus saving tim[e and]
avoiding the harsher climate and more difficult terr[ain of]
the river route. Still, the area between Tientsin and P[eking,]
primarily flat and sometimes marshy lowlands with [scat-]
tered villages of mud huts, was almost unbearably h[ot in]
the summer of 1900. Seymour's forces would ha[ve to]
trudge through miles of wheat fields in the blist[ering]
summer sun.

From the first day it appeared that Seymour [had]
made some questionable assumptions. The two-thous[and-]
man force, traveling in five railroad cars, met little B[oxer]
resistance except for a few skirmishes at the village o[f Lo]
Ra.[4] But repair of the railroad line proved time-consum[ing,]
and at the end of the first day the expedition had o[nly]
managed to reach the railroad bridge at Yangts'un, twen[ty-]
five miles north of Tientsin. On the morning of June [11,]
as the allied troop train crossed the railroad bridge to [the]
west bank of the river, Seymour's forces encountered [the]
troops of General Nieh Shih-ch'eng's Front Army. T[he]
latter offered no opposition but simply exchanged friend[ly]
greetings and taunts.

Problems continued to impede progress, howeve[r.]
Moving westward toward Lang Fang, the expedition[ary]
troops were slowed down by track repairs and constantl[y]
harassed by bands of Boxers operating from the whea[t]
fields along the line. By evening they had reached Lan[g]
Fang, only halfway from Yangts'un to the capital, whic[h]
was still forty miles away. Provisions were running short[,]
and Seymour left small detachments of guards at each rail[-]

had seriously underestimated the difficulties he was likely to encounter on the way to Peking. He was a career naval officer, with little experience in land warfare, and was obviously out of his element. Moreover, his capacity to lead was hampered by the inherent ambiguity of the situation. As commander of a multinational force, his was a position of seniority more than of command.

For two days Seymour and his forces remained stranded at Lang Fang while the admiral attempted to decide what to do. Harassment from Boxer bands armed with spears, swords, and even clubs did not cause many casualties—indeed, the losses on the Chinese side were much greater—but they added to the difficulty of opening communications with the rear. His reconnaissance forces had been attacked on June 13 by a Boxer force at An Ting, and to the rear there had been attacks on the railway station at the village of Lo Fa, halfway to the railway bridge at Yangts'un. Later, Seymour would contend that "an immediate dash to save the legations was the only course to pursue." At Lang Fang, however, retreat seemed advisable. On June 15, after one more abortive attempt to send a supply train back for provisions, Seymour decided to return to Tientsin on foot.

THE ATTACK ON THE TAKU FORTS

In the warships off the coast at Taku, the news of the Seymour fiasco caused serious concern. The rumors that the Chinese government was willing to risk hostilities with the Western powers now seemed to be proving all too true. Information from the mainland suggested that the court was now actively preparing for war. General Nieh Shih-ch'eng, one source reported, had been instructed to move his troops toward Taku. Mines were being laid at the mouth of the Pei Ho to impede the entry of Western ships toward Tientsin. Rumors abounded that Chinese forces planned to launch a massive attack on June 19, the anniversary of the Tientsin massacre of 1870.

On June 16 the admirals decided to take action. At a conference held on the Russian flagship and attended by military commanders of all the powers except the United States, they decided unanimously to send an ultimatum to the Chinese demanding the surrender of the Taku forts which protected the entrance to the Pei Ho. The Chinese fortifications at Taku consisted of several forts lying astride the Pei Ho at the conjunction of the river with the

An artist's view of the Taku forts (*Leslie's Weekly*, July 28, 1900, p. 67)

Gulf of Chihli. They had been destroyed by the allies during the Lorcha Arrow War and rebuilt shortly afterward. If the Chinese did not surrender the forts by 2:00 A.M. the following morning, the powers would open hostilities.

An attack on the Taku forts would be difficult, since the mud flats at the mouth of the river made it impossible for deep-draft warships to approach close enough to the fortifications to bombard them with their heavy guns. The major warships of the powers were forced to remain ten miles away. After dark on the evening of June 16 nine shallow-draft gunboats (French, British, Russian, and German) entered the river and took up positions adjacent to the forts. Just after midnight the Chinese garrison opened fire on the small flotilla in the river. The allied ships responded, and, after several hours of intermittent firing of their light guns, they sent landing parties across

the mud flats to storm the Chinese fortifications. By the early morning hours Chinese resistance had collapsed. With fewer than two hundred casualties (according to one estimate, sixty-four were killed and eighty-nine wounded), the Western powers had won the first major battle of the war. Chinese losses, many of them a result of the allied bombardment which blew up powder magazines within the fortifications, were estimated at three thousand.

The Western assault on Taku settled the gnawing controversy within the Chinese government over whether or not to go to war. Even as late as June 16 the court had considered the possibility of a compromise. At a meeting of the Grand Council on that date, Manchu nobles in attendance were virtually unanimous in advocating firm resistance, but a few councilmen were hesitant, asking how China could expect to resist all the great powers at one time. When K'ang Yi replied that the Boxers were invincible, someone commented that, to the contrary, as a force for the defense of the dynasty they were completely unreliable. It was Tz'u Hsi herself who settled the argument:

If we cannot rely upon the supernatural formulas, can we not rely on the hearts of the people? China is weak; the only thing we can depend on is the heart of the people. If we lose it, how can we maintain our territory?[5]

To her listeners the meaning was clear. By the "hearts of the people" she meant the Boxers.

In the end a compromise was reached. Unaware that Seymour's forces had already retreated, the council sent two men to persuade the admiral to return to Tientsin. In the likely event that this bid for peace was unsuccessful (and it was: the two emissaries were unable to get through and were forced to return to the capital), preparations would be made for war. Viceroy Yü Lu and the generals in the capital area were instructed to resist any attempt by Western forces to approach Peking. Similar instructions were sent to General Tseng Ch'i in Manchuria, where Russian troops were massing. Moreover, the council made the fateful decision to incorporate Boxer units into the regular army. The Boxers were now formally to be considered defenders of the state.

Events were now in motion that made war inevitable. On June 17 the empress dowager summoned the members of the Grand Council and announced that she had just received a four-point ultimatum from the great powers. As conditions for a peace settlement, the foreigners were demanding that a special residence be set aside for the emperor; all revenues of the Chinese empire be collected by the foreign legations; and all military affairs be placed under foreign control. The ultimatum made a fourth demand, most significant of all, which Tz'u Hsi did not announce at the time but which would come out later: Tz'u Hsi was to abdicate her position and the emperor was to be restored to active rule.

The ultimatum was obviously designed to humiliate the court. Indeed, its fourth demand attacked the empress dowager where she was most vulnerable. Tz'u Hsi played the situation to the hilt. She was outraged at the effrontery of the barbarians in their attempt to interfere in the internal affairs of the Celestial Empire. If the court accepted such demands, China could not survive, she declared. Should we not fight to our last breath? she ranted. When one of her advisers brought out a declaration of war that had been drafted earlier, she approved it on the spot.

Most members of the council were too cowed by Tz'u Hsi's imperious behavior to question her decisions. Jung Lu was not, however. Absolutely loyal to the empress dowager and long a favorite at court, he was allowed, within limits, to raise objections. Jung Lu had not reached and maintained his position of influence without learning the limits of his power, however, and he exercised his privilege with caution. In this case, he was troubled because Tz'u Hsi's plans appeared to include a direct attack on the foreign ministries. War was one thing, but an attack on the legation quarter was another, and Jung Lu appealed to the empress dowager not to permit it. To attempt to kill a diplomatic representative, he pointed out, was to insult a country. If the foreign ministers in Peking were massacred, all of the great powers would unite in a war of revenge against China.

Jung Lu received some support from others at court. Hsü Ching-ch'eng, ex-minister to the tsarist court at St. Petersburg and now head of the Imperial University in Peking, and Yüan Ch'ang, a minister in the Tsungli Yamen, pleaded for caution. The latter argued that the ultimatum had to be a forgery, since the foreign diplomats were too experienced to believe they could interfere so blatantly in the affairs of the empire. Moreover, he said, it would be folly to rely on the so-called "magical powers" of the Boxers. He had himself visited the legation quarter and seen the bodies of Boxer troops who had been repelled by foreign bullets. So much for the vaunted invulnerability of these "defenders of the dynasty."

The pleas of the moderates aroused Tz'u Hsi's anger. She declared that she had taken all that she could stand from the barbarian devils and commanded Jung Lu and his allies to hold their tongues. She did agree, however, to hold off on a declaration of war and to send an ultimatum demanding that the foreign envoys and their families leave China. In the meantime she ordered Yüan Shih-k'ai to send units of his Peiyang Army to the capital in preparation for possible hostilities. Representatives from the Tsungli Yamen were sent to inform the legations that, if the Western powers wanted war, the diplomatic corps would have to leave China. Sir Claude MacDonald answered for the allies. Admiral Seymour was not coming to Peking with hostile intentions, he said, but solely to protect the lives of the foreign residents in the capital. MacDonald would not agree to halt the relieving force.

The ministers were puzzled by the Chinese ultimatum, for the so-called "four-point ultimatum" received by Tz'u Hsi had not been sent by the allies but was indeed a forgery, concocted by Prince Tuan and his allies to incite the empress dowager to declare war on the barbarians. When Jung Lu learned, a few days after its receipt, that the document was spurious, he informed Tz'u Hsi. She launched a tirade against the perpetrators, but by then it was too late to avoid the consequences.

Still, although war seemed imminent, neither side had irrevocably opened hostilities. The Western assault on Taku settled the issue. On June 19, when the court received a memorial from Yü Lu reporting the Western ultimatum to surrender the Taku forts, Tz'u Hsi concluded that the powers were determined to resort to force. The legations were informed that diplomatic relations were broken, and the foreigners were told to leave the city within twenty-four hours.

On the same day China declared war on the foreign powers.[6] Imperial troops were given a free hand to open attacks on all foreign forces in north China. Prince Chuang and K'ang Yi were appointed to command the Boxer forces—thirty thousand strong in the Peking area alone. An additional forty-four hundred units, each consisting of up to several hundred men, were assigned to Prince Tuan to guard the capital.

SEYMOUR RETURNS TO TIENTSIN

Admiral Seymour's plan for the return to Tientsin was to retreat to Yangts'un by rail, repairing the line on the way, and then to reorganize his forces for an advance upriver. From Yangts'un he hoped to find junks to transport heavy weapons and the wounded back to Tientsin via the Pei Ho. The remainder of the military column would accompany the junks along the west bank.

By June 18 the retreating columns had managed to return to the rail-river junction at Yangts'un. On the way from Lang Fang they had been constantly exposed to attacks by the Boxers. Moreover, the German units deployed to protect the rear of the column were harassed by five thousand imperial troops under the command of General Tung Fu-hsiang. This was the first time that regular troops had engaged in open combat with Seymour's forces.

At Yangts'un Seymour abandoned the train and seized several native boats for transporting the wounded, provisions, heavy field guns, and ammunition. In mid-afternoon of June 19 the allied units began moving downriver. Unfortunately, the drought throughout north China had caused the river level to drop, and the seized junks had trouble navigating. This problem was compounded by the Westerners' lack of familiarity with the unwieldy Chinese river craft. At the beginning of the march all the heavy equipment had to be left behind. Soon the junks were abandoned entirely and the wounded were forced to join the rest of the troops along the river bank. As the forces progressed, they cleared the Boxers by rifle and bayonet from several villages along the way. At the end of the first day they had traveled only eight miles toward Tientsin and relative safety.

Progress over the next few days continued to be agonizingly slow, and by the afternoon of June 21 the advance units reached the Hsi-ku arsenal on the west bank of the river about three miles north of Tientsin. The allied units were short of ammunition as well as food and water; the arsenal was a welcome sight. In late afternoon two groups of allied forces, one British and the other German, crossed the river and seized the arsenal with little opposition. Inside they found several guns and over fifteen tons of rice. Seymour decided to spend the night at Hsi-ku. He sent out several messengers to inform the allied forces in Tientsin that his troops were just north of the city, but none was able to get through.

Secure in the arsenal, Seymour decided to remain at Hsi-ku, care for the wounded, and await assistance. On June 23 Chinese forces tried to retake the arsenal, but the defenders, well armed and well stocked once again, were able to repel them. Captured Chinese soldiers reported that General Nieh Shih-ch'eng's army was discouraged. It had attacked Seymour's small units with twenty-five battalions for several days without success. A total of 62 of Seymour's forces had been killed and about 230 wounded.

On June 25 help for Seymour's besieged forces finally arrived. Nearly two thousand Russian troops under Colonel

Shirinsky, newly arrived from Port Arthur, moved upriver from Tientsin and relieved Seymour's garrison. After destroying the arsenal, all units returned to the city of Tientsin.

AMERICA ENTERS THE CONFLICT

The attack on the Chinese fortifications at Taku had been a joint action of all the powers present off the north China coast except the United States. Throughout the planning and military phase the Americans had held themselves aloof. On June 14, when queried by the British as to American plans in the event of hostilities at Taku, Admiral Louis Kempff, highest ranking officer in the American squadron, had replied that he was "not authorized to initiate any act of war with a country with which my country is at peace." The next day, when allied forces occupied the railway station near the forts in preparation for the eventual move to Tientsin, American troops had not participated in the operation, nor had they taken part in the actual attack on Taku. Admiral Kempff had taken literally Hay's June 10 telegram to Conger calling for a cautious policy in China. Kempff did send upriver the American warship *Monocacy,* a gunboat built during the Civil War, to provide a shelter for the foreign community at Taku during the bombardment. Ironically, it was the first ship to be struck by Chinese shells during the assault on the forts.

Admiral Kempff's attitude reflected the McKinley administration's caution regarding the crisis. The first reactions to Kempff's reticence in the American press were somewhat critical; some observers remembered that another American naval commander in China, faced with a similar situation, had said, "Blood is thicker than water," and joined in an allied naval operation against the forts. [7] Even President McKinley questioned Kempff's decision, but he soon revised his opinion. In a message to Congress he stated that a hostile demonstration by the powers

Cartoon of Uncle Sam and President McKinley attacking the murderous Boxers, entitled "Is this Imperialism?" (*Harper's Weekly*, August 28, 1900, cover)

would simply serve to intensify antiforeign feeling in China and encourage the Boxers to take action against Seymour's relief force. And, of course, American participation would have unleashed widespread criticism of the administration's misuse of executive authority to launch yet another imperialist adventure.

  Still, McKinley's administration had been sufficiently concerned about events in north China to make some preparations for possible hostilities. In early June a battalion of the 1st Marines was dispatched from Cavite in the

Philippines, arriving off Taku on June 18. On June 16 the 9th Infantry Regiment under Colonel Emerson Liscum was ordered from Manila; it was due to arrive in China on July 6, to be followed shortly by the 6th U.S. Cavalry, scheduled to embark from San Francisco on July 1. These moves were officially interpreted as missions to protect American lives and property, not as acts of war. Hay still sought to draw a clear distinction between joint military action and American diplomatic action.

The ambivalence within the McKinley administration accurately reflected the mood throughout the country. On the one hand a rising wave of anti-imperialism was sweeping the nation. The takeover of the Philippines at the end of the Spanish-American War and American actions against the Filipino forces of Emilio Aguinaldo north of Manila had inspired a distaste for colonial activity among a significant proportion of the nation's citizens. Any belli-cose action by American forces in China would certainly be interpreted in these circles as the beginning of a new American adventure in Asia. To a considerable extent, these anti-imperialist views were taken up by the Democratic party, in opposition since the ascent of McKinley to the presidency in 1896. This was undoubtedly a factor in dam-pening the enthusiasm of some groups in the Republican party for further action in China during the first weeks of summer.

Indeed, vociferous forces within the country were prodding the administration to take stern action to protect American interests in China. The strongest advocates of an active posture, perhaps, were religious groups involved in the missionary effort which was now imperiled by Boxer activities in north China. If McKinley did not act to pro-tect American missionaries, a French diplomatic observer warned, he would be the object of "Biblical maledictions" from every pulpit in America. More broadly, of course, an active American foreign policy in Asia had support from many groups throughout the country, not least in the "yellow press" which had been partly responsible for fomenting the just-completed war against Spain. As one popular American weekly of the period commented, "That America, once having decided to move, is to back up her plan, whatever it is, with enough troops and ships is gratifying to everyone in the East. Let those who are inclined to cavil at the new role of the country in the world's affairs remember that the moment is rapidly approaching, if it has not arrived, when the future of the world's civilization will be at stake. Will it be a world in which the English-speaking race, with its high standard of life and liberty, will prevail; or a world in which the despot and the slave—shall we leave out the 'e' and call it Slav?—will dictate the future of the sphere?"[8] It was under the influence of such criticism in the press that McKinley had reluctantly dispatched the 9th Infantry Regiment from the Philippines to north China. In a private discussion with French Ambassador Cambon, Secretary Hay said that the regiment would be the last American unit to be sent to the area. Time would show that this was an unduly optimistic assessment of the situation.

THE VICEROYS STRUGGLE FOR PEACE

In central and south China, the viceroys viewed the escalation of the crisis with increasing nervousness. When the situation deteriorated, moderates in Peking under Jung Lu attempted to persuade Liu K'un-yi to intercede along with Li Hung-chang, probably the man with the most influence at court, to encourage the empress dowager to suppress the Boxers. Li, however, was a cautious man during a crisis. He refused Liu K'un-yi's invitation to take action, saying that, since the empress dowager was for the moment determined on her course of action, any persuasion on his part would be futile. Rebuffed by Li Hung-chang, Liu K'un-yi turned to Chang Chih-tung, and on June 14 the two sent a joint memorial to Peking urging the suppression of the antiforeign movement and suggesting that Li Hung-chang be appointed to negotiate a settlement with the great powers. Otherwise, they warned, China would be subjected to a disastrous foreign invasion. Unfortunately, the memorial did not arrive until after the fall of the Taku forts. By then it was too late to avert war.

Once war had been declared on the powers, of course, the viceroys found themselves in a delicate situation. Any move on their part to conciliate the foreigners could be interpreted by the court as treason. Still, convinced that war was futile, they were inclined to do their best to ignore the declaration of war and to avoid hostilities in areas under their control. They did not publicize the government's edict and increasingly drew together for mutual support.

The desire for compromise on the part of the viceroys did not go unnoticed in Western capitals, and soon after the brief Taku campaign the Western naval commanders in north China issued a statement designed to assuage their concern:

The admirals and senior naval officers of the allied powers in China desire to make known to all viceroys and authorities of the coasts and rivers, cities and provinces of China that they intend to use armed force only against Boxers and people who oppose them on their march to Peking for the rescue of their fellow-countrymen.[9]

For their part, in other words, the allies did not consider themselves to be at war with China.

The viceroys rushed to take advantage of this conciliatory statement, and jointly memorialized the throne to suppress the Boxer movement in north China. Liu told Jung Lu that he would be willing to march north to fight for his country, but that to slaughter a few helpless foreigners would be an act "totally lacking in humanity." The thrust of their memorial thus paralleled that of the admirals' statement, and for emphasis the viceroys sent copies to world capitals.

The viceroys' attempts to isolate the rest of China from the unrest in Chihli Province met with the general approval of the foreign community in central and south

China. The trouble in the north had had a noticeable effect in the Yangtse Valley area—trade had slowed down, factories stood idle, and steamship service to other areas of the nation had been discontinued. To reassure the local populace, the foreign consuls issued a statement declaring their willingness to cooperate with the local authorities in maintaining law and order. Foreign warships in the Shanghai harbor (there were eight at the time) took up positions for possible action as "a measure of precaution," but avoided hostile actions. The British consul-general in Shanghai offered troops to help suppress antiforeign activities, but the local authorities rejected assistance, stating that such foreign aid would only "inflame the situation."

In response to these gestures from the foreign powers, the viceroys decided to offer to keep the peace by their own actions throughout the Yangtse Valley if the powers would agree to maintain order in the foreign concessions area in Shanghai. On June 26 the viceroys presented the foreign consuls with a nine-point draft proposal calling for mutual efforts to maintain peace in the area. The consuls objected to only one point in the proposal—that the viceroys would not be held responsible for disturbances caused by the entrance of foreign warships in the Yangtse River unless the ships' entry had been sanctioned by them. On June 27 the consuls responded by saying that they had no intention of landing forces in the Yangtse Valley so long as the rights of foreigners throughout the area were maintained, but that they demanded the right to take whatever action was necessary to rescue foreigners subjected to threats from antiforeign elements.

So long as the area remained quiet, the problem was hypothetical. Still, unless something could be done to halt war in the north, local measures to limit the spread of hostilities would probably prove futile. Obviously, the viceroys, while doing their best to exert a calming influence in Peking, would have to open private communications with foreign capitals to assure them that a negotiated settlement was indeed a possibility. Li Hung-chang gave active consideration during the last week of June to making a trip north to argue for compromise. Though he did not follow through on this plan, he did, on his own initiative and without informing Peking, send telegrams to foreign powers assuring them that the action at Taku had not been ordered by Peking, and asking them if at all possible to keep diplomatic communications open with the Chinese government.

Chang Chih-tung pursued the will-of-the-wisp of peace through his own contacts in Japan. He suggested to Tokyo that, if the great powers agreed not to advance beyond Tientsin or to threaten the capital, the empress dowager would be assured of their peaceful intentions and would then be able to suppress the Boxers and their supporters at court.

In Peking the moderates were not so optimistic. Late in June Jung Lu wrote to Chang Chih-tung confiding that he and his allies, Prince Ch'ing and Wang Wen-shao, had no influence over the militants who were now strongly in control at court. One moderate in the government was so discouraged about the trends in Peking that he asked Yüan Shih-k'ai, governor of Shantung Province, to march on Peking and stage a coup to get rid of the militants. Yüan had been firmly suppressing antiforeign activities in Shantung and was considered an ally of the moderate faction. But when he was asked to dispatch some of his best troops to Peking, he found excuses for delay. Yüan was solicitous of his own neck and sensed that the time for decisive action was not yet ripe. The problem at Peking was internal, he replied, and required internal treatment. With obvious reluctance, he eventually did send a newly organized unit, but it arrived too late to affect the fighting there.

Chapter Six

The Siege at Peking

While generals and diplomats in world capitals pondered over what action to take in China, the residents of the legation quarter watched with mounting anxiety as their last ties to the outside world were broken. By the second week in June Peking seemed on the verge of chaos. Boxers were entering the capital by the thousands. They wandered at will through the city looting and burning, inflamed to a fever pitch of anti-Western feeling. According to observers, many were youths from the neighboring villages; others appeared to be regulars of Tung Fu-hsiang's Kansu Army. The latter had apparently come to the city at the express will of the empress dowager.

The government seemed powerless—or reluctant—to take action to maintain law and order. Since the rampaging Boxer squads made no distinction between high and low status, native or foreigner, those inhabitants of the city who could afford to do so began to leave, taking their precious belongings with them. Terror and violence ruled the streets of Peking.

Indeed, the impression that the court had no intention of curbing the violence was not far from the truth. As the crisis worsened, the empress dowager appeared content to let events unfold unchecked and to give the militants free rein. In fact, two of the leading antiforeign officials at court, K'ang Yi and Duke Lan, had actually attended the conflagration at the Christian church on the night of June 13, and Tz'u Hsi had watched from the imperial palace as the flames brightened the night sky.

As the noose tightened around them, the foreigners tried to strike back. Scouting parties sent out by the legations frequently encountered and attacked roving bands of Boxers on the streets of Peking. On one occasion a patrol composed of American, British, and Japanese soldiers discovered a group of several dozen Boxers looting a temple in the eastern section of the city (one source says the foreigners broke in while the Boxers were preparing Chinese Christians for human sacrifice on an altar). According to the somewhat laconic account by Lancelot Giles, a student interpreter at the British legation, every one of the Boxers was killed "almost without resistance."[1]

Attacks on that scale were hardly sufficient, however, to protect the foreigners from the seemingly thousands of Chinese stirred to an anti-Western frenzy by the Boxer activities and the attitude of the court. Indeed, sober heads in the diplomatic community were painfully aware of their vulnerability to attack. They were isolated in an inland capital over a hundred miles from the sea; they were viewed with increasing hostility by the local populace and by the Chinese government, whose own intentions were shrouded in mystery; and their entire armed force consisted of fewer than five hundred officers and enlisted men of mixed nationalities.

Not the least of the foreigners' problems was the relative indefensibility of the legation quarter itself. Backed on the south by the Peking city wall—a brick rampart fifty feet high and approximately forty feet thick which surrounded the entire Tartar city—the diplomatic quarter

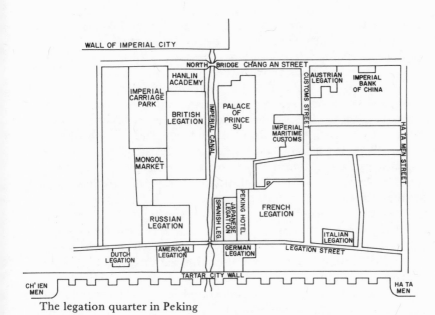

The legation quarter in Peking

comprised an area a bit more than two thousand feet square. The city wall to the south offered some protection, but the remaining three sides were open to street traffic and were dangerously vulnerable to attack from the outside. Along the eastern and western boundaries, though, there were several features which might be utilized to form a defensive perimeter. On the east the French and German legations and the building housing the Imperial Maritime Customs were all stout edifices that could form the cornerstones of a defensive line running along Omann Street, one of the major north-south thoroughfares in the city. The two legations located east of this line—Austrian and Italian—presumably would have to be evacuated. Along the western boundary the backs of the Russian and British legations and, at the juncture of the wall, the Russo-Chinese Bank formed a natural defense line against attack. To the west of this line was the imperial carriage park and a small Mongol market; these would have to be cleared to provide adequate visibility for the defenders against any attacking force. Beyond the market and the carriage park were some of the major ministries of the Chinese empire, along with the legation of the Netherlands, which was too isolated to be given adequate protection. To make the eastern and western perimeters reasonably secure from attack, the foreigners would have to block off the street accesses to the legation quarter. The main problem was Legation Street, which ran directly through the quarter about six hundred feet north of the wall.

Another difficult task for the foreigners would be the defense of the northern perimeter. The northern boundary was Ch'ang An Street, a major thoroughfare which ran along the south wall of the imperial city. It offered easy access to the heart of the legation quarter, particularly in the center where the imperial canal ran directly south from the imperial city to exit at a water gate along the Tartar wall. If attackers penetrated into the legation area along the canal, they could split the quarter in half. In that event defense of the legations would be a virtual impossibility.

Even along the south wall the defenders faced no easy task, for along the top of the wall ran a parapet about forty feet wide. To protect the legations the foreigners would have to control the wall virtually from the Ch'ien Men in the center to the Ha Ta Men, about halfway from the Ch'ien Men to the southeastern corner of the Tartar city. If the attackers gained control of the wall, they would be able to rain rifle and cannon fire at will into the heart of the diplomatic quarter.

Even if the foreigners had been able to secure a defensive position, their weaponry would have proved inadequate to the task. The only fieldpiece available was an Italian one-pounder which, although accurate enough, could do little damage, since its shells were so small. In addition, there were a few rapid-fire machine guns — the Americans had a Colt, the Austrians a Maxim, and the British an old five-barrel Nordenfeldt which often failed to

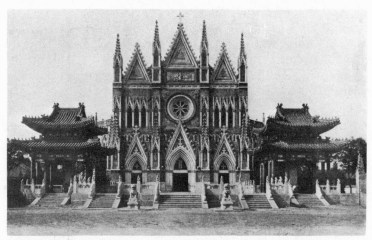

The Catholic Peitang Cathedral in Peking, refuge of Bishop Favier and the Chinese Christians during the siege (*Leslie's Weekly,* August 18, 1900, p. 128)

work. Ammunition was in relatively short supply, and certainly not sufficient for a long siege.

The population of the foreign community numbered slightly more than 470, including 149 women and 79 children. The quarter was guarded by a military contingent of approximately 450 men, 21 of them officers of various nationalities. The largest forces—slightly over 80 each—were the British and the Russians. There were 56 Americans and about an equal number of Germans, 75 French, 37 Austrians, 39 Italians, and 25 Japanese. Of this number, 43 had been sent to the Peitang Cathedral to guard the Roman Catholic converts there. This total, absurdly inadequate to protect the quarter from the several thousand regular troops and Boxers at large within the city, would eventually be supplemented by 75 civilian volunteers recruited from among the 245 male residents. Called the "Carving Knife Brigade" in reference to the variety of weapons at their disposal, this ragtag group performed valuable service in the defense of the legations throughout the siege.

THE BEGINNING OF THE SIEGE

At four o'clock on the afternoon of June 19 Tz'u Hsi made her official response to the allied attack on the Taku forts. At that hour all the foreign legations received identical messages from the Tsungli Yamen: because of the attack on Taku, a state of war existed between China and the powers. The diplomatic representatives and all of their dependents were instructed to leave Peking within twenty-four hours and retire to Tientsin, from whence they could be evacuated from China. Recognizing the danger of attack, the Tsungli Yamen (prompted by Jung Lu, who had pleaded with the empress dowager to recognize that the sanctity of diplomatic representatives was a cardinal point of agreement among the nations of the world) offered to provide an armed guard to escort the foreigners to safety.

The diplomatic community was divided on how to react to the Chinese ultimatum. Many strongly suspected the court's motives, and some were absolutely opposed to trusting its guarantee of protection. After heated discussion, the ministers decided to play for time. They refused to move from Peking until more guards were provided for their protection, and they demanded an interview with the Tsungli Yamen for the following day. Early the next morning, June 20, the ministers of the various legations gathered at the French Legation. By 9:30 A.M. they had received no reply from the Chinese government on their request for an interview, and the German minister, Baron Klemens von Ketteler, announced that he would go alone to the office of the Tsungli Yamen, several blocks to the northeast of the legation quarter, to obtain an answer. Von Ketteler's behavior was no surprise to his colleagues. Since his arrival in Peking he had earned a reputation for swagger and arrogance. A few days earlier a Boxer had driven a cart into the legation quarter and begun to insult the foreign bystanders while making threatening gestures with his knife. While most had watched nervously, von Ketteler had marched out into the street and begun flailing at the Chinese with his cane until the latter fled.

Von Ketteler's fellow ministers made a half-hearted effort to dissuade him from going, but failed, and von Ketteler and his interpreter, Heinrich Cordes, left in two covered sedan chairs to make their way to the Chinese foreign office. As they passed north on Ha Ta Men Street with von Ketteler in the lead, a Manchu soldier standing alongside the road suddenly pointed his rifle into the minister's chair and fired. Von Ketteler was killed instantly. Cordes, to the rear, froze in horror, then jumped from his own chair and ran. He was wounded by rifle fire in both legs but managed to stumble through the tangled web of streets to the American Methodist Mission, about a mile to the east of the legation quarter. When word of the murder reached the diplomats, they were outraged. A search party was immediately sent out to locate von Ketteler's corpse and bring it back to the German legation, but Chinese soldiers refused to let the foreign troops look for the body, which in any case had disappeared.

Until von Ketteler's murder the envoys had been badly divided on whether to evacuate the foreign community to Tientsin. American Minister Edwin Conger, in particular, was seriously considering accepting the Chinese offer and ordered American families to prepare for departure. He began making these arrangements despite pleas from his subordinates that a foreign exodus from Peking would place the thousands of Chinese Christians in the capital area (including several hundred at the American Methodist Mission) at the mercy of the enraged Boxer hordes rampaging through the streets.

The murder of von Ketteler settled the issue. There would be no movement without adequate protection provided by the allied armed forces. It was now strongly suspected that the German minister's murder had not been an accident, but had been deliberately planned by the court. (Evidence eventually suggested that there was at least some justification for this belief. Several months later German troops apprehended a Manchu soldier who confessed to the slaying; the soldier claimed that his superior officers offered him a reward for shooting the minister. By then the point was somewhat academic. In any event, he was executed on the spot where von Ketteler's murder had taken place.) In the afternoon of June 20 the Tsungli Yamen sent a note to the legations, inviting the ministers to reconsider the ultimatum and to consider means of leaving the capital. The note made no reference to the killing of the German diplomat.

In all probability the murder of von Ketteler played a significant role in the crisis. Whether or not it had been deliberately planned by court reactionaries, von Ketteler's murder was not simply one more step in a rapidly deteriorating situation. China had now committed an irrevocable action: it had inflicted harm on a diplomatic representative of one of the great powers. There appeared now no way out of the stand-off short of war. At 4:00 P.M. on June 21, when the twenty-four-hour ultimatum expired, Chinese troops opened fire on the legations. The siege at Peking had begun.

PREPARATIONS FOR DEFENSE

Within the legations there was no further excuse for delay. During the preceding days flimsy barricades had been erected on the major thoroughfares through the legation quarter and at the bridge crossing the Imperial Canal on Ch'ang An Street along the northern rim of the area. The foreigners now set to work to strengthen their defenses. Sandbags and paving blocks were hastily brought up to strengthen the barriers between the quarter and the outside world. Bomb shelters were built to protect troops along the defensive perimeter, and loopholes were cut in walls to permit the besieged forces to fire on the surrounding Chinese troops.

Other serious problems besides defense strategies

demanded immediate attention. The extent of the foreigners' responsibility for the fate of the Chinese converts at the American Methodist Mission had been argued fiercely within the diplomatic community. Now that the foreigners were going to stay, the converts would not be abandoned, willy-nilly, to the vicissitudes of fate. Still, should they be protected by the legations? American Minister Conger, whose behavior in this respect shamed many of his countrymen in Peking, ordered that the American missionaries at the mission be escorted to the legation quarter for protection, but that the Chinese Christians there—over eight hundred—be instructed to fend for themselves.

Fortunately for the latter, more humane counsel prevailed, and it was finally agreed that the converts would be brought to the quarter and housed in the palace of Prince Su—the Su Wang Fu—a spacious structure directly across the Imperial Canal from the British legation. A party of twenty American marines was dispatched to the mission during a lull in the firing that first afternoon. They escorted the entire party—seventy foreign missionaries and some eight hundred Chinese—to the legation quarter without incident. The Chinese joined more than two thousand converts already huddled together in the palace—all dependent for their survival on the ability of their foreign protectors to stave off the impending attacks. On the following day the American mission and two of the abandoned legations beyond the foreign defense perimeter were burned to the ground.

Once the initial steps had been taken to block off points of easy access to the quarter, the major problem for the foreign community was lack of organization. In light of the diversity of the population within the legation quarter, and of the bitter internecine quarrels that divided the various powers, organizing for defense was no easy matter. First to be decided was the question of leadership. Defense of the legations obviously required the specialized experience of a trained military expert; yet, according to protocol, it was the minister who had the primary responsibility for the protection of all national interests, including the lives and property of all citizens residing in the area. Fortunately, a few of the diplomats present had prior military experience: British Minister Sir Claude MacDonald had been a career officer in the Scot's Greys before entering the diplomatic service, and American Minister Edwin Conger was an ex-infantry officer who had seen combat experience during the Civil War. Also, Conger's first secretary, Herbert Squiers, had served fifteen years in the U.S. cavalry.

Given the circumstances, however, it is hardly surprising that there was a certain period of experimentation before a reasonably stable chain of command was established within the besieged area. At the outset, command was seized by the highest ranking military officer among the foreign community—the Austrian naval officer von Thomann, commander of the Austrian cruiser *Zenta*. Von Thomann happened to be in Peking on vacation when the crisis erupted. As events would prove, he was not a fortuitous choice for leadership, but the other military officers within the quarter were all younger men of low rank and not enough experience to take command.

No amount of combat experience, however, would have eased the precarious situation in which the besieged foreigners found themselves. The military problems of providing for the defense of the legation quarter seemed nearly insurmountable. In addition, there were problems of food and water, of shelter and sanitation, and of dealing with nearly three thousand Chinese crammed into the palace of Prince Su. Here the organizational abilities of Sir Claude MacDonald were quickly demonstrated. As *doyen* of the diplomatic corps in Peking and representative of the premier imperialist power in Asia, MacDonald easily claimed the civilian leadership of the foreign colony. He immediately began to form a committee structure to put some order into the defense of the legations. Committees were also formed to take responsibility for all the diverse needs of the community—food, health and sanitation, distribution of labor, fuel supply, water, and fire defense. A parent committee, the General Committee, under the American missionary Tewkesbury, was formed to advise Minister MacDonald.

The most vital problem was maintaining a defense perimeter adequate to protect the legations from outside attack. To some degree, the buildings in the quarter could be used as a bulwark. But the streets offering access into the area needed to be sealed off, and stout barricades had to be built which could withstand cannon fire from the Chinese while allowing the defenders to fire outside. With respect to these problems the foreigners were fortunate. Responsibility for fortifications was handled by a committee under another American missionary, Dr. Frank Gamewell, who had been educated as an engineer at Cornell University before entering the missionary service. According to accounts of the siege, Gamewell was superb at his job. Under his supervision the community set to work to provide for its own safety. Here, as nowhere else, the spirit of cooperation and innovation was demonstrated. In response to Gamewell's call for sandbags, sandbags, and more sandbags, the more resourceful women in the community sewed sandbag casings out of whatever fabric was available in the area—clothing, silk and brocade furnishings, and draperies. The women manufactured an average of two thousand sandbags a day, fifty thousand over the entire period of the siege.

Another serious problem was food and water. The foodstocks of the legations were inadequate to withstand a long siege. Fortunately, there were several local grain retail shops within the quarter, and their supplies of wheat and rice were requisitioned for the duration. Such luxuries as meat and vegetables were soon in short supply, and before long the community began to slaughter its horses and mules for food. As for water, there were eight wells within the legation area. While the water was not especially clean, it could be made potable by boiling.

The "International Gun," an artillery piece constructed and used with great effectiveness by the legations during the siege at Peking (*Leslie's Weekly,* December 15, 1900, cover)